HOW BROADWAY WORKS

HOW BROADWAY WORKS

Building and Running a Show From the People Who Make It Happen

Sharon Grace Powers

APPLAUSE
THEATRE & CINEMA BOOKS
Essex, Connecticut

APPLAUSE
THEATRE & CINEMA BOOKS

An imprint of Globe Pequot, the trade division of
The Rowman & Littlefield Publishing Group, Inc.
4501 Forbes Boulevard, Suite 200, Lanham, Maryland 20706
www.rowman.com

Distributed by NATIONAL BOOK NETWORK

Library of Congress Cataloging-in-Publication Data Available

ISBN 978-1-4930-5994-2 (pbk. : alk. paper)
ISBN 978-1-4930-5995-9 (electronic)

∞™ The paper used in this publication meets the minimum requirements of
American National Standard for Information Sciences—Permanence of Paper
for Printed Library Materials, ANSI/NISO 739.48-1992

To Marie, my mother, Hanna, Leo, Doris, and Tara, who believed in me when I didn't believe in myself.

Contents

Foreword

This book is a tribute to the hundreds of *artists / artisans* behind the curtain who collaborate to bring a theatrical vision to a Broadway stage. There are basically thirty Broadway theatres and as many people doing the same jobs as these book contributors. What this book relates is the essence of how a show is brought to and runs every night on Broadway, and although each production is unique, the general pattern is the same.

Also, I want to share with young people who dream of working on Broadway that there is much more to a Broadway career than acting, singing, or dancing. They can find many, but not all, of the theatrical career possibilities in this book. All the jobs discussed are creative, fulfilling, and necessary to create a home for an actor on the stage. For any given Broadway production, there are fifty to more than seventy-five people backstage who work with the performers onstage to make the show run smoothly.

If a young person's ambition is Broadway, then moving to New York is essential. Even if they have worked for some years in regional theatre, they will face starting all over again. Broadway is a small community, and it is about making contacts, showing *what* you can do, *how* you do it, and *how well* you fit into the environment. Ultimately, though, it can be a matter of luck. Theatre is perhaps one of the most *collaborative* environments, but Broadway theatre is a special mosaic. New York is a hotbed of talent, and the competition is extraordinary and at the highest level.

Many of the contributors to this book had experience acting in elementary or high school. What they discovered was they were not particularly suited to performing but had other talents that were necessary for the theatrical storytelling process. Storytelling can be as simple as relating something that happened to you during the day or telling a spooky story around a campfire or as elaborate as a Broadway extravaganza.

In a Broadway production, the term "creatives" usually refers to the writer, composer, lyricist, director, choreographer, and designers. It is true that the words and music on a page are the impetus for any production and it takes the performers to bring those words and that music to life. It also takes a director's vision of how they want to tell the story that gives the overall concept for a production. However, there is a vast array of individuals who bring their imaginations and talents to complete the picture we see onstage—drapers, seamstresses, dressers, wigmakers, stagehands, carpenters, painters, mixers, orchestrators, conductors, to name a few. They are the backbone of a theatrical production.

Interacting with everyone who became part of this book, I came to the conclusion that everyone involved in a production is a "creative" to some degree. The behind-the-scenes people take what is an idea in someone else's mind and find a way to transform that intangible vision into an actual physical reality. It requires creative thinking and problem-solving to convert an amorphous idea into something concrete. There were three words that attracted these artists/artisans to theatre that were consistently mentioned to me: storytelling, collaboration, and problem-solving.

Thank You

So many books in theatre are written about an actor or a single designer. Not much is written, if anything, about how the individual parts of a Broadway production fit together and make it complete.

This is a very deep heartfelt thank-you to everyone who contributed to this book. They all referred me to someone else whom they thought could fill out the picture. If someone could not follow through because they were overwhelmed when work began again in earnest after COVID-19, I was able to call upon someone to help me find a replacement. They reviewed what I wrote to confirm accuracy according to their experience. They were generous with their information and their time.

Ironically, sheltering in place with COVID-19 became the most productive period for this book since everyone was available to be interviewed!

Evan Adamson, Gregg Barnes, John Lee Beatty, Brian Blythe, Peter Bogyo, Sam Brooks, David Brian Brown, Jane Cardona, Jeremy Chernick, Katherine Chick, Sarah Cimino, Elizabeth Coleman, Michael Curry, Jessica Dermody, Jeff Fender, Carin M. Ford, Christopher Gattelli, Gwendolyn M. Gilliam, Alexander Gottlieb, Taylor Green, Charlie Grieco, Kimberly Grigsby, Emily Grishman, Kai Harada, Matt Hodges, Nevin Hedley, Allen Lee Hughes, James F. Ingalls, David Kaley, Polly Kinney, John Kristiansen, Tommy Kurzman, Zane Mark, Katherine Marshall, Michael McElroy, John Miller, Ben Moss, Aaron Porter, Gene O'Donovan, Margaret Peot, Austin Rodriguez, Peter Sarafin, Michael Starobin, Victoria Tinsman, Paloma Young.

1

General Management/Producer

General Manager

When we did *Caroline or Change*, [original Broadway production] the cast and crew were on stage and all the producers came. In order to get the show done, they [the producers] had to go out and get a lot more money from a lot more people. There were more producers than there were in the cast. That's the way it is these days.

–Gene O'Donovan, founder of Aurora Productions Inc., production management company

The lead Broadway producer is the head of a sprawling theatrical company and basically is responsible for *everything*. As the quote says, there are *many* financial investors to a Broadway show, but whether the lead producer is a hands-on producer or not, everything flows from them. The lead producer believes in the play or musical enough to take a huge gamble on a new production. Each production is a new start-up entity, most often an LLC, which the lead producer creates, assembles the departments and staff, assembles the right artistic team, and proceeds to raise money to mount that production. Unless it is a revival, which still can take some years, new material can take a decade or more to mount as a Broadway production.

Initially, the producer hires a lawyer to set up the LLC and to obtain a legal option on the play or musical. The next question is how much will the production cost? Then enters the general manager (GM). A GM is the producer's chief business and financial representative, with whom the producer consults on a daily basis throughout the production.

The lead producer has a vision for the show they have optioned, and it is the GM who oversees the execution of that vision. The GM usually has worked with the lead producer before so a mutual understanding and trust has been established. Essentially, the GM sets up the superstructure of a production, manages every facet of the show, and makes sure everything stays within budget.

Being a GM of such a sprawling enterprise requires a vast arsenal of theatrical knowledge and how a theatrical production works. The GM creates the initial budget, which includes obvious items such as sets and costumes, but all the not-obvious expenditures such as insurance, payroll taxes, legal filings, personnel, crew, and marketing as well. The GM must be conversant with all the many disparate aspects of a show.

There are at least thirteen unions on Broadway, and the GM needs to be familiar with each of their complexities. They are consulted about anything that has a financial or business implication for the show, such as whether the summer performing schedule of shows should change because many New York City people are away for the weekends, and how the unions would affect a Sunday performance (an additional premium).

Contract negotiations can be split between the lead producer and the GM, depending on the producer's choice. Producers have different strengths, so sometimes the producer prefers to negotiate contracts, especially if it is a big star. Otherwise, the producer relates the parameters for a negotiation and the GM handles the negotiation with the agents or the artist's representative. However, the producer has the final say about the artistic team they think will be the best team to make the show a success, from director, to designers, to stars, to the production management company.

To learn how to be a GM, one can go to college and major in business or arts management, but it is a long and involved process. For someone who is interested, one way is working in a GM's office where all that activity is happening. Peter Bogyo, the well-known Broadway GM and author of the seminal book *Broadway General Manager: Demystifying the Most Important and Least Understood Role in Show Business*, began as an actor and knew nothing about the GM's role, so he decided it would behoove him to work in an established GM's office.

> I went to work for my first general manager starting as the second assistant, became first assistant, then the office manager, then eventually I apprenticed for, and got into ATPAM, the manager's union. Along the way, when I didn't know anything about this field, I made a list of questions and was sensitive enough to wait until an appropriate time to ask the current company manager, "Can you explain this?" I read everything I could, from budgets to contracts, and tried to understand them.

Accumulating this knowledge and the skills took several years. Even with a college degree, practical experience in the middle of the action is more substantive than academia alone.

A professional accounting firm is hired, which meets with the GM once a week to go over profit/loss statements, discuss accruals, amortization, and royalty issues. The GM does not need to be an accountant, but they must be able to comprehend accounting terminology and what it means.

Another critical hire after the lawyer, the accounting firm, and the GM is the company manager (CM), whom the GM traditionally hires and who comes on board shortly before rehearsals begin. The CM works closely with the GM, is based in the GM's office, and is the liaison between the GM, the producer, and the production. The CM is the primary intermediary between cast, crew, box office, and administration and interacts daily with those constituencies. The CM reads all the contracts to understand individual agreements, sets up and dispenses the payroll to cast and crew, and manages royalty payments. The CM handles hospitality and coordinates any travel issues for the company, pays company bills under the GM's supervision, handles house seat requests, and reviews the backup in the theatre's weekly settlement statement, through which the show is paid for the previous week's performances, net of theatre expenses taken off the top. There are no specific college programs for learning to be a CM, but backstage and theatre experience, plus arts and business administration, are helpful.

One difficult part of the job is the CM must be in-house for *every* performance, six days a week, eight shows a week, with little off time between the two shows on matinee days. The CM is the contact person for the production stage manager when any problem occurs during a performance. Although the production stage manager deals directly with all performance issues, the production stage manager reports any problem requiring administrative assistance to the CM, who then informs the GM.

While a GM is not officially affiliated with a union, CMs are members of the Association for Theatrical Press Agents and Managers (ATPAM), which is a union affiliated with International Alliance of Theatrical Stage Employees. There is a substantive apprentice program for becoming a CM, requiring two years of work weeks and both a written and oral exam, which is an all-day exam. The traditional and most common path for becoming a GM is by first serving many years as a CM.

The Broadway League of Producers

The Broadway League is a trade organization of theatre owners, operators, producers, presenters, GMs, and various supply businesses that service the entertainment industry, including Broadway and their national touring shows, as well as presenters of touring productions in cities throughout North America. It is the collective bargaining agent for Broadway producers (representing the show) and theatre owners (representing the house), and it negotiates union contracts on their behalf. The Broadway League's producer members individually hire their own GMs, production management companies, marketing companies, and legal firms for a production. The League itself has a relatively small staff, but it is its *members* who provide a multitude of jobs for young people interested in working in theatre.

Another mission of the League is that it works hard to promote, market, and support live theatre, and is a co-producer of the annual Tony Awards, along with the American Theatre Wing. During the past several years, the Broadway League has made a concerted effort in New York City and surrounding communities to establish outreach programs to increase diversity at all levels of production and services. Not everything is performing.

There are a variety of community and intern programs reaching out to communities of color to introduce jobs that exist in theatre. There are many workforce development programs, including a high school partnership with the New York City Department of Education for the Broadway Shadowing Program, Careers on Broadway, Audience Development, year-round internship programs, and more.

There are accounting firms, law offices, insurance companies, and advertising agencies that specialize specifically in theatre, and they all require different skills and have many niches. If someone loves live theatre, there are many opportunities to participate, and all of these jobs are necessary and critical to the production of a play or musical. For anyone interested, they can contact the Broadway League for their outreach initiatives.

Producing Entities

There are several producing entities on Broadway, many of which abide by the contracts negotiated by the Broadway League. Disney is perhaps the most visible and up until now has operated independently from the Broadway League, negotiating their own contracts with the unions.

Every Disney show is structured as a department within the corporation, and staffing for non-artistic positions is in-house. The in-house administrative staff moves from show to show, such as production managers, GMs, and marketing and legal services. The artistic talent is hired outside the corporation for each Broadway show. Disney is such a huge organization that there is a support system in place which can bring immense resources to each show. Although a show can close on Broadway, if it is known there would be touring companies after Broadway, the schedule and staffing is built into the original budget. Some people can work on one Disney production for several years.

Interestingly enough, not long ago, the president of Disney's theatrical division became chairman of the board of the Broadway League, which could be an indication Disney may eventually agree to abide by the Broadway League's negotiated contracts.

Also in the last few years, the three major theatre owner entities—Shubert, Nederlander, and Jujamcyn—have also, at times, taken the lead in producing a show, especially if it will be booked into one of their theatres. The theatre owners have even started having an in-house department specifically to develop shows as well for just this purpose.

2

Production Management Company

Production Manager

When productions were simpler, the production master carpenter oversaw the physical aspects of construction of the stage set and supervised the load-in of the set onto the stage. That job evolved into the technical director's (TD's) job. The invasion of big British musicals like *Phantom*, *Cats*, and *Les Misérables* to Broadway in the late 1980s to early 1990s brought the production manager (PM). American dance and opera already used PMs, but theatre did not. While the British transfers hired PMs, TDs were still prominent in Broadway productions.

As the entire Broadway production structure increased, the TD position expanded to incorporate budgeting, financial elements, and part of the general manager's (GM's) duties. That led to the TDs referring to themselves as PMs, which evolved into production management companies. There are a handful of companies that specialize in this area for Broadway productions and a few owned by women. The company is usually hired by the GM of the production unless a producer makes a personal request.

The responsibilities for a production management company have grown exponentially. Their staff can be as many as twelve employees, some of whom are PMs, some associate PMs, and

7

assistant PMs. Plus there is a support staff including interns and office staff. The production management company grew out of the need to generate a more consistent income, instead of one show with a sporadic pre-production schedule. By enlarging the staff, a production management company can manage two or three shows at once that are in various production stages and handle the massive amount of paperwork for each.

The PMs assigned to a show prefer to be part of the production from the very beginning so that technical issues can be discussed and dealt with early in the process. When production management companies are brought onto a production, the first thing they do is write the production calendar, which lists dates when and where everyone on the technical side of the production must be. They figure out the technical budget, prepare pink contracts (production contracts) for and hire the production stagehands, liaise with the union, order and organize trucking, and plan the load-in and load-out schedule.

The PM assigned to a show is the hands-on person overseeing the technical details of the show. On a play, there can be a PM and an intern. On a musical, it can be a company principal, a PM, an associate PM, and an intern. An intern position is an opportunity for a novice to be exposed to professional theatre and meet people. Interns work long hours for very little money, but some companies pay an intern a modest stipend to help living in New York City.

Prep

When developing a Broadway show there is never one rule for anything. Most shows start with several readings, then workshops with minimal sets, and tryouts at a regional theatre with the intent of transferring it to New York. The Globe Theatre and La Jolla Playhouse in California have been tryout destinations for several Broadway shows, also Off-Broadway. Although each tryout theatre has its own production staff, the Broadway production management company has a supervisory presence to consult on concerns that could impinge on the Broadway production (i.e., how set pieces are used or how they will function in the Broadway house).

Once a show is Broadway bound, the prep time on a play can be four months *before* it moves to the theatre and a musical can be several months. If a play is a star vehicle, it is usually a limited run. A musical is often open-ended. One PM worked on *Shrek* for three years before it ever got to a theatre, and *The Book of Mormon* took nine months.

Production prep time is not necessarily full time. The PM receives some payment for prep time, but the work is sporadic until the show nears a full Broadway production.

The set designer produces many drawings and a model which are used in the scene shop bidding process. At the same time, the PM and the set designer consult with the lighting and sound designers for their concerns. Once the drawings are approved by the GM/producer, the production management company takes the set drawings and creates a set of technical drawings with building specifications. After collecting the shop bids, the production management company creates a spread-sheet for bid comparisons, which is given to the producer and the GM.

Set Production—Offsite Shops

Scene Shop

Scenery is built at independent offsite scene shops. The set designer, associate designer, and the PM visit the scene shop frequently, supervising every step of construction to avoid mistakes. Each shop has a reputation for a specific specialty (i.e., general construction, mechanical expertise, painting). (The bidding process is discussed in the set design section.)

Once the show is awarded to a scene shop, there is a "kick-off" meeting. The set designer, PM, and scene shop representative sit down and go through *every* piece of scenery in the show. There are pages and pages of set drawings. The technical drawings specify how every piece of scenery is to be built and broken down. Each item is explicitly discussed, negotiated, and agreed upon. The budget is at the forefront. This is a very long session and takes hours or days.

The PM writes the *text* for the technical (construction) drawings. The written text describes how the PM would like the particular pieces of scenery built, what materials to use, how the pieces are broken up for shipment to the theatre, and how they will be installed. The shop draws information from that text as they proceed to build the set.

Then the shop creates the *technical* drawings for the set. Upon completion of the drawings, the PM reviews them for accuracy and for any needed changes, and has more discussions with the designer. Any changes are reviewed again before anything is put forward for construction. The PM also participates in the bid process for sound and lighting as well.

Broadway stages are relatively small, so sets are constructed in sections then assembled once loaded onstage. Gene O'Donovan, who founded Aurora (a well-established production management company), was introduced to the magic of theatre by accident:

> A friend asked me if I wanted to work at a scene shop loading trucks. We [three friends] all went out and loaded the trucks. I had never even thought about the scenery business before, much less theatre. When I got there, I just thought it was magical, even though I was loading trucks. If you've never seen a piece of scenery before, how it comes apart, how it's put back together again, or what the process is, it's a wonder. I was just really engaged by it. That *was* the beginning for me.

To complete the construction of the set and before it is delivered to the theatre, the scene shop marks the back of every piece of the set with a code. It is sort of a puzzle to guide the stagehands in assembling the pieces onstage. These markings must absolutely be accurate or the setup onstage is chaos.

Another element in set design is referred to as "*soft goods*"—curtains for windows, drapes, or proscenium curtains (the curtain you see from the house). These items are supervised by the designer and/or the associate and the PM, but they are fabricated in a different shop. If these items require paint to complete the design, they are painted in the scene shop.

Scene Shop Carpenters

Most Broadway sets are built because it is more cost-effective for a long run of eight shows a week. A limited-run play might rent specialty items like a hospital bed. The budget governs these decisions.

In the past, scenic painters painted moldings, arches, brick walls, and windows. Modern advances in stage lighting can reveal that kind of detail as fake. So the trend on Broadway is using *real* materials and *real* wood in the construction of the sets. Real concrete has been poured in theatres. Scene shop carpenters build anything that needs to be built, including flats, which mask the immediate back and sides of the stage and then stretch canvas over them.

Scene Shop Painters

Once the set is built, the shop scenic painters add depth and color to the completed set pieces. The painter follows the designer's set drawings to create the effects desired, whether atmospheric, translucent, gauzy, or a seedy interior. Many shop painters studied fine art and know an infinite variety of tricks and techniques to produce those effects. A thorough discussion of scene painting is in the set designer segment.

When the set is delivered to the theatre and installed on-stage, the scene painter might touch up the set before opening night. Producers do that sparingly because of the expense.

Production and House Stagehands

Stagehands are the technical people who work behind the curtain before, during, and after a performance. The stage craft union governing Broadway is Local One under the International Alliance of Theatrical Stage Employees (IATSE) umbrella. The two Broadway organizations that have complex contracts with

Local One are the Broadway League and Disney. Each has strict requirements and rules. The whole process of who and who does not get hired is mired in these contracts.

Broadway is one of the entities under Local One jurisdiction. Everyone working in a Broadway house must be in a union. A show would not get onstage without stagehands. However, there is a delicate interaction between the show producer/GM and the theatre owners regarding stagehands.

A Broadway theatre comes with a *house crew* (head carpenter, head electrician, and head props person, and sometimes a flyman) hired by the theatre owner. They are considered the *local* crew. The house heads hire the additional crew to install and run the show.

The show/producer has the right to hire the *production* stagehands or pink contracts, but those hires are *not* part of the local house crew. They are *supervisors* of the local crew. However, there is *always* a house head in each department (carpenter, props, electrician). The house heads hire the crew (based on the needs of the show and the number requested by the PM) to install and run the show under the supervision of the pink contract (production) crew, and there are different contracts for the production and house crews with two different pay scales.

Depending on the type of show (play or musical), the number of pink contracts can be larger or smaller. A musical can have seven or eight pink contract positions, and a play can have four. It is the PM who basically distributes those pink contracts according to the needs of the show. It can include the carpenter, the props head, the electrician, the deck automation operator, the deck Audio 2, and first line spot, among others. All the hires must be approved by the GM/producer.

In addition, the PM is in charge of not only managing the entire technical staff and overseeing equipment, but they also are responsible for maintaining the crew levels (i.e., replacements) and backup crews and training new crew members in the job they are replacing. Likewise, each pink contract must have a backup counterpart for emergencies.

Although most flying scenery on a show is automated today, the position of flyman is written into a show contract whether there are flying pieces or not. If there are flying pieces that person is a *house* flyman and one of the *house* crew heads. A flyman handles scenery that is lowered to the stage from the air space above the stage and then returns that scenery piece back to that space when not needed. Today some plays have morphed from stand-alone sets to "mini" musicals. On a musical there is *always* a house flyman.

If there are no flying pieces, then that flyman can be moved to another department. On most musicals, the fly automation operator is a pink contract. If the house head is capable of doing the job of a pink contract, the GM/producer can designate that person to do the job (without a pink contract) which reduces the number of production pink contracts. That recommendation is made by the PM.

The house crew and their hires are paid by the theatre owner and reimbursed by the production. The pink contracts are negotiated by the PM usually with conversations among the crew, PM, and GM, and are paid directly by the production. Salaries can slightly vary between shows.

The house electrician is strictly limited to one or two cues during the show, because their primary responsibility is anything electrical affecting the theatre itself. The house electrician cannot have cues if something happens in the theatre. If more than the house electrician is required for the show, the production must hire more electricians. Succinctly, the running crew is the keeper of the theatre and preps, cleans, maintains the house, and protects that physical space, but they also can work the run of the show.

Once the production is working in the theatre, at the end of the day it is the responsibility of both the house stagehands and the pink contracts to make sure all equipment is cleaned up, props are put away, and the theatre is left in an organized manner for the next day. However, it is the pink contracts who make sure it all happens as it should. One could look at it as housekeeping, but it is also a safety and legal issue because there are so many departments and people working in the theatre at any given time. Working backstage is hazardous.

Formerly the pathway for joining Local One was arduous, but it has improved over the years. A stagehand can be a member of another local in another state which gets them into the union, but not necessarily Local One, which is specifically for Broadway. Now a person can get into Local One by either becoming an apprentice or by getting on the organizational list by working in a Local One jurisdiction (television, theatre, events, The Met Opera, Lincoln Center, 92nd Y) for a few consecutive years.

There is a room called the Replacement Room at the union where each morning stagehands show up and as calls from production offices for day work come in the union sends people out. Some days are busy, and some days are not. However, it is a way to get work, make money, and get onto the union list.

The Load-In

Once the sets are completed, they are trucked to the theatre. As previously mentioned, the production management company initially had created the calendar schedule for the entire process for when the set should be finished, when the set is to be delivered, when the set is to be moved into the theatre, the order in which and how it is set up on the stage, the timing of the setup, and how many people are required. The reverse is true when the show's run ends.

The production management company also organizes the load-in staff. The union contract designates a minimum of seventeen people for a musical and fourteen for a play. The number depends on the complexity of the show. The production management company determines to which department those hires are assigned.

When the big job of set load-in and setup begins, it can take three weeks for a play and one getting ready for the cast. The extra week can be used for a dry tech to see how set changes happen before actors are onstage. For a musical it can be a month and a half to three months, depending on the size of the show.

Production and house stagehands unload the pieces onto the sidewalk, move them inside, and pile them on the stage.

When you are in the Broadway theatre district, you often see stagehands loading or unloading a set. They also seem to be idly waiting around, but sometimes their day runs from eight in the morning to midnight. They have an eight-hour minimum and overtime as needed. If the production is large enough, the PM, in conjunction with the pink contract heads, will inform the house heads when additional stagehands are needed. The house heads will hire the additional crew who are temporary hires.

Once all the set pieces are loaded onstage, the stage crew follows those code markings on the back of the set pieces to assemble the set. This takes hours and a lot of coordination. After the set and furniture are in place, stagehands spike the stage, meaning they put plain or glow tape (phosphorescent tape) on the stage floor to mark where the furniture is to be placed for each scene during the performance, which is often when the lights are low. It is also a guide for an actor to find their mark onstage.

Technology, automation, and money have transformed the art of stagecraft. In the past, a production had as many men as were required to make the largest move in a show. Now a production tries to have as small a crew as possible. Today very large heavy moves are mechanized. Motors can lift a nine-thousand-pound piece of scenery, and this mechanization has introduced another job category of theatrical engineers. An "engineer" is not a member of the union. The engineer is either from an outside engineering company or someone in a shop who is a licensed engineer. Not every piece of scenery requires an engineer's stamp. The PM will have noted which pieces of scenery need certification on the technical specifications at the bids. Again, this is a legal and safety requirement.

Before the cast moves to the theatre, the entire crew has a dry tech where they run through all the set, sound, and light changes for the show to minimize any glitches.

Cast Move to Theatre

From the prep time to the load-in to the theatre to the time when the cast comes onstage, the PM has been the boss of the theatre site and the production stage manager the boss of the offsite rehearsal site. Their parallel tracks of autonomy reverse. When the cast moves to the theatre, the PM takes on a support position supervising the entire stage crew and the production stage manager runs the entire production.

When the cast moves to the theatre, the producer can buy a number of ten out of twelve-hour days, which involves cast and crew. The technical crew arrives at the theatre around eight o'clock in the morning to work before the cast arrives for a half-hour call at 12:30 and continue until the evening. If anything technical needs adjusting, the crew is present. After rehearsal for the day, the director gives cast notes and the PM gives crew notes. This continues until the production opens.

Before previews begin with an audience, there is the real tech rehearsal where the cast is in costumes and makeup, and the entire production runs through the show from top to bottom until the show runs smoothly. This can take weeks for a large musical.

When the show opens, the PM is no longer needed on a daily basis, but their job is not over. The production management company is still responsible for the correct running of the show and for the maintenance of any technical issues in all departments every performance. As mentioned earlier, the PM oversees crew replacements and handles stagehand union problems.

Load-Out and Recycling Show Sets

In the past when the entire set was broken down and dismantled, it would take all night and was called "strike night." Today it is called load-out and can take weeks. Load-out is supervised by the production management company in dismantling and restoring the theatre to its original condition when the production arrived. For example, in the run of the musical *Matilda*, the orchestra was not in the pit but in the theatre basement. The stagehands had to build the orchestra room, make sure it was ventilated, air conditioned, and heated. When the run ended, the orchestra room was dismantled and returned to its original condition. A hole had been cut into the stage floor, so the stage had to be repaired. When a new production enters a theatre, it is completely empty, and that is how it must be when the production leaves.

Over the last twenty years, the concept of conserving or recycling has become part of the Broadway scene. For a producer to retain sets without the possibility of another production is financially prohibitive. Formerly after load-out, unused set pieces were heaped onto a truck, shipped to Secaucus, New Jersey, and thrown into a landfill.

Today, a producer sometimes stores a set if other productions are planned. There is a huge place in Orange, Connecticut, called Eagle Storage where many truckloads of old Broadway shows are stored. If it turns out there is no tour, the producer will either rent it or sell it to other theatre companies. With *Spamalot*, the producers knew they were going to have several companies, so the sets were stored and eventually sold to a theatre in Maine.

When sets are not saved, there is now an organization for recycling sets called the Broadway Green Initiative. The producer directs the production management company to oversee the disposal process. Today almost 85 percent of the material goes to a recycling center and gets reused. This is a much smarter way to use those materials.

3

Sets

Set Designer

When the curtain goes up, what the audience sees onstage is the result of the set designer's vision executed by many people. Since the early twentieth century, set design has become an increasingly important component of a play's production. The set designer's job is to create a "home" for the play or musical to further the script's story, time, and place. That "home" is where the actors live during the performance.

Although universities and colleges have excellent theatre programs, a set designer can come to their profession from studying painting, architecture, or even English literature. Internships in community and regional theatres offer opportunities for a young set designer to apply and develop their skills.

The set designer is one of the main creative engines for a production and is hired by the producer early in a production usually after the director. The call can come through their agent, the producer, or the director. The set designer for Broadway must be a member of Local 829, United Scenic Artists, which is under the umbrella of International Alliance of Theatrical Stage Employees. The union specifies a minimum prep time for a set designer of six weeks for a play and two months for a musical, but for Broadway it can take longer.

All set designers work with a design associate who is also a member of Local 829. The associate is recommended by the designer and paid by the production on a weekly basis. The associate designer is the designer's right-hand person and basically helps execute and represent the design when the designer is engaged with other members of the production.

Once hired, the set designer reads the script and meets with the director, producer, and general manager, who explain the production's overview, the dates involved, and the budget allowance. The budget framework is crucial for the set designer to avoid wasted hours and creative effort on ideas that are not feasible.

Initially, the set designer's primary interaction is with the director, whose time is finite. These meetings are limited yet intensely valued by the set designer. The director presents their thoughts about the production, as well as some insights into the author's intent.

Once the job is confirmed, the designer rereads the script with attention to the set needs and the directorial concept. Usually, a script dictates specific design elements such as period, time, place, a character's look, and age. Sometimes there are no stage directions, so the designer prepares a list of questions to discuss with the director. Although the script usually establishes parameters and the director has a vision, it is the set designer's imagination (together with other department designers) that creates an overall visual concept for the production. This concept can include the color scheme that affects the mood, costumes, and lights.

It is important to remember that the theatre stage is an empty vessel. The script is words on paper and director's ideas are in their mind, but a stage set physically exists, must be appropriate for the play or musical, and must function practically for all participants in the production in front of and behind the curtain. The more information the designer can obtain in advance, the better they can do the job.

John Lee Beatty mentioned that when he was working on *Time Stands Still*, he attended a reading at which he heard Laura Linney read her part and when he left he knew what the scenery should look like. He "sort of nailed the look from listening to her voice." It also helps if the playwright can articulate what is *in* their head to the designer, because words can mean different things to two people. When working on Lanford Wilson's *Talley's Folly*, Mr. Beatty said, "[Wilson] said, 'moonlight through broken shutters' and that was about it. That was a great set description, and the show *WAS* [sic] like 'moonlight through broken shutters.'"

Broadway theatres are a hundred years old. The house and lobby areas have been restored, renovated, or updated but the stage, backstage, and orchestra pit usually have not. Stage dimensions are an integral element in set design, and most Broadway theatres are consistent in size. The prosceniums are usually between thirty-six to forty-feet wide with a twenty-seven to thirty-foot depth. That is a relatively small workspace. Some stages are even smaller and are most appropriate for intimate plays. The St. James Theatre until recently had a depth of far less than thirty feet, yet the big, flamboyant original productions of *Oklahoma!*, *Hello Dolly*, and *The King and I* all played there.

In the past when out-of-town tryouts were the norm, the production did not always know for which Broadway theatre it was destined. One designer used a smaller sketch pad for his design floor plans figuring the set would fit into a Broadway house when it transferred. If a design did not fit, it could require alterations and additional expense. Today the Broadway theatre is usually predetermined, so designers can design accordingly.

One of the creative challenges for the Broadway set designer and the shop builders is how to make lavish plays or musicals work in such small spaces. On a large Las Vegas stage, the *Titanic* (the ship) can easily roll downstage in one piece. For Broadway, scenery is built in small sections and then reassembled onstage like a puzzle. The set designer understands the theatre's stage size and that they will start with a *totally empty* stage.

After consulting with the director, the designer begins the *preliminary* sketches, which generally define the acting area, backstage area, and storage space for furniture and props. These drawings include everything that appears onstage that is not costumes, lighting, or sound. The drawings must be as accurate as they can be up to that point in the production process.

During this preliminary period, the designer confers with several departments. The lighting designer is concerned with the practicals (lights that are fixed on scenery) and how much space lighting is going to have or *not* have. The sound designer needs to know where the speakers can be placed, if there is room to hide them, or if there will be a conflict with the lighting rig. The set designer shares the set color scheme with the costume designer and lighting designer so there is color cohesion for the production. The set designer works with the props department, which joins the production early as well.

The production management company assigns a production manager to the show who meets with the designer early and is responsible for monitoring the technical aspects of the set design. If a design idea is unworkable, the production manager helps find a solution.

As with absolutely everything involved in a Broadway production, during the entire set process there are *many* revisions before approval is given. After a final design review by the director, author, and general manager/producer that works for all relevant departments, the set design is approved.

Now the set designer drafts a set of *final* drawings for *everything* that appears onstage, aided by the associate. In addition, the design staff makes a three-dimensional cardboard or cutout model following the ground plan of the set. A ground plan is the set design shown from a bird's-eye view with all the flats and set pieces in place in correct scale on the stage. Accuracy is key because once the bid is awarded to a shop and building begins, mistakes can require a change order costing added expense and revisiting the entire approval process again. All this material is provided to the shop reps at the bidding sessions and are legally important. Set designer John Lee Beatty said final set drawings need to include:

> Every bit of scenery, props, masking fabric, and every little step to get on and off the acting area. When doing a Broadway show, you are renting a piece of real estate from the front of

the stage to a back wall. Sometimes you do not get a working house curtain or the pipes on which to hang the scenery. Everything that appears on that stage that is not a costume, lighting, or sound is scenery. I must make sure I've drawn and anticipated everything because when we go into the bid process with six or seven shops competing, everything has to be on those drawings or there are cost consequences.

After final approval, the production management company takes the designer's drawings and writes a set of technical specifications as to how each piece of scenery must be built, how it must go together and come apart, and how it must function once it is in the theatre.

The incorporation of computers into theatre design was inevitable, but it is a huge aid to visualize the set. The increased sophistication of the software programs can animate how set pieces move in and out of a scene. The development of three-dimensional printing can create miniature furniture to dress the set model, as well as build the scale scenery itself, which enhances the design presentation to other production departments.

In addition to computers, technological advances in theatre assist a set designer in creating more spectacular sets. With the proliferation of movies becoming Broadway plays or musicals, the audience is more visually aware and anticipates key movie elements to be reproduced onstage. This is all still evolving.

After all the materials are completed, the next step is the bidding process. The sketches, model, and a complete set of design drawings are presented to the six or seven scene shop companies who bid on the job. The shops take all the material away for about a week and return with their estimate. If all bids come in and the price is too high, there can be negotiations and/or adjustments to the design to fit the budget. Legally, all parties must agree on which shop is going to build the set.

There are many factors that go into the decision of awarding contracts. For example, scene shops, like actors, have different talents and one shop can be known for mechanical or carpentry skills, while another is better for painting.

When the bids come in, several days pass while the general manager/producer, the designer, and the production manager review them. Previously, most scene shops were located in New York City or in New Jersey, but due to the real estate boom, shops have moved further and further away. A show could be built in Calgary, Alberta, Canada; another show could be built in and transferred from Australia.

After the bid is awarded, there is something called the "kick-off" meeting, where the set designer, the shop representative, and the production manager sit down and reaffirm what was agreed to in the bid. This is a legal issue and can take hours. Every piece of scenery is scrutinized as to how it is to be built, how it is broken down for transport, and what the load-in order of each piece is. With such limited stage space, the wrong load-in sequence can cost the show many thousands of dollars.

The set designer, the associate, and the production manager frequently visit the scene shop to observe the work and give notes. Visits are usually more frequent on a musical than on a drama because there can be as many as twenty set pieces in a musical versus three for a drama. Whether a designer is more hands-on or relies on their associate, set construction is followed very closely for adherence to the designer's vision.

Occasionally changes to the set design can occur after the bidding process has been approved. It can be caused by the designer forgetting something in their drawings or during rehearsal there is a change in a scene. Suddenly the designer is told that a scene has been moved from indoors to outside, or a railing is required that affects the set design. Then the designer must go through the entire process of drawing the railing, submitting it for a bid, and getting the producer's approval for the additional cost. That is when the producer's contingency budget (money set aside for such emergencies) is used. This is rare but, as mentioned, adaptability is necessary.

Even with the advancement of technology, it cannot replace human experience and imagination. Aside from knowing the stage environment, an experienced Broadway set designer understands how something onstage looks from the audience's perspective. Matt Hodges, a former props designer, gives an example:

We were doing a show where it took place in a mansion in the Hollywood Hills overlooking Los Angeles in the 1950's. John Lee [Beatty] said, "Outside the windows why don't we get those little LED Christmas trees and put them sideways, strap them to the back railing, and it will look like the cityscape." And we're like, "Ok?" So we ordered 10 of the LED Christmas trees, put them up sideways, and it looked like nothing. Then we went into the audience and saw all those little points of light, and it looked like the distant Hollywood Hills. In the context our imagination takes over and that's the magic of theatre, right?

Even with computers, the "art" in theatrical design and painting has not entirely diminished. Some designers still produce their original hand-painted renderings in watercolors, which can be fed into the computer by the associate. Younger designers often create their renderings in the computer. However, what really attracts a set designer to live theatre is that they can draw their idea, see it come alive onstage, and have it seen by a large audience.

In addition to the set, the set designer is responsible for the props department and all the props used in the production. Where previously rehearsals used folding chairs and imaginary furniture, today a simulated set with real furniture is often created for the actors. Some props are purchased in duplicate to facilitate the rehearsal, for example a bookcase with books. This allows the actors and director to experiment with staging, timing, and scene changes.

The set designer observes early rehearsals to see what needs to be adjusted. The associate designer takes notes of any changes that affect the set design or props. As John Lee Beatty explains:

When I observe a rehearsal and watch an actor stumble over a chair, I might suggest a footstool instead. Or the size of a chair may not work for the actor. Can the actor get out of the chair easily or does the scale of the chair work for the actor? Once with Rosemary Harris I brought in three appropriate chairs and had her sit in all three to see how she looked. She caught on, and really got into how she could turn, sit down, get up in each version.

The designer goes to the final rehearsal run-through to track any last-minute changes, because the set must be ready when the actors move to the theatre the next day. Items that were not needed in rehearsal, like props such as ivy, draperies, and pictures, can be pre-dressed onstage before the actors arrive. The actual props used in rehearsal are moved to the theatre quickly.

While the actors are still rehearsing, the shop is completing the scenery construction. The set designer's goal is to approve all scenery *before* it leaves the shop for delivery. Prior to load-in is what is called the pre-hang, which involves hanging intricate hardware or spotting lines to hang the scenery a certain way before the completed set is loaded-in.

Following the pre-hang comes the load-in (in England it's called a put-in). In the 1980s, a load-in for a play was two days with everything set on the stage. Now productions are more sophisticated and complicated, a load-in can be two weeks for a play or more for a musical. The set designer and/or the associate are present for the load-in to resolve any issues or problems that crop up, like doors not opening or closing properly.

After the load-in and installation of all the scenery, there is the dry tech, where all the departments run through the play without the actors to practice the technical aspects of the show such as the set transitions, lighting cues, sound cues, and the timing of computerized wenches if any are being used for set pieces. This activity means hopefully only one long day for the entire stage crew and the designers often starting at eight in the morning and going until 11 PM or midnight.

The first day the actors are onstage is very difficult because, as Mr. Beatty says, "that is when fantasy and reality collide, and you find out which things are going to work, need to be adapted, or are just *not* going to work." There is a semi-tech rehearsal to check actors' positions, their spacing (which needs adjustment after being in a rehearsal room), and potential problems. Then prior to audience previews, there is the *real* tech rehearsal period. This is when the actors, lighting, sound, costumes, makeup, scenery, orchestra, and props people try to go through the show until they get it right. A complicated musical can be in tech for one or two months and a play for up to two weeks. As tweaking is still going on with the show, it can be a period of utter mayhem and exhaustion. But all this effort goes into making certain the show runs smoothly.

Scenic Painters

There is a rich history in scenic painting from the time when moldings, balustrades, paneling, and brick walls were painted on scenery. Advances in lighting technology have made some illusions look fake. Most of today's scenery is built, but painting is still an indispensable element of set design.

Many scenic shop painters come from a fine arts background and are fine artists in their own right. They have knowledge in three-dimensional skills such as sculpting, plastering, and gilding, and certainly know all types of paint such as pigments, acrylic, oil, and tempera. Colors are mixed to match the colors specified by the designer. The palette can be bold and bright for a musical or dark and mysterious for a drama, or vice versa.

Some set designers prefer certain scene shops and their painters because the designer knows the artists understand their artwork. The set designer has chosen the set color schemes and approves the work of the shop painters. Seasoned designers are well versed in the subtleties of paint. If they want the backdrop to look more Monet than Manet, they can communicate with the shop painter as to how to achieve that effect.

Arnold Abramson of Nolan Studios was a legendary scenic artist. He taught at Yale and ran the best paint shop on Broadway in his time. John Lee Beatty recalls when working as a scenic artist:

> As a scenic painter I was allowed to work on Raoul Pene Du Bois drops but I wasn't allowed to paint on Oliver Smith drops, which I would have loved to have done. There were people who painted Oliver Smith shows and they knew how to interpret his little, unbelievably beautiful watercolors. Sometimes he would do just a little squiggle here, a little bit of paint, and they would have to interpret the rest, but they could do it in his style. I mean you really need to get into the head

of what he [the designer] wants and not necessarily *exactly* what he painted. Back then when I did a Du Bois drop, I was having trouble mixing the colors right. Another painter who had done other Du Bois shows told me a secret of how to mix the colors perfectly. There are secrets and tricks, but that paint world is not nearly as important now because you have more built scenery, the lighting got brighter, and you couldn't hide illusions as easily.

Today another technological advance is a set designer can design and paint watercolors for backdrops, have them scanned into the computer, adapted, and then printed on a very large format printer! So although some art gets lost, other art evolves.

In production, the set designer's department initially experiences the problems, but as onstage rehearsals progress, problems move on to lighting and costumes. Eventually every department experiences the hot seat. Alas, sound is in that position last!

Associate Set Designer

An associate set designer is the designer's right-hand person. According to Evan Adamson, an associate on Broadway, "There is no guidebook as to what it means to be an associate. The role and duties will vary based on the project and designer with whom the associate is working."

Each set designer has a different approach to the creative process and style of working. An associate should possess a wide range of abilities in order to complement those different work styles. Some designers closely incorporate the associate in the creative process from the beginning of the design process. The relationship between the designer and associate fluctuates based on the needs of the production, schedules, and current project. Whatever the relationship, the primary responsibility of the associate is always to support the set designer and oversee the implementation of the design. Often the associate will need to represent the designer and make design choices when the designer is not present.

Associates commonly have studied scenic design or fine arts in college. Prior to the early 2000s, the design process was completely analog, using hand-drawing, hand-painting, and hand-sculpting techniques. These crafts are still practiced and utilized, but today's younger generation of designers also rely heavily on digital design tools, as computers have become mainstream. Set design abounds in many media, but the storytelling and the immediate audience reaction in live theatre is ever the rewarding end product, regardless of the tools used in the process. As Evan Adamson said, "I'm always thinking, throughout the process, that the drawings and models are all going to materialize in three dimensions and that motivates my work and commitment to the process. Specifically, the arc of a design going from a piece of paper to a three-dimensional structure on stage is thrilling."

Many Broadway associates are set designers themselves and work in regional theatres, community theatres, and other venues throughout the country. They are members of the United Scenic Artists Union, Local 829. It is the same union for film, television, theatre, and events and falls under the International Alliance of

Theatrical Stage Employees umbrella. This same union covers regional theatres and other forms of live entertainment. In the past there was a testing regimen for joining, but today the union has instituted an apprentice program.

The associate set designer is appointed to the position by the designer; however, they are technically hired and paid by the production. The set design associate on Broadway is contracted for a certain number of weeks, which can vary based on the size and scope of each production. The number of weeks they are paid for is often less than the number of calendar weeks listed in the schedule. Payments begin when their work commences.

Ideally the associate is brought in early to begin their collaboration with the designer and attend initial meetings with the director to become familiar with the creative discussions and production objectives. This type of pre-production work can be irregularly scheduled and spread out over time, which allows for ideas to gestate and evolve.

During pre-production, before cast rehearsals begin, the associate's time and duties change intermittently based on the production's needs and schedule. This pre-production period can span several months, requiring a day or two in one week and six days in another week. If the design process continues over the course of several months (or even years), the associate often takes on other projects they work on concurrently. Consequently, an associate often is involved with three or four shows simultaneously, all of which can be with different designers. Collectively, this provides them with a steady income and builds their reputation and credits.

A young scenic design graduate has several avenues to gain experience and start their career: working as an apprentice at a regional theatre, an internship at a design studio, or creating their own designs for smaller scale productions. These scenarios provide opportunities to learn the professional and business aspects of theatre design, make contacts, refine their skill set, and have their talents noticed.

Once officially joining the production, the associate's work begins in earnest. Working closely with the designer from the beginning allows the associate to have an intimate understanding of the designer's goals and what the other production departments need. In the late 1990s and early 2000s, computers became more commonly used in the Broadway design process. Today, they are the norm and expected. Design sketches and renderings, architectural drawings, and digital crafted models are all examples of materials that the associate set designer can provide and develop. It is important that the associate stays up to date with the ever-evolving technological advancements, such as upgraded software programs and applications.

Despite the critical role of computers, there is still a strong reliance and practical use of hand-drawing, hand-painting, and model making in the design process. When drawing initial scenic sketches, the set designer draws at a drafting table where the scale is small, the pace is quick, and the outcome is expressive. Working with and understanding scale is an essential part of every designer's process. In the beginning, drawings can be hand-drawn in a small scale, for example, a quarter inch equals a foot. As the design progresses and evolves, the associate converts the hand-drawn information into a digitized format, using various computer applications. Through this workflow, the drawings become more clarified and the scale is enlarged to a half inch equals a foot. This enlargement and refinement improves precision and makes interpreting this information easier for the shops when fabricating the scenery.

Throughout this process, it is important that the associate preserves the *intentions* of the design. Color, scale, and composition are integral factors of every design, and their preservation is paramount regardless of whether design is created by hand or computer.

Relatively recently, three-dimensional printing has become an alternative approach to model making. This technology continues to improve but the turnaround time is rather slow, considering the pace of the design process for Broadway, where meetings and presentations can occur daily. As three-dimensional printing evolves, hand-crafted models remain an essential skill and important means in the design process. Evan Adamson recalled:

Having a background in fine arts, when I was starting my
career, I initially approached the computer skills of set design
with a very hands-off attitude. I was more comfortable using
my hands to paint, sculpt, and draw. Once I saw the power
and benefit of the computer programs and how 3-D modeling
and printing could be used, I adapted and added those tools
to my skill set. It's important to be well-versed in both hand-
crafted and digitally generated methods.

As mentioned under the set designer section, a physical set
model is still part of the process and is used in meetings. With
computers, a digital three-dimensional model of the set can
be made and viewed on a computer and it can also be printed
and made into a physical model. In addition, the digital three-
dimensional models can be used for animation. An associate can
make animated pre-visualizations illustrating what the set will
look like, how the set pieces move onstage, and how the sets
turn around or open up. The digitized model can demonstrate
how a scene transitions from one scene to the next, which is ex-
traordinarily beneficial for a director to see and that can affect
their direction: "Oh, I see that's going to fly up and that's going
to zip down into the floor."

The digitized three-dimensional models became a lifeline for
theatre design during COVID-19 when everyone was in lock-
down. As design associate for the recent *The Music Man* starring
Hugh Jackman, Mr. Adamson was able to animate the entire
show digitally so that design conversations could continue with
the director and producers. It allowed the design process to
continue when the physical model became valueless because
everyone was forced to work remotely.

Although it is a labor-intensive process, it is an incredibly
helpful tool for communicating a variety of things to the design
and directing teams. Being informed in advance of what are essentially ideas at this phase gives everyone in the production
the advantage of experiencing those ideas virtually before the
set is built and installed in the theatre. It saves money, time, and
ultimately serves the production in ways that are different from
a physical model.

The associate attends rehearsals, visits the scenery fabricators regularly, and converses with all of the other departments, essentially becoming a "keeper of all information," much like a script supervisor on a movie. They record any directional changes or physical conflicts that can affect the set. If the company is in the theatre for only four weeks and suddenly a set piece has an issue, the shop must be contacted to assess and determine if changes can be incorporated. As much as possible, the associate tries to keep adjustments within the approved budget and avoid any added cost. If requests are made that are major and require additional expense, the designer, producer, and general manager are contacted and a creative and budget discussion ensues for approval before proceeding.

Producing scenery is a monumental process from design to construction, requiring the efforts of many people who rely on each other to make sure the result is correct. The designer, the associate, and the production manager independently visit the shops to monitor the set build; however, the associate often spends more time visiting the shops than the designer. The associate oversees the building and painting process, and communicates all progress to the designer. The production manager is responsible for making sure the finished set meets the technical specifications and is within budget. Once the set leaves the shops, there is considerably less room for error and adjustments.

When the shop work is completed, the set is transported to the theatre for load-in, and the production manager supervises the entire process. The set designer and associate are present to check the set assembly and answer any questions. The days are long, stakes are high, and decision-making and solutions become critical to manage stresses and emotions that are unavoidably present.

The difference between a play and a musical is the same for every department. A drama is typically less complex, having fewer moving parts, and fewer sets or changes.

Many musicals are multifaceted spectacles filled with moving scenery, special effects, and full stage transformations that happen in just a few seconds. Over the course of a two-hour show, the audience might see a dozen or more changes, all of which have been carefully planned and extensively rehearsed in order to look effortless. A musical has more aspects to manage, and the performance is a whirl of activity onstage and backstage.

During technical rehearsals, work is happening in the theatre all day, from 8 AM to midnight, during which the associate and set designer are present. After rehearsal, there is a work notes session for the crew. Each morning the production manager and stage crew implement as many set changes as possible from the previous day's work notes. The cast rehearses during the afternoon and evening, and the technical staff works around them. The designer or associate consults with the director continually to sort out new ideas and changes. The associate relays that information to the production manager and/or the scene shop.

As previews near, the full tech rehearsal occurs where all departments work through the show with the actors, refining and improving the quality of the show with each pass. It is a time to resolve any glitches. This phase can last a few weeks or even months for a large musical. The company tries to complete as many run-throughs before previews start to ensure a smooth show when the audience is present.

With the influx of English production transplants to Broadway, it is usual that the English set designer has an associate designer who is based in the United States. This is a great value to the English set designer, because the associate has a more direct line of communication with the shops and a familiarity with various local processes and practices that are different from the United Kingdom. Once the design is approved for Broadway, the English designer might return to England to work on another production and then return to New York periodically to visit the Broadway production. The associate designer is even more critical to the process when the designer is unavailable or physically absent from the theatre. In that circumstance, the associate designer is responsible for managing the set fabrication, interacting with and answering questions from the shops and other production departments, and constantly communicating with the absent designer. With the time difference, those update conversations can occur at 5 AM New York time (11 AM London time).

The associate designer's job usually ends on opening night. At that time the show is frozen and the artistic and design process is no longer occurring. A rare exception can be if an automated piece of scenery malfunctions during a performance. Automated scenery is scenery not manually pushed or physically operated. Instead, it is driven by motors and computer systems. Some heavy scenery may require an engineer's stamp of approval, and the production manager indicates which ones do on the technical specifications for the bids. Sometimes the engineer can be from an outside company or be a licensed engineer who works in the scene shop. In any event, the designer and the scene shop are brought in as the matter is resolved.

4

Props

Production Props Supervisor

I came from props originally. I think of all the artisan disciplines in theatre or live entertainment, props is a really unique one, because the props people need the skills of everyone. They need to be able to build things out of wood, so they need carpentry skills. Now props make things light up, so they need lighting skills. They need to be able to scenic paint. They need to sew and upholster.

–Jeremy Chernick, special effects designer

The props department of a Broadway show has changed dramatically over the last couple of decades, and it is no longer just teacups and doilies. The job is extensive and encompasses many components. Movie studios and music publishers have found a new revenue stream by putting some of their back catalogs on a Broadway stage. The effect is to whet an audience's appetite for reproducing the spectacle they have seen in film or an arena. In so doing, people who create props for Broadway must be inventive and masters of problem-solving. In addition to building and sourcing, props designer Matt Hodges reflected:

You're styling a show. You're talking about pleats, curtains, color choices, and how to faux finish things. You're making little design choices that are informed by character, period, and style. You might be discussing what is appropriate for 1993 versus 1980. You are involved in very artistic detailed things, but you're also just having to unload the truck, move the couch up the stairs, and track the budget on Excel.

As Peter Sarafin, a production props supervisor, said, "Our industry is one of the toughest jobs and when you find someone who can handle the stress and is good at it, it's a good thing. To be honest, so many young assistants fold. They just can't handle it."

So what are props? Props are everything that is movable onstage and not physically attached to the set. Today the majority of props used on Broadway are either built or bought. Even for a limited run of a show the props may be built rather than rented. To rent something for ten weeks runs up an expensive tab. It becomes less expensive to build something that will endure the wear and tear of eight shows a week for a four-month run. A prop like hospital equipment needs to be rented, but the fee can be negotiated.

Today, as live theatre competes with action movies, there are many areas of props that are produced by separate entities, such as special effects (pyrotechnics) and puppets which, more often than not, the props department physically handles during the show. Puppets are designed, constructed, and delivered to the production, where most often the props department takes care of the day-to-day maintenance and operation of the puppets. Seldom is there a dedicated puppet supervisor on a show because the cost of salary and benefits is prohibitive.

As shows grew bigger, what used to be called the props master (still used in regional theatres) on Broadway is now called the production props supervisor. The production management company is the one who initiates the call to the props supervisor, but the supervisor can be recommended by the set designer or the director. When hired, the props supervisor works under the direction of the set designer but is their own entity. The props supervisor is in daily contact with the set designer and the director, so all three relationships are vital from the very beginning of the production process (readings and workshops). In the past, men dominated the props department, but today the props personnel includes many women.

The production management company wants the prop person to know how to do everything. The supervisor must be an organized person who can run a budget, run a schedule, be imaginative to solve problems, and be artistic in materializing the set designer's vision. The supervisor needs to know how long it will take to build a prop, how much it will cost, who to call to source it if necessary, and to advise management if a duplicate prop is wise to make. In addition to a weird range of skills and a vast amount of information, the props person needs to use Excel and track a budget with a lot of receipts. When all is completed, the supervisor delivers everything to the theatre and works with the crew to get it through tech and ready for the show.

In the past, a props person fell into a gray area. Many props department people were actually non-union and had their own workshop for sourcing or building. Befriending the stage crew helped the non-union props person to complete their tasks on the stage. If feathers were ruffled, the crew could prohibit that props person from touching anything onstage. This placed the non-union props department in a sort of limbo because to work backstage required being a union member.

More recently, a new wave of Broadway designers wanted their prop person to be a designer and be outside with them in the theatre during tech to look at things and not be backstage moving things around. Running the props backstage is an entirely separate complicated job run now by the head of props. The new designers demanded the top props person backstage be a different position; however, the producers were not receptive to hiring and paying benefits for a second person. So the gray area continued.

A few years ago, the Broadway contract for the stagehand union Local One was renegotiated and required that *all* people in the props position be at least in some sort of International

Alliance of Theatrical Stage Employees (IATSE) union. For those prop people, it meant they finally got paid for overtime and gained elusive benefits.

There are several unions a prop person can belong to, but they definitely need a union card to physically touch anything on a Broadway stage. There are many locals throughout the country, but Allied Craftsmen and Technicians is perhaps an easier union to join. Allied Craftsmen and Technicians is a Manhattan-based local under the IATSE umbrella. It was created for people who needed a card on Broadway and covers a wide range of behind-the-scenes employees. To apply, a person needs some credits, a letter of recommendation from a member, and a résumé. Local One, which is specifically for Broadway stage-hands, is perhaps the most difficult to join. No matter the union, to work in a theatre on Broadway one must be part of IATSE.

There is an artistic side to props, depending on the relationship with the set designer. If there is a previous working relationship between the supervisor, set designer, and the director, there is already a certain established trust in their artistic opinion. Often props personnel come from a fine arts or artistic background and can discern the difference between a light fixture from the 1930s and one from the 1920s, which is a real asset for a set designer's vision.

Props people could be called tinkerers or jacks-of-all-trades. They usually have a very broad exposure in many areas, but one invaluable asset they possess is an intuitive skill of how things work, what the designer wants, how to build it, how to make it function, and how to fix it when it breaks.

A props person does a little bit of making and schlepping. Further up the ladder, it is more about managing a team of people across several shops. Once the supervisor is working on a Broadway show with a budget of several thousand dollars, they are not just overseeing. They might do work on little projects as the bigger ones are being built. As Matt Hodges said:

> I feel every prop master still has a little shop where he can still bang something out if he needs to, but the bigger the shop is, the more you're managing a much bigger project than you are

making. I doubt there is anyone who has skipped the process because you have to know *how* to do all those things even if you're not doing it. A lot of times you're not sending the drawing to a shop. You're involved in exactly how the shop is going to build it, making sure they do it the way you as a designer want them to, and ensuring it's delivered properly.

As props became more complicated, in addition to being a person who could source items, the supervisor role evolved into more of a designer of props. The props supervisor takes the set designer's drawing and figures out how to create the prop as a tangible functioning object and designs the technical side of how the prop functions. For most props people, that aspect is the creative fun of the job. Then the supervisor's crew maintains and repairs it during the run.

The props supervisor is not considered a full designer even though they design the set designer's idea. They do not receive a royalty for their creative efforts, but they receive what is called a maintenance fee. Basically, the maintenance fee is a day's pay every week of the run, so if something goes wrong that the crew cannot repair, the supervisor fixes the problem. That can accrue to a month of days over six months and if it takes two or three weeks to repair a prop, that work has been paid for by the maintenance fee. If the damage by use in the show is more extensive, a separate repair bill can be submitted.

One of the major issues for props in a long run is durability. Eight shows a week takes a toll on props. Actors use them, and things get dropped and thrown around. Props are made to be as strong as possible to sustain the abuse a run imposes. One challenge is engineering a prop to be strong without making it heavy. Another challenge is if a show uses perishables. The props department has to judge the amount of food products or drinks to have on hand for a performance.

Every show is different for the props department. A play could be all about antique furniture and styling, another is all foliage, another is special effects, found objects, or everything is specifically built. It is never the same, which is one of the job's attractions.

The props department interacts with *all* the production departments. The supervisor functions as sort of the middle person between the artistic side of the director, the set designer, and the production side (the production company), and everyone who is building or shopping the props.

Once hired, the first thing the props supervisor does is read the script, watch readings, and have discussions with the set designer and director to understand their show concept. The supervisor gathers as much information from the set drawings and models to formulate a props list and discern what are props or parts of the set. The general manager has already prepared the show budget, which includes the cost allotted for props, so the supervisor works with the set designer and the production management company to validate that their budget projections meet the budget allotment. The delivery time frame of any specialty items, like special effects or puppets, must be included in that estimate.

Initially, when the props supervisor joins a Broadway show, they may have an assistant who may or may not be in a union. The assistant mainly does much of the running around outside the theatre during rehearsals, tech rehearsals, and previews. They are essentially the liaison between the props supervisor and the production world at large. It is an important position as it can be a training ground for future props supervisors. If they are not union, once the rehearsal moves to the theatre, they are not allowed to work *in* the theatre and are not part of the stage crew; the position usually ends at opening. Any rehearsal equipment needed is then handled by the head of props, the assistant props (if there is one), or the house props person.

Additionally, the props supervisor recommends the head of props, which is a union position employed by the production and hired on a pink contract. They are beholden to the producers, production manager, and props supervisor. The head of props runs the show and manages its day-to-day maintenance. On a big show, the head of props can have an assistant who is also a union member, hired on a pink contract, and part of the stage crew. The props head may be working in the studio helping build the props and joins the company formally when the production nears load-in to the theatre.

A prop supervisor is sometimes working on another show concurrently, so often the supervisor has worked with whoever is hired as head of props and relies on them to operate backstage props and manage any emergencies during the run. Once the production moves into the theatre, the supervisor oversees the props run crew.

Since props expanded, it is not possible for one or two people to produce all the props for a show, so many props supervisors have their own shop, where they have a team of four or five people who build the props but are paid through the production until the show opens. In that situation, the props supervisor can monitor the props being built while their assistant is acquiring rehearsal props.

The supervisor is also responsible for and oversees the building of any props required for rehearsals. An actual set is not required, but the rehearsal room is marked off with tape indicating rooms or where furniture might go. Other times, especially with big musicals, rolling stair units are necessary for dancers to practice the choreography or kitchen countertops that are integral to scene work are needed. The set department is not involved in building or buying the props.

If the props supervisor does not have a shop, they must have an arsenal of shop sources and be skilled in figuring out who can build the prop, who can deliver on time, who fits into the budget, and who has the right aesthetic for the job, and they must supervise the building process. This is where relationships are essential.

Another quality for a props supervisor is communication, whether they own a shop or source the work out, they must be able to clearly transmit the set designer's wishes and organize the logistics of delivering the item to the theatre. So much is determined on whether things are completed on time and correctly. For example, if the show needs a vintage refrigerator, the props assistant must find one. If it is to be attached to the set, the delivery of the refrigerator to the scene shop weeks ahead so it is fastened to the set and ready for load-in must be guaranteed.

Throughout all of this activity, the props supervisor is in constant communication with the person assigned by the production management company monitoring the budget and expenditures. Once the budget is approved, the production management company either supplies petty cash for small prop items or cuts a check to pay the shop building large or specialty items. The props supervisor is responsible for every penny that is spent and for making good decisions on that spending, and ultimately the management company is accountable to the producers.

Depending on the size of the show and the production timeline, the props department can be working a couple of months on large custom-made items entailing time to design and build. So much money is on the line for Broadway that when there is a concrete decision for a show opening, everything happens fast. Today because of the cost for a Broadway production, everything is compressed and rehearsal schedules that were a month and a half are now often only a month.

Mock-ups of props are used in rehearsal, and the props supervisor holds off finalizing anything, knowing it will change. If a prop needed in specific scene requires time to build, the supervisor can be forced to ask the director to jump ahead to that scene, so the staging can be set early. There is only so much planning that can be done when there are so many moving parts that must be coordinated together. If a custom-made piece is finalized, but on day one of rehearsal there is a change, that change could cost ten thousand dollars, which is a waste of money. Peter Sarafin, who designed props for *Bullets Over Broadway*, said:

> One of the more complicated things we ever made was a Model T Ford for *Bullets Over Broadway* where we took the engine out and put an electric engine in it, made custom gears and the car was actually driven around the stage. I think that was the only prop ever that just worked, never had to mess with it. It was just perfect. But everything else always needs adjustments.

Tech rehearsals are always messy periods in a Broadway production. All the technical crews come together onstage to find out what does or does not work. A speaker juts two inches out further than planned, so now a particular prop is two inches too wide. Even with specific drawings, there is just no way to avoid these issues. It is one reason why it takes weeks in the theatre before previews begin while the crews work from 8 AM to midnight to solve the problems. Items are sent out for repairs in the afternoon and brought back the next morning. This back-and-forth problem-solving repeats for four or more weeks, and somehow it all works, the curtain goes up, and no one knows quite how. It definitely takes a village to bring everything together. It is a very challenging and laborious period.

Plays are generally simpler for props because there are fewer moving parts, but there are other constraints, especially with a period play. Although there are no musical distractions, props assume a stronger significance. Everything is in the details. Actors in a play relate to their props as an integral part of the time, the place, and their character. Actors in a musical relate to their props as well, but they have the added razzle-dazzle of music and dance so the relationship to the prop is not quite as intimate as in a straight play.

In general, musicals have a bigger budget than plays. Some props people prefer musicals because they are more complicated and the problem-solving is more challenging. Others prefer plays because as Matt Hodges said, "They are more realistic. It's like dressing a realistic setting."

The props supervisor's job is usually finished when a show closes. If the show is going on a national tour (first tier) and the original producer is involved, the supervisor will make sure the props are packed correctly and go to the right places. If the supervisor is involved with other projects, they rely on the head of props to handle that process. If time allows, the supervisor will be involved even with a second national tour. However, if a non-union company like Troika buys the prop package, a union supervisor is too expensive for that company, so the supervisor can be hired for a week or two to educate the new show crew how all the props work.

When a show is successful like *The Book of Mormon* or *Hamilton* with multiple tours, a props supervisor can be part of that show for two or three years. Being absent from the Broadway loop for two or three years could make it more difficult to re-enter that loop, but the job is so tough that there are not a lot of people who want to do it.

Sometimes the original supervisor is engaged with other shows, so they will pass the national tour on to a younger associate, giving that person the opportunity to move up the ladder. As far as load-out goes, the supervisor is involved if some things were borrowed from another theatre or rented. Those items have to be sorted and returned in good condition.

If a show is not going on tour, the props are dealt with in two ways. The producer may put everything in storage hoping they can sell the props package to a second-tier tour, but after eight shows a week a lot of it is reduced to garbage. According to props supervisor Peter Sarafin, "Our stage crew has held it together with screws, glue, spit, and gum for two years because a producer doesn't want to pay for something new to be made and it just needs to be trashed."

The same result happens to antiques that were purchased as props. The wear and tear reduces them to rubbish. Matt Hodges said, "It is sad especially when you find wonderful antiques, but I came to the realization that the second I buy it, it's not an antique anymore. It's a prop. The cost of making a gold candlestick that costs $900 is less that the cost of a modern show making one for $3,000." If the supervisor has a shop and a prop is salvageable, it might be given to that supervisor for future use. If there is no life left to the show and everything is going into trash, sometimes the actors, designers, or producers will take things.

Although most props are built by hand and ingenuity, currently computers have a place in props creation on Broadway. Supervisor Peter Sarafin was a fine arts major in college studying painting. He said of his experience at the art school in Ohio that he attended: "They really drove into your head that we were not going to be Picasso and we were forced to learn Photoshop, Illustrator. They emphasized that 99% of us were going to work in some sort of commercial visual art field and we were all mad about it. It was the greatest thing that was ever done for me." Now he uses Photoshop and Illustrator to create paper props, banners, and even artwork. There are other technological developments in the foreseeable future for theatre when pricing reduces, such as CNC (computer numerical router) used for cutting various materials in carpentry, larger printers for three-dimensional printing, and more sophisticated projection capabilities.

Head of Props

The props department on a Broadway show may be the most versatile department in an entire production. It is a combination of tinkering, problem-solving, organizing, multitasking, and imagination. In high school, Austin Rodriguez combined high school with a vocational school that taught theatre technology (lighting, sound, and a little in costumes). During that time, he also did props backstage for Cathy Rigby's touring production of *Peter Pan* where he discovered his true calling:

> As I built props and started to create and run shows backstage, I thought this is definitely the most fun you get to have. You know the lighting guy has to sit behind the light board for a whole show. Costumes is great, but I really didn't like to do laundry at that point. With props I got to do everything. Props are crazy problem-solvers. When it comes to small little intricate things that do a trick or magical trick, they always come to us.

On Broadway props people today belong to a union affiliated with IATSE, not necessarily Local One which is specifically New York City. There are locals throughout the United States and all are affiliated with IATSE. The production props people are hired by the production company on a pink contract.

There are theatre house props people who also are union members, but they are paid by the theatre and answer to the Shuberts or Jujamycyn or whoever is the theatre owner. Before the props are loaded into the theatre, the house props people are responsible for fixing all the auditorium seats and sweeping and cleaning the stage, especially after lighting, carpenters, and general stage crew have been working.

The title for the person who runs the Broadway show is the head of props. The head of props is responsible for *all* props once they arrive at the theatre. Many head props people also build props outside at one of the shops before they join a production. Head of props is also referred to as props master, which is a term used mostly in regional theatres.

Head of props is hired by the production company but can be recommended by the designer, the director, the production company, or the production props supervisor. Technically, the props head is contracted to begin work on the first day of load-in to the theatre. If it is a big show, the props head can have an assistant who is a union member and helps run the show.

The production props supervisor's assistant has already been shopping for small accessories or hand props for rehearsals. Depending on the relationship with the supervisor, the head of props can be shopping for large props such as a sofa, cabinet, or bookcase. These large items may be purchased in duplicate so the actors can have one set during rehearsals and the duplicates are preset in the theatre in preparation for the actors' arrival.

The production props supervisor is responsible for building all the props and transporting them to different places. If the props are mobile enough, they are delivered to the rehearsal space so the actors can work with them. The larger prop pieces like big pieces of furniture or set dressing are delivered to the theatre before the cast arrives.

One of the primary tasks for the head of props is prepping and organizing the space backstage. They must carve out space for dressing rooms, and determine whether shelves, mirrors, or furniture are needed. Shelves have to be built and planned to keep egress for the cast and the crew. The orchestra pit has to be furnished with chairs, music stands, hooks on walls if the musicians require them, and lockers for the instruments have to be determined. A space for any perishables in the show needs to be established. During this prep period, the props department is supplemented by the services of house and production stagehands.

The production props department waits for all the set pieces to be moved in and definitely set before bringing in the props to avoid moving the props around each time there is a change.

Slowly the props are loaded into the theatre and put onstage. Props coordinates with the wardrobe department to load in the costumes and all their boxes. The stage sweeping and cleaning by house props is ongoing, so the stage space is tidy and safe for when the actors enter the theatre.

Once the scenic department is finished building and installing their items and the lighting department finishes setting up their equipment, the props and wardrobe departments figure out the remainder of the space. The props head has observed the building of the props. This gives them the opportunity to calculate the size of an item and the space it requires for backstage storage. The props are delivered before the cast moves onstage.

As mentioned previously, Broadway theatres backstage are small, so *all* space is considered, including flying something in the air. Some of the small props are used in rehearsal, but eventually they are moved into the theatre. All of this requires preplanning for tech, and it is a mad scramble.

The primary space for wardrobe is somewhat predetermined by where the washing machines and dryers are already located backstage. However, the props head, wardrobe supervisor, and stage management consult to solve several other wardrobe challenges. For big musicals, more space is necessary for the issue of quick changes backstage. Is there room for quick change booths, which props would build, or can a make-shift curtain be used? Should some costumes be stored by hanging them in fly space above the stage?

Depending on the production, there often are prop shelves in the wings for storing the smaller props for the actors to pick up for a specific scene. To avoid confusion, there are tape markers on the shelves indicating where a prop belongs when it is put back. The head of props is responsible for making sure the props are in place on the shelves before each performance, and very often, actors will check their own props to reassure themselves their props are in place. The stage manager or an assistant stage manager can also double check the props shelves before a performance. Returning the prop to the table or shelf can be the actor's responsibility or a crew member.

When tech begins, it is the first time the entire production is in the theatre. Up to this point, it has been theory; now everyone has to work out their job for real. For props the first scene usually drags on because lighting is getting their first chance, so it gives props and the actors the opportunity to figure out what needs to be stage left or stage right. Sometimes this is done in the dark, while the lighting is adjusted. If need be, while they are teching onstage, props will wear head lamps to work backstage in the dark to hang set dressings. If props needs to make noise for their work, they wait for the cast to have a ten-minute break. Austin Rodriguez said, "We're never married to anything. We're just like, 'What can we do to just start?'"

During tech when the cast is onstage, the crews work around each other. The crew work time is 8 AM to 11:30 AM, lunch, and then back when the cast is onstage. Props need to be repainted, touched up, or repaired, and the morning time is usually when that happens.

When the show is up and running, the props department establishes a preset time to make repairs and maintain the props before setting the stage for the performance. That can be an hour before the show starts. They have tools, adhesives, tape, and a set of tricks to make repairs quickly during the show or during preset.

Often there is a work call every week or every other week where props, carpentry, electric, and sound do their maintenance to make sure the show looks like it did on opening night. Traditionally, it is scheduled for Wednesday morning before a two-show day between 8 AM and 11:30 AM, which gives them three hours to catch up.

In addition to all the duties for the props department that have been listed, props are called in after the show is open for rehearsals for understudies and swings. If the actor needs to work with a prop, a props person must be present. Scheduling for this is coordinated with stage management and how many props people is determined.

The props department is a totally catch-all department. Besides organizing backstage space, supplying and building the props, and repairing and maintaining the props during the run, sometimes the props head and assistant operate the puppets during the show.

Since *The Lion King*, the use of puppetry on Broadway has increased. When the puppet designer creates the puppet, the designer determines the number of people necessary to operate the puppet. Technically, the rule on Broadway is if the puppeteer is not seen, it is considered a prop and a stagehand operates it. In *Beetlejuice*, the props head and the props assistant ran the sandworm puppets. If the puppeteer *is* seen, then it is operated by an actor. On some very large shows, like *The Lion King*, there is a puppet department dedicated to maintenance of the puppets. Normally, it is the props department.

When the puppet designer delivers the puppets to the theatre, the designer teaches the people who will operate the puppets how to run and maintain them. Austin Rodriguez says: "You get inside and figure it out through the rehearsal process. So you learn what every pulley, piece of elastic, and mechanism does so you can make sure that puppet is working and ready every night."

As technology gets more sophisticated and in some ways more affordable, and Broadway shows get bigger and bigger and bigger, no matter how simple a show is, some wildly magical device is incorporated into the production to aid the storytelling. Computers make it possible to put a servo motor into a prop to make it move remotely through a computer.

Affordable LED lights made the idea of an infinity mirror in *Beetlejuice* possible, emulating the Tim Burton film. For the infinity mirror, the props department developed the concept of using different LEDs that are made with microchips for each LED, which were then hooked up to a controller inside the box which spoke wirelessly to the lighting board. The lighting programmer programmed the lighting board which could operate and control all those lights individually.

Once a show closes, wardrobe and hair/wigs pack their own boxes, but props provides the muscle to move their boxes. Sets go hither and yon, and can be saved, sold, or stored. The head of props synchronizes with the production props supervisor and the production management company to figure out where the props are to go. A lot depends on the future life of the show.

In the past, sets were often sent off to a landfill unless they were to be used for a road company. There were several productions of *Spamalot*, so the scenery was stored. It was eventually sold to a theatre in Maine. Today, there is an entity called the Broadway Green Initiative which has changed the entire thinking of how sets from a closed show are handled. Now if a show's set is not saved, it goes to the Broadway Green Initiative where almost 85 percent of the material is recycled and gets reused.

After a run, most props are well worn. Some props are stored in a warehouse for a future production (i.e., a *Phantom* production) or rented. Some go back to the shop where the props were made. Some are sold to smaller theatres. Props that are going to be trashed can be distributed to cast, crew, and anyone in the production who thinks they can use them.

Once the show ends and the props are moved out of the theatre, the props contract ends.

Puppets

> His work [Michael Curry] is just beautiful. I think the most beautiful part of his work sometimes is the mechanisms and how things are built. Getting inside some of those large puppets you're like, "This is so beautiful and it really can move easily." I was inside this giant puppet and it was tricky because of the small amount of walking space you could trip easily. But as far as moving a person on and off stage and being able to control a puppet with a person on top of it, it was *very* easy. He's a great designer and all his puppets are amazing.
>
> –Austin Rodriguez, head of props

In the world of entertainment, puppetry has a very long record from the Chinese shadow puppets to early hand puppets and marionettes. For the world of Broadway theatre, history was made after a tryout of *The Lion King* debuted in Minneapolis in 1997. It was one of the earliest wide uses of puppets as a storytelling device in a Broadway show up to that point. Since the 1990s, the development of technology, materials, and the influence of cinematic fantasy has encouraged and made possible the ability to incorporate more spectacle onstage, arena shows, Super Bowl, opera, and Las Vegas. With *The Lion King*, Disney found a new revenue stream in adapting some of their lucrative animated films to the stage. Straight plays such as *Equus* used a form of puppets with the skeletal framework of the horses in the original production. Since then, more plays like *War Horse* have also found the use of puppets effective in the storytelling process.

The director can request a puppet designer or the producer can choose them. Oddly enough, the puppet designer frequently joins the production as early as the composer and writer. The show can have a fanciful character that cannot be played by a human, and it is a concept needing exploration in the very early stages of development. Occasionally, the puppet designer concludes using a puppet is not appropriate. The puppet designer Michael Curry commented:

One of the things I do is try to find the correct use of puppetry. The early part is exploration and we often experiment with human characters playing a fantastic character. We experimented with many of the small puppets in *The Lion King* as full-body costumes. Zazoo was a 6′2″ man at one point in a costume and it just didn't work. In 1996 the idea of exposing puppeteers on the stage instead of hiding them was radical. We wanted the dancers to do the work in the show so the troupe was consistent. I often don't hide the trick of puppeteering. I think that's another level of performance that the audience enjoys. It's like getting two performances.

A puppet designer can be a member of Local 829, United Scenic Artists, which is under the umbrella of IATSE, but it is not a requirement that a puppet designer on Broadway be a member of a union. Some puppet designers work as set designers as well.

The puppet designer receives a small fee to explore the use of puppets for the production, then a fee for designing them. Fabrication of the puppets is a separate fee, and the show can take up to a year-and-a-half to form itself and get onstage. As a designer, they receive royalties from the production and subsequent productions under the same producer.

Many shows have already appropriated a budget for the construction of the puppets, so the designer knows what the funding is before designing. Other times they submit a budget before finalizing the design. It does not affect the imagination, only the parameters within which the designer employs materials and complexities. Fifty thousand dollars is different from one million.

How a Broadway show comes together is not a perfect science. A few collaborators have early discussions about what the story is. If it is Disney's *Frozen*, the story is known. Other shows are very open slates where there are roughly two levels of engagement. One is called pre-production where everything is thrown on the table and tried in workshops. No bad ideas. Once all that is collected and honed into a plausible collage, the second level is with the producer where the design elements and specific details are deliberated.

The use of puppets in a production is to serve the storytelling of the show; otherwise, they are unnecessary. During early development of a show in workshops, the puppet designer works with sets, lighting, costumes, and the production manager, but primarily with the director. The first mock-ups are made with cheaper materials as the design and concept evolve. However, by the first day of rehearsal with the cast, about two months before moving to the theatre, the puppets must be somewhat finished prototypes. The puppets are delivered to the theatre by truck or plane, whether they were made in Oregon or Brooklyn.

There are many types of puppets from the traditional that use rods for control, hand puppets where the hand moves the puppet from inside, and marionettes, which use strings and levers. Then there are wearable or structural costumes which were used in *The Lion King*, worn and manipulated by dancers. There are shadow puppets which are flat with a light source behind adapted from an ancient Chinese tradition.

Since a puppet in a Broadway production is a character in advancing the story, movement is an essential factor in its creation. Whether it is rods, strings, levers, or actors, the puppet needs to be able to move. The designer Michael Curry says: "Movement is very difficult because the physics and engineering that go behind the movement is very complicated. Especially to make something that interacts with an actor that works every night, eight shows a week."

Constructing a puppet for a Broadway production takes knowledge of physics and engineering techniques to create a structure that has mobility and durability. With all the physical movements of dance, it also must be lightweight. The advances of some plastics like carbon fiber (often used in the aerospace industry) are super lightweight and compatible with a dancer or actor operating the puppets. Then there are metals like aluminum, titanium, and stainless steel that are used for the inside of a puppet shell. All of that shell is then covered with an aesthetic cover of paint, fabrics, or feathers, depending on the need. Over the last twenty years, all these materials have contributed to the feasibility of integrating puppets into Broadway productions.

Building a puppet is expensive, especially when it needs to endure eight shows a week for hopefully a successful run. By rehearsals the aggregate idea for the puppet has been determined through trial and error in workshops and approved by the director, but the prototype is not totally complete with the colors and finish. The rehearsal time is still a discovery process for minor adjustments, though there are usually no substantive changes. During rehearsal the designer refines the *scale* of the puppet for the person who will be handling it and for that person to learn its operating intricacies.

Some puppet designers have their own company and staff for building their puppets, which gives them a greater amount of control over their product. The designer can work on several shows at the same time but will have an assistant designated for a specific show to follow through in the designer's sporadic absence.

Calculating how to get the puppet on and off the stage and where to store it is like figuring out a Rubik's Cube. The playing and backstage areas of a Broadway theatre are very small, so most puppets are put on a big rack that gets pulled up into the grid above the stage so the floor underneath is clear. It takes well-choreographed maneuvering backstage during and after a show that resembles another dance form.

The puppets are intricate structures, but not so complicated that the operators cannot learn to work them. Depending on the size of the show and the number of puppets, the designer will spend five or so weeks training the designated operators how to manipulate the puppets. The designer may work with the choreographer because often the operators are dancers and part of the storytelling, not just working a puppet.

There is usually not a specific puppet department on a show unless the show has a large number of puppets, such as *The Lion King*. Then there is a position called the puppet master who maintains and repairs the puppets during the day. They are usually affiliated with the puppet fabricator and do not run the show. It is another expense, so producers prefer not to add that to their budget.

Most often the responsibility of maintaining the puppets during the run of the show falls on the props and wardrobe departments. The props department repairs the mechanics of the puppet, while the wardrobe department repairs any tears of fabric or other coverings on the outer layer of the puppets. However, the first line of defense for noting anything amiss with the puppet is the actor or props person operating the puppet. The actors/dancers fill out a report nightly listing anything that does not seem quite right. They can sense if there is a change with the device when they are operating it. The operator knows if a string is broken or a rod is damaged. Hopefully, any needed repairs can be done before anything happens in front of an audience.

Although the designer can be engaged on other shows, they are still obligated to be an advisor on the show for its run, so to some extent the job does not end until the show ends. The designer receives the nightly report of the show from the stage manager, so they are always informed of the status of the puppets. With a long run (or with tours), like *Frozen* and *The Lion King*, those puppets need replacement and refurbishment along the way. Puppet designers supervise that work either in their own shop or an outside shop.

A puppet designer can occasionally have some part of their design that is patented and copyrighted, but it is the show producer who fully owns the copyright to the designs. When a show ends, most of the puppets are completely used up. Occasionally, things go to a museum, but others are demolished including the molds.

Michael Curry initially was a fine artist creating moving sculptures. Fine artists often work alone, and the New York art gallery scene can be a rather sterile environment. After coming to the attention of the theatre world, Michael Curry found theatre very conducive to his sensibilities:

> I have worked in film and TV, where there are 60 people in a room trying to talk about one thing. Theatre is kind of a beautiful collaboration of a *wonderfully* small group (six to eight people) who trust each other and are *very* creatively open. Ideas can be thrown out without embarrassment, so it's a safe environment. As a fine artist I was working alone. What I really like about theatre is the collaboration.

Special Effects

Special effects (SFX) in theatre has different definitions, and theatre productions present very specific challenges. On Broadway, often SFX blends between departments or departs from other designers who cannot cover it. So whichever department SFX is assigned during a production is dictated by the script or the vision of the creative team.

SFX are seen in many venues, including film, television, circuses, and spectaculars. The realism of SFX in film and television has had a significant influence on the use of SFX in theatre. Today the audience expects a certain realism onstage that they have seen on the screen as opposed to something more stylized. This makes the job of an SFX designer more challenging and more creative.

Two early practitioners were Chic Silber, still active with *Wicked*. Gregory Meeh, who worked prolifically in the 1980s with *Phantom*, *Les Misérables*, and *Beauty and the Beast*, recently came out of retirement to work on *Paradise Square*. Both men were active in several mediums, including opera, dance, circuses, and modern dance, then theatre beckoned their particular talents. SFX became more of a feature on Broadway as technology developed and London shows like *Phantom* and *Les Misérables* arrived with all their use of spectacle. Today there are still only a few people who do SFX, and one person who inherited the Silber-Meeh mantel is Jeremy Chernick. Austin Rodriguez told me, "If you need rain, smoke or fire in a show, call Jeremy." Today the SFX field has a growing number of young women in the field. As with many designers, to survive in a freelance environment, they all work in diverse industries.

At first SFX was only a moment in the production, maybe four seconds long, but then *Phantom* came along and it had an ambience running throughout the show. There was a low fog appearing and disappearing on cue. There were sparks and a big explosion when the chandelier fell, so that involved pyrotechnics. What and how could those effects be repeated every performance? That fell under SFX.

Like props, SFX is problem-solving, entails multiple abilities, and works with many departments to produce an effect that may last three minutes or a whole show. On *Frozen*, the show is highly computerized and everything in the show is synchronized with lighting. The SFX designer had to turn the creative concepts into equipment, feasibility, repeatability, and durability. Not all shows are so heavily computerized.

An SFX designer is hired as an independent artist and may not belong to a union. They are hired specifically for each show. If it is a single moment in a show, SFX will be lumped into another department. If there are many SFX or SFX that are continuous throughout the show, there will be a designated person for the SFX department to run the show.

The SFX designer does have an assistant who is hired based on the show's need, the assistant's skills, and availability. Since some SFX designs are cued through a computer similar to lighting, having an assistant who is a lighting programmer is a great asset. That assistant can translate the complexity of what the equipment does and how it runs into an understandable language when they input that data into the computer.

How an SFX designer is hired on Broadway varies. A director may request the designer, occasionally a choreographer, or other designers on the show if there is a weird SFX they cannot handle. Sometimes it is the production management company. The designers are paid by the production.

The SFX designer receives either a design fee or a consulting fee, depending on whether the SFX are just a moment, a few slight moments in a show, or whether SFX are a large component existing throughout the show, and if they are involved from top to bottom through tech. Most shows have a budget for SFX, which evolves on what the task is, and the designer works within that budget. Constructing the SFX is separate from the design or consulting fee.

Straight plays tend to use SFX more frequently. According to Jeremy Chernick:

> I do a lot of drama because of the violence. I do a lot of musicals because of the razzle-dazzle. But my favorite is comedy

because it's so rare that I get asked. If I can be involved some-how in creating a joke or a punchline, it's like the *greatest* for me. It's so rare that what I do gets a laugh, but if it can be crafted that way, the laughter is the best payoff. That's some-thing special.

The SFX designer first reads the script, meets with the director, and sometimes wonders why they were hired. Most often when reading the script, the SFX are incredibly obvious, so the designer makes notes before meeting with the director. Other times the show is already in rehearsals, and the designer is called about a specific point in the play to inquire if they can create what they *now* imagine or make what is currently planned better. Some-times the show is already in previews and asking to add some-thing at that time usually is a sign the show is in trouble.

Although it is best when the SFX designer is brought in early when the first creative conversations are happening, that is not always how it works. Early will result in the effects being the most integrated and seamless in a show. A large part of SFX is hiding how the effect happened and where it came from so the audience's attention is not distracted from the story. If the designer is involved in the beginning, they can collaborate more thoroughly with the set designer about how and where to hide things and how it all will work.

The SFX designer works mainly with the set designer, props, and lighting; scenery and lighting are the primary anchor points. Often the choreographer or director can also be the driv-ing force. Like everyone involved, directorial changes during rehearsal are a given and everyone has to pivot. Sometimes for SFX it costs money and sometimes it does not. Sometimes there are designs that are difficult to change, so if the production gets too close to the period when final decisions must be made, SFX will be more assertive with the cut off time to move forward so the assignment can be accomplished.

SFX are referred to as "special" because they can be danger-ous. Once hired, the SFX designer does a system of schematics in-cluding drawings, lists of equipment, and narrative descriptions.

There is a bid process for SFX just like other departments (i.e., sets, costumes, lights, and sound). The SFX design goes out to a variety of shops that specialize in certain elements. Sometimes rental houses can provide supplies required for a specific kind of special effect, such as fog needed to cover the stage. That machine is usually rented from a lighting shop. Sometimes the SFX can be built by a scene shop, by a prop shop, or by the designers themselves.

On Broadway, the SFX team consists of the designer, an assistant, a person backstage who runs the effects, and a programmer to program the computer console. The size of the team depends on the size and complexity of the effect requested.

The SFX assistant aids the designer with the drawings, list making, organization, and communication with various other production departments. They are often extremely knowledgeable and skilled in a variety of SFX technologies.

Besides the schematics, the designer also does camera or in-person demonstrations to explain their idea. The SFX team will go to a little studio or a rehearsal space with the cast and crew to demonstrate the planned SFX. This is necessary so there are no shocks or surprises. Many SFX can be explosive.

In some cases, the SFX team goes to rehearsal for a few days to work with the actors to replicate the SFX and confirm they are on the right track. By the time the production moves to the stage, a lot of the SFX have already been through technical rehearsals. SFX can be hazardous, so all of this preparatory work is vital to make sure everyone is informed and reassured that all the effects are safe. Once in tech, there is just too much going on and no time to stop to figure it out.

In working out particularly intricate SFX, it is more like choreography. Jeremy Chernick recalls:

Sometimes I have to say to actors when they work with me, "For these few moments, it would be better if you stopped acting because what you are doing is so choreographic, also slightly dangerous, and we need total focus. You can turn the acting back on later, but for now we're going to count it out. It's just going to be beats. On beat one we do this, on beat two we do this, on beat three we pull the trigger, on beat four we react, on beat five we're complete." Once they learn that, it gets inside of them and they can continue.

The person who runs the show is determined by the number of SFX in the production. There are Local One stagehands who can work with an SFX designer, especially if there is anything with fire or pyrotechnics. Those two elements require a certified person to run those effects, and Local One has a handful of members who have that certification. Frequently there is a designated person, usually from the lighting department, who is in charge since many elements are triggered by lighting cues. Mostly it is run by any department that the SFX touch. Sporadically a props person will cover something, especially if there are actor-motivated SFX.

Each show contract is different and has different requirements, but generally the SFX designer's job ends opening night. The designer does receive a royalty for the run of the show, like other designers, which ends when the show ends. It does not carry over to a future production with a new producer. The SFX designer does not participate in the load-out.

5

Costumes

Costume Designer

When I designed my first Broadway show, we were in tech for five weeks. If the director said, "The light isn't focused in the right spot and I don't like the gel color," a bunch of union guys had to roll out a cherry picker, climb up the ladders, and change the light position and the gel. Now they do that in a second with the computer. *For the costume department, we are essentially rooted in an old-world craft.* I can't call the costume shop and say, "I need a new Elizabethan gown in the morning." I know that process is going to take a month, require three fittings, and cost money. A click of a mouse won't change it.

–Gregg Barnes, costume designer

Costumes are one of the first things the audience sees when an actor takes the stage and perhaps one of the most complex labor-intensive departments in a Broadway production. From the moment a designer creates a sketch to when an actor puts on the costume, there are numerous skilled people who have contributed to that one garment.

Shows, especially musicals, can be in development for years. When a costume designer is initially approached varies, but they are usually recommended by the director, who reaches out early to explore a designer's availability for a block of time. On occasion a producer has a preference. The costume designer negotiates a designer's fee upfront through an agent or lawyer and after approval of the producer and director, is hired very early in a Broadway production, usually after the director.

Once formally hired, the costume designer reads whatever script exists at that moment. With a revival, the basic script is set. With a new work, the script will have dialogue and scene structure, but there might be vast descriptive sections of what is planned, or no second act yet. During this early period the designer and director meet to discuss the production's vision and concepts, if any, for the costumes. The costume designer then rereads the script making a preliminary costume chart with the budget in mind. A costume chart is a list of each character, what costumes they wear, and how they move throughout the play. Some shows have forty costumes. *Aladdín* had approximately three hundred.

Creating costumes may be an old-world craft, but computers are a tremendous research aid. After the chart, the designer starts researching whatever imagery might be appropriate to flesh out the initial design concepts. The details from that research can lead down ten thousand different paths. All that information is then assembled into a cogent design vision for the show.

The chart and research are then presented to the director hoping to ignite the director's imagination. If there is a spark, the designer revisits the director with simple sketches or photographs for further discussion and consensus. Readings and workshops are concurrently taking place, but the designer is essentially working alone at the drawing board.

Costume Sketches and Approval

Costume designers each have individual creative methods. Some produce hand-painted renderings which can take six to eight hours to complete, but these allow the design ideas to evolve. Others sketch on the computer, which has a different advantage. If the designer created a red dress, but the director prefers green, the color can be changed instantly on the computer. Gregg Barnes, who still draws his designs by hand, opined:

> For me there is something creatively necessary about confronting a blank piece of paper, developing the shapes, exploring the textures, balancing the palette of the sketch or the scene. To draw and paint is really a labor but is an essential part of my process. It informs everything I do next. I know that when I go into the fitting room, if I deviate from the sketch, I know *exactly* what I'm doing. I know potentially what I'm going to lose and what I'm going to gain. I think you can look at it as if I were a playwright who labors over the arrangement of the words. My point is that you draw a red dress because it *should be* a red dress. Let's face it, a pencil or a mouse are both tools to get something down on paper to start the process. Everything is valid.

To understand where the production is going the designer watches a video of a reading or attends a workshop rehearsal as the production develops. Costume designer Paloma Young said while watching a very early rehearsal on one show, she realized what she originally designed was not going to work. So this early period for the costume design process is very fluid.

Everything begins with the script, but modern theatre scripts tend to be more cinematic with few stage directions. A new show is a totally blank design page and rarely has a lot of practical information pertaining to costumes. Costumes require time for an actor to get out of and into during the performance, so stage transitions can be problematic. All these considerations are part of the design process. In one regional theatre, help came from a director who previously directed the show being staged. Gregg Barnes recalled:

> I was designing a production of *Dream Girls* at a regional theatre and the gentleman who directed it had done it before. I brought in my chart and he said, "Great but you have to understand that in order for us to land in Scene 8 without any

transitionary time, you've got to have them [the cast] completely dressed in Scene 5. Everything in Scenes 5, 6 and 7 is overdress, so they can just throw it on the floor and they're ready for Scene 8." If he hadn't told me that, I would have been designing all of those scenes in isolation.

Costume Team

A Broadway costume designer's team consists of an associate and assistants. There is some departmental inconsistency in the Broadway structure. Unlike set designers or lighting designers, whose associates are paid by the production early on, the costume designer's associate and assistants are not formally paid by the production until all the designs, sketches, and charts are on paper. The costume designer designs the production without help from assistants (unless they are on the designer's payroll). The producers pay the costume designer's team to *implement* the design. Until then, while the costume designer is designing alone, they are responsible for paying an assistant to copy research and get art supplies. A set designer's associate who is paid by the production can work intermittently with the set designer early on, but they are hired for a specific number of weeks. Those early sporadic individual days are counted as part of the negotiated weeks.

Some costume designers have a studio with a full-time staff and others have an ad hoc staff. Being hired early, especially in a musical, the costume designer's prep time is long, and they work mainly with the team independently.

Every costume designer on Broadway has an associate who is an indispensable part of the team. When the designer is officially hired, they notify their associate to block out time for the production schedule. Often the designer will hire the associate to help with all the pre-planning before rehearsals start, and unlike sets and lighting, the associate is paid by the designer or works for free until officially joining the production.

Over the last twenty years, the position of costume associate has morphed into essentially being a project manager. They work with the designer in preparing the budget, scheduling fittings and meetings, tracking the budget, and making sure the costume production does not go over budget. The designer or the associate are also responsible for communicating and overseeing all the individual artisans constructing the costumes.

Designer's Fee

The costume union provides a baseline for the type of show in question, but the designer fee is negotiated upfront through an agent or a lawyer. In addition, the costume designer prepares a costume budget, which is separate from the design fee.

The design fee is not a significant amount when a show can take three to four years to open. Consequently, a costume designer works on several shows concurrently at different stages of development, just as other department designers. However, costumes require hands-on attendance, so taking on additional jobs is limited. The designer must weigh the obligation and timeline of each project and how much work it entails. An Off Broadway show with 4 actors and 10 costumes can be interspersed with a large musical that has 250 costumes. Organization is important to manage multiple shows with multiple research avenues.

Costume Budget

The second budget is the costume budget covering the costume construction. Most general managers/producers do not discuss the costume budget with the designer, preferring to wait for the designer's estimate, when the producer can say, "Oh no that's way too much."

When the designer brings the associate onto their team, the two review the sketches and do a preliminary budget. They figure out how many assistants are necessary to execute the work. From experience, they can evaluate the price range of each costume and know the cost of certain items, such as shoes. The budget includes extras for each garment, such as fabric painting or beading. This preliminary budget process takes weeks.

The production budget can set a separate staffing budget for the assistants, which can be broken up however the designer deems best. Gregg Barnes points out:

Of course the producer says upfront, "Don't worry about the budget. We just want you to dream." Then you learn the budget is 70% less than fulfilling this dream you conjured. You try to work out a way to accommodate the budget and retain most of the dream. There's an artistic element to this but there is also a very *very* not to be underestimated business side. If somebody gives you a million dollars to get their show into the theatre, only to find out they hate the clothes for the opening number (that you've spent $200,000 on that are to be thrown out and redone), nobody's happy. So that informs the process as well as how big your team is.

There is a lot of dialogue back and forth to agree on a costume budget. The surest way to not have a career is to go overbudget.

The costume budget must be approved by the general manager/producer, and the design has to be approved by the producer and director.

Cast Fittings

Few shows go directly to Broadway without having a tryout at some regional theatre or Off Broadway. Until a show approaches an actual production, the costume designer is doing preparatory work. Once the production is in the tryout phase, a Broadway production is anticipated, a cast is hired (which normally will be the Broadway cast), and costume building will begin (tryout costumes will be used for Broadway). Finally, the costume designer works with actors.

This next phase for the costume designer is fittings. This phase is different for a musical and a play. A musical allows a long prep time so sketching and fittings do not necessarily coincide. With a play, the actors are often doing their character prep work while the designer is analyzing the script and preparing the costume chart. The play prep time is relatively brief at approximately four weeks.

Tryouts are not only to assess the play or musical; they are immensely helpful to a costume designer in revealing a costume's functionality or shortcomings.

Once the show is in rehearsal, the costume designer has an initial fitting with an actor where the sketches agreed to by the designer and director are presented. There is a delicate balance for the designer to get a sense of the actor's clothing preferences and their sense of the character. Departures from the sketches can happen. An actress does not feel comfortable in a sleeveless dress, so the director is notified before the designer makes any change. Choreography in a musical can necessitate certain design adjustments for the dancers to execute the choreography but the change goes against the costume period. The costume designer must find a solution to serve the choreographic needs and yet not deny their period design. The costume should enhance the character and further the story. There is some flexibility, but the designer understands that 10 percent of their design is going to change before opening.

Tryouts

It has been emphasized that everything changes until opening night, but this presents a serious issue for costumes. The costume budget has been approved and, by an out-of-town tryout, most of that budget has been used. Anticipating the unforeseen, costume designers try to set aside emergency money. The creatives suddenly decide they hate the opening number or move a musical number from one act to another. As Gregg Barnes muses:

> You have to be facile and quick on your feet, because they're not going to give you another half a million dollars to solve the problem, which may have nothing to do with what you designed. They cut a scene or they're going to take the lead's 11 o'clock number and do it in the first act. You're thinking, I've spent all the money on the 11 o'clock number and it's not appropriate for her to come out in a red bugle beaded pantsuit in the first act. So I need something spectacular, but it has to be rethought in a different way. So the jigsaw puzzle continues.

Another issue is often the director does not see the entire cast in costume until tech, so there can be more tweaks then.

Construction of Costumes

Building costumes for a Broadway production is no simple feat. A few of the artists/artisans are discussed in this book, but they all contribute to the garment. The designer and associate oversee and coordinate all of these pieces while dealing with opening deadlines, directional and choreographic changes, and egos.

There is an amazing amount of collaboration among many individuals to produce one garment. Each step has its own requirement, which when finished is fed into the next production phase. The draper who makes a mock-up, the cutter who makes the pattern, the beader who creates the beading piece to go on a costume, the sewers, stitchers, fabric painters, milliners, and tailors. Each individual facet is fed into the production line to complete the costume.

It has been mentioned that costumes take time to produce. Costumes also have to be strong and sturdy to survive an eight-show week. The original production of *Peter and the Starcatcher* was tried out at the La Jolla Playhouse which has its own costume stock. The designer, Paloma Young, had access to that costume stock, other nearby theatres, and a lot of thrift shopping. A lot of the costumes were thrift store buys and not specifically constructed. As Ms. Young recalled:

> The clothes were distressed and super broken down to look all raggedy like sailors and orphans. The show is quite physical. You've got a bunch of non-dancer guys doing really intense physical lifts and tumbles. The costumes continued to deteriorate and get very very sweaty. On Broadway even though we had looks that we loved, we needed doubles of everything. On a two-show day you can't take a sweater that is drenched with sweat, take it off for the dinner break, and put it back on and have it be cold. Everyone is going to get sick. There are lots of union rules about it too.

When a show runs eight shows a week, costumes need to be more pragmatic and functional. It is generally a combination of build and purchase for any show, because costumes are provided down to underwear.

Marketing and Public Relations

Marketing a Broadway show is vital, and often public relations wants an early start for their ad campaign. Interviews with the principal actors and posters need scheduling. For *Mean Girls*, the marketers wanted to create an iconic symbol, but the costumes were not finished. Fortunately, it was modern dress, so the actresses wore plain pink dresses with the title *Mean Girls* over their figures for the poster. Once the show opened, the poster was redone with the show costumes.

Social media is another headache for a Broadway production. Sometimes a young internist with limited experience is assigned to social media and posts poor quality or out-of-focus pictures of the designer's renderings. Now for artistic self-preservation, designers create public relations packages ahead of rehearsals. The package is given to the general manager to forward to the marketing company. The designer gives permission to use their name on specifically approved renderings for the advertising campaign.

Social media usage has instigated social media training for the actors and the stage crew to educate them how not to be controversial and to respect their fellow actors. This has gained more significance since more stars and celebrities are cast in Broadway productions. The designer is also pivotal in this effort because when a star is in a fitting, the designer basically asks the actor to undress. It is important to create a world in which the star feels safe and knows that when their photo is taken, they are protected from some young intern having access to it and selling it to some magazine. When Josh Groban was performing in *Natasha, Pierre & the Great Comet of 1812*, everyone had to turn off the location on their phones and tweets because the company did not want his overzealous fans to know where he was rehearsing.

Designer Royalty

Once a show opens, the designer receives an additional weekly compensation. It is a weekly fee negotiated with the general manager/producer, the designer's agent, and the designer's accountant. When the show recoups its cost, then the designer participates in the production profit-sharing structure that has been successful on Broadway. If a show has six companies under the original producer's umbrella, that royalty becomes six times the original amount. That is rare because not every show is such a hit. That royalty/profit-sharing continues as long as it is under the umbrella of that original production. *Beauty and the Beast* ran fourteen years and *Phantom* ran twenty-eight years. As soon as the show is licensed to regional theatres or schools, that royalty ceases.

Ownership of Designs

In essence, the costume designer and set designer are not copyright protected. The producer owns the physical costumes, and the costume designer owns the designs, but the designer cannot physically sell the designs to profit from them. If the designer's drawings are used in a book, they must give their permission for usage. If the production has touring companies under the original producer, then the designer gets a royalty for the costumes. When the show is licensed to regional theatres and high schools, they do not. If the regional theatre *rents* the original costumes, the designer receives a rental fee.

Social media presents another hazard for designing copyright. With social media, a designer in a licensed production (i.e., regional theatre) can actually copy the original designs down to where a patch pocket is applied (which happened with *Peter and the Starcatcher*), but the original designer does not get money or credit; this happens quite often.

This is still an unsettled issue for set, lighting, and costume designers. The design is their intellectual property, but they are not compensated for that creativity except in the original production. The only thing that can be copyrighted is something on paper, for example a costume design or a light plot.

Multiple Jobs

As mentioned, the design fee is nominal and the commitment to a show can be several years until it is in production, so depending on the size of the project, a designer will be involved in several shows at the same time. The shows can be at different stages in development, but it requires excellent time management. Once a show opens, if it appears to be a hit or near a hit, there is money to hire the associate to represent the designer if questions arise while the designer is engaged on another project. If the show is struggling and there are cast changes, financially no one extra can be hired so the designer must oversee the changes.

With *Aladdín* there were six different companies around the world, so the associate was the person who oversaw all the different companies. For a big hit like *Beauty and the Beast* or *Phantom of the Opera*, which ran for fifteen and twenty-eight years, respectively, it can be a career stabilizer for some people.

Cast Change

If there are cast changes, the designer manages those changes even if they are out of town through their associate. Often the designer attends the show during the run and makes notes or has fittings with understudies or swings, which can be considered part of the additional weekly compensation. If it requires extensive additional time shopping and attending new fittings, the designer can request a day rate for the additional work.

Cast replacements often are similar to the original actor so the designer only needs to tweak the costume. In *Aladdín*, it is fairly certain a Jasmine is going to be a woman and Aladdin is going to be a man. If it is modern dress, the replacement can be so physically different from the original performer, such as taller, thinner, heavier, a different ethnicity, then the designer must reexamine the design. The spirit of the show is always honored, because again with social media and chat rooms, "everybody knows everything and if you change a shoe, they want to know why."

Union

The costume designer belongs to the Scenic Artists Union Local 829, also under the International Alliance of Theatrical Stage Employees (IATSE) umbrella, based in New York. There are different contracts for Broadway, Off Broadway, film, and television. There are three branches of the union (Eastern/New York, Central/Chicago, and Western/Los Angeles). There is geographical reciprocity if someone works in one branch but is a member of another branch. They get paid but the local union forwards the money to the designer's home branch.

There is a certain hierarchy in the union. The costume union is not as strong as the set designer's union even though they all belong to the same union. The designer Paloma Young related:

> For years costume designers had the short end of the stick in many ways and every time a new contract was negotiated everyone (lighting, sound, set designers) got the same bump up, but the costume designer remained less supported with a lower functional wage than their peers. One April during the high Broadway season, the union had their meeting on Monday, the near universal day off. I didn't have a show on Broadway that year, so I attended. I looked around and the room was filled with twenty-five men who were lighting, sound, and scenic designers. I thought to myself there's a reason I am here on what would be the day off, because the costume designers are working right now. They are shopping and meeting with shops. It's also the day they have the longest access to the costumes for major alterations. There's a lot of invisible labor happening outside of the theatre for costume designers whereas most of the work on the other design elements happens inside the theatre once tech starts. Recently the union has made significant inroads in improving protection and compensation for costume designers and their assistants in a targeted way.

In the early 1980s, the union made a concerted effort to expand the base, primarily because the membership was very small and to include health insurance and retirement a bigger pool was needed. Today the entry requirement is an exam and presentation of a portfolio.

Costume Design Associate

The costume design associate can be suggested to the designer by the management company, but more frequently the associate is recommended by the designer. The associate is essentially the designer's right-hand person, and their production relationship is very unique because they work so closely together to produce the costumes and their tasks can be interdependent. Costume design associate Alexander Gottlieb reflected:

> One of the great benefits from the associate/designer relationship is that, as an associate, you get the opportunity to learn from established designers about their early beginnings, the experiences that shaped the trajectory of their professional career, and about all the designers who have come and gone and made an impact on the American theatre. The arc of my own career is shaped by the experiences and expertise of the designers with whom I've worked and the friendships that have evolved with the many wonderful vendors I encounter.

When the associate is hired and formally becomes part of the production varies and can depend on the designer's work method. However, before the associate joins the production, the designer has already had meetings with the creatives and has assembled preliminary design drawings based on those meetings.

Until the associate is officially on contract and part of the production, they are paid directly by the designer or work for free as pre-production. Like the set design associate, the costume design associate is hired for a specific number of weeks. If the associate begins work before a formal contract, that intermittent work can usually be accrued as part of the contracted weeks.

The costume department on Broadway is different from any other department in the production. Whereas the scenic department has the production management company and a production manager who supervises staffing and budgets for lighting, projection, sound, and scenery, for better or worse, the costume department operates with a lot more independence in setting its own agenda and managing its own budgets.

The costume department creates bid books, spreadsheets, and technical drawings/research. It manages the costume timelines and deliveries with their builders and vendors. The department is independently responsible for fully facilitating/ managing the manufacturing of the costumes for the entire show and is beholden to the general manager. It is a team effort, but the bulk of the administrative work is part of the associate designer's job.

Whenever in the process the associate comes on board, they contribute to research, determine sources, and assist in the aesthetic framework of the show. The aesthetic vision includes the designer's choice of costume style for the show, the fabrics, the accessories, and how all those items are employed for the costumes. It is the associate designer's job to be fully immersed in that vision and to advance the refinement, execution, and facilitation of that aesthetic to the stage. That is why the relationship between the designer and the associate designer is so critical.

Most often the associate begins early with the designer in the pre-production phase of the production and can aid the designer in research. As the production progresses, the associate is responsible for creating and managing various documents necessary for the costume department. At the same time, the associate is managing the team, the budgets, the expenses, the costume building, and the tasks multiply as discussed throughout this segment.

Some of the paperwork includes costume charts, which are anything that is costume related, such as numbering or labeling costume sketches, dressing lists, and costume plots per scene/act.

There are costume bibles, which are organized binders of all the costume-related fabrics, accessories, and materials that are planned for each specific costume and can include photos/ drawings of how a costume is constructed including any special rigging, paint and yarn samples, color names for custom fabrics, trims/buttons with vendor names, and any relevant information for the costume. If it is purchased clothing, the bible would include tag information, pricing, and scene number. It lists all the behind-the-scenes, factual information about what was used to create the designs. Also there are bid books which are distributed to the shops for labor estimates and discussed later in this chapter.

There is no cardinal rule as to when the rest of the costume team commences work, and the size of the costume team is determined by the needs of the production. It can be anywhere from three to seven people. A big show can have an associate, one or two assistants, and one or two additional production assistants. A play can have an associate, one assistant, and one production assistant. A small play can have one assistant.

An associate and all the assistants are members of the United Scenic Artists Local 829, which also includes scenic, projection, sound, scenic painters, and allied trades. The union has baseline minimum salary designations for different levels of associates and assistants, but sometimes an associate can negotiate their salary above the minimum, depending on the job and the production, including their contract, the rate, the title, and the length of time (number of weeks) for the contract. The traditional entry for a design member candidate is an application, a portfolio review, and letters of recommendation. There is not really a journeyman program, but for anyone wanting to join the union it does require some experience. Technically, the associate is a negotiated assistant working under the assistant designer contract to implement the design.

In addition to the costume associate, there are union assistants who participate in a multitude of pre-production activities once they are on contract. Anyone who does work that involves the aesthetics of the show must be on a union contract, which means a union assistant can participate in fittings, source ready-made items, pull research, swatch fabrics, help set up bibles, and/or coordinate meetings. They help find and set up office space, if the designer's studio is not sufficient to act as the home base for an entire production.

In addition, the team consists of non-union production assistants whose tasks and responsibilities are steps above interns. The non-union assistants usually do pick-ups and drop-offs, and on occasion they make charts, document things, or set up fitting times. They do many of the same tasks as the union assistants and often accompany the union assistants on their shopping journeys, thereby learning the shop sources in midtown and which stores handle specialty items. They help build bibles, furthering their knowledge of what goes into building a costume, and they can help the associate with petty cash and tracking the expenses. Despite all that work, they do not select samples, so their work does not directly impact the costume aesthetics. It is similar to an apprentice where they can learn what skills are required to perform the tasks of assistants and associates and simultaneously hone their own skills.

Through their work on a production, non-union assistants are on track to become a design membership candidate (DMC), a relatively new designation, which developed from the industry need to protect the many non-union assistants who were doing union-level work, but had not yet applied to the union or taken the exam. The design membership candidate program allows a person to continue to refine their craft while under the protection of the union. Although they are non-union, the position is essential for the department and for the future of the industry. If a production is willing, these positions contribute to the next generation of costume professionals.

Budgets

There are two budgets for which the associate is responsible: the staffing budget and the physical costume build budget. The negotiations for these budgets vary depending on the production and general management. On occasion the two budget negotiations can intersect, but general opinion is that the breakdown of each budget should be separate so management has a clearer understanding where every dollar is going.

Staffing Budget

One of the primary budgets the associate creates is for staffing, but that process depends on when their contract is confirmed by the producer/general management office.

Generally, the associate consults with the designer to determine what is appropriate for each show. Whatever plan is crafted, the goal is to make sure the department has coverage through previews. Ideally the associate would like to negotiate the assistant budget early; however, there is one constant in a Broadway production and that is each production is different and so too is each general management/producer office. There is no hard-and-fast rule of when the staffing budget is negotiated.

Sometimes general management tries to predetermine the assistant budget, which oftentimes does not work out, requiring a diligent back and forth negotiation between the costume department and the general manager. Sometimes the assistant budget is negotiated in the designer's contract stemming from those early creative discussions. That negotiation is usually handled between the designer's agent and the management office and then executed by the associate. In other cases, the general management will ask the designer and associate what they think the assistant budget should be and how it will be used, and from there the negotiations begin.

Creating the staffing budget is complex, because much depends on where and if the costumes are in the build process and when delivery is expected. The first task the associate does is make a schedule calculating how many weeks are projected that the costume staff will need to complete the costumes. A musical can require twelve to sixteen weeks, sometimes up to more than twenty weeks for a very big musical. Even if a play is not as complicated as a big musical, an associate on a play can vary widely. Recently the general management for a play with a cast of six with two costumes each wanted the associate for ten weeks, illustrating that the system is ever-changing.

Next the associate sets up a calendar estimating how many assistants are necessary, how their labor should be divided (in joint assessment with the designer), and when they should be brought onto the production. There can be a primary first assistant who has more responsibilities and would need to be around for tech, previews, and even some pre-production. There can be an assistant delegated to handle shoes, who starts just before rehearsals to fit everyone for whatever footwear the actors need and then may not stay all the way through tech. The split of labor also determines how many weeks an assistant works or how many weeks the assistant will be off during a slow week. All of that planning is put into the calendar from which the associate estimates the staffing cost. All of this information is presented to the general manager, and an animated discussion ensues as to what can be cut and what is absolutely essential until an agreement is achieved.

Costume Budget

From the costume charts and designs, the associate and designer work to establish a costume budget, which is for the actual building of the costumes and can occur before creating a staff budget. This is a comprehensive budget that includes fabrics, materials, and any additional labor related to the manufacturing process not included in the shop makers' price. This budget can include things such as space rental, office supplies, shipping, alterations, and overall contingencies. The budget should also try to include unforeseen costs, for example, if shoes were purchased for a dance number but the choreography changed requiring different shoes or design changes that require new fabrics. The budget is usually very detailed and according to associate Alexander Gottlieb, "From personal experience I have been taught to present the budget as transparently as possible to show general managers and producers where every dollar is going."

Much like bids for the scenery, the costume budget is submitted for bids to a variety of shops. The associate begins by investigating fabric costs and interacting with shops to gather cost estimates for the costume construction. A crucial part of that process is creating a bid book. Bid books are made for each shop based on conversations with the designer about where they would like the costumes made. Although there are a few full-service shops, most shops specialize in specific skills, and all designers have their preferences and relationships. Bid books include all the sketches for which the costume department is requesting price estimates and a cover sheet laying out what is included with each design, such as a bodice, skirt, petticoat, etc. If the designer is thinking of additional treatments such as fabric painting, beading, or any other specialty, that is included so the costume shop can give accurate pricing. Also included in the bid book is any peculiar costume requirement or trick a costume needs to execute, such as a breakaway coat.

The designer and associate meet with the shops, present the bid book, and talk through the show and the designs. It is vital for the costume shop to hear from the designer in person what is important about their design as it pertains to the show. The associate also outlines the timelines for the first and final fittings, deliveries of fabrics, and when the completed costumes are expected. At the same time, the associate might also plan for swing and understudy manufacturing schedules and if they need to happen during the main build period or during previews. In some cases, several shops can bid on the same designs, and it would be up to the designer (in conversation with the associate) to make the final decision as to what to put in the budget and to which shop they would like to award the bid. Final approval comes from the general manager/producer.

In developing the costume budget, the associate is responsible for anticipating every item that is to be worn in the show by the cast, the understudies, and the swings, including a general contingency. On occasion the shipping and other external costs are negotiated separately as part of the overall production budget and therefore not relevant to the costume budget conversation. Again, this is on a case-by-case basis.

The amount of time an associate spends researching costs, dealing with financials, and negotiating rates, budgets, fees, and contracts with the shops to come up with the budget varies with each production. It can be four weeks or move very quickly. Sometimes it can take quite a long time. The associate can work with the designer off contract many months before pre-production even begins to arrange all of this. It all depends on how much production build time there is and how much the general manager/producer are willing to pay. There can even be occasions when an associate assembled budgets completely off contract and was never reimbursed because they wanted to get the budget details sorted so as not to delay the costume build period.

Finally, when the pricing has been assembled, the budget can be firmed up. Then the designer (usually with the associate to fine tune the details) negotiates the budget with the general manager/producer. This entire budget process depends on the producer, who quite often knows exactly how much they have allocated for costumes in the production budget, but they like to see what the costume team will present on their own.

Organizing a costume budget for Broadway is a complex operation, but getting the budget to an agreeable amount with management can also take a very long time. There have been times, though rare, when costume building has begun even before the budget has been entirely approved. Generally, after the bids are awarded and contracts are sent out, deposits are paid so the work can begin. With the costume budget approved, the designer and the team can move forward with the physical process of costume building and actually buying all necessary fabrics, materials, and accessories.

As mentioned elsewhere in this book, the number of actor fittings are limited by Actors' Equity, the acting union. An actor can be seen for fittings only four times before rehearsals start and before management must pay the actor for additional fittings. So after taking measurements and a trip to the shoe maker, the costumers have only two more chances to see an actor under union guidelines. Thus, the associate tries to structure fittings with those rules in mind and transmit the actors' information, measurements, and prepare the first fitting before rehearsals begin.

Although the associate position is a pivotal role in the costume department and no matter how close the designer and associate are, it is essential that the designer is present in the formative fittings and costume build stages not necessitating the associate to step in. In scheduling fittings, the associate works around the designer's other commitments or responsibilities to the other departments so the designer is present for almost 100 percent of the fittings/shop meetings. In an extreme case where the designer is really not available, for example, a fitting overlaps due to the rehearsal schedule, the associate and designer can be forced to split up and reconnect afterward to discuss what happened and what is needed to move forward.

This is an example of why the associate should be in tune with the designer's wishes and ideas. They might act in a design capacity in the designer's absence by managing the team and keeping track of any fabric or trim that still needs sourcing for fitting. However, the associate ensures that swatches are available in the fittings and the designer is present to answer any important design questions. The associate's job is primarily to anticipate and react rather than make executive decisions, unless otherwise instructed/discussed with the designer.

In addition to creating the budgets, the associate is responsible for tracking the cost of daily or weekly costume expenditures. The designer is focused on the costume designs and production issues, so it is critical for the designer to be informed if the department is on or over budget.

Costume Building

The costume building process has several layers. There is shop sourcing for materials and accessories, selection of same, maintenance of receipts and expenses, fittings, and specificity as to what a union or non-union person can do.

Shop Sourcing

Before rents in Manhattan became so expensive, there were a multitude of shops in the garment district for fabrics, accessories, and general supplies for costume construction. Today there are fewer shops, some are in Queens and New Jersey, and with the internet there are trim and fabric sources outside the United States, which have expanded possibilities and choices.

Shopping

The costume associate and the assistants are in constant motion running, shopping (especially if it is a modern dress show), or returning items.

The union assistants shop for samples of fabrics (swatching), buttons, trims, laces—any items the designer needs to select to complete a garment. If a silk dress is red, the assistant shops every fabric store and brings back red silk swatches. There is an expertise in any task and what makes a proficient swatcher is not the number of swatches they bring back, but the thoughtfulness of the swatches being gathered. Because not all costume shops provide their own fabric service, the designer relies on the associate and the assistants to be their eyes out in the world accumulating samples using their own study of costumes, building techniques, fabrics, etc., to bring back meaningful and relevant swatches.

The swatching assistant meets with the designer and associate to review the designs and learn the designer's wishes for each costume. How does the designer want the costume to feel, to move onstage, to portray the character, and to support the storytelling? It is crucial to have a dynamic team that can perform this incredibly important job, which is essential to the process. Usually, an assistant contract performing these tasks can exist until the show is frozen.

Accountability to General Manager

Maintaining receipts of purchases is a huge clerical job that is managed by the associate. Each general manager has their own method for handling purchases. An adjustment variable can be whether it is one production or several productions of a show.

The costume department can be assigned credit cards, especially for modern dress shows, where the costume team does almost all the purchasing. The associate instructs their team how they want the receipts assembled and organized for presentation to the management office for reconciliation. Some offices have the credit card statements internally audited by the associate to make sure all receipts are accounted for.

If an associate is managing receipts for several productions of a show, the company can establish a petty cash float. The associate is then responsible to recap and submit those receipts when the float gets too low to assure there is enough cash available for whatever the show needs. On very large modern dress shows, there are constant purchases to manage. In such an instance, an associate might hire a non-union assistant to manage the receipts, make sure everything is entered daily into the expense sheet, and track returns clearly so there are no questions for the general management office about how the money is spent.

Fittings

Once a cast is set, actor fittings are scheduled and measurements are taken. When everything is built from scratch, the measurements and fabrics are transferred to the shops executing the garment. The draper has already created preliminary costume patterns from the sketches, so muslin or inexpensive cotton fabric mock-ups are made for the fittings. Discussions of style, design, line, and fit take place.

Even as the associate joins the designer for the fittings, they are holding daily team meetings about the tasks ahead, swatching fabrics, occasionally taking the designer to the fabric stores, shopping for accessories, meeting with the hair department to make sure the hats fit over the wigs, talking with the shoemaker, trying to balance the budget, and making sure everyone in the department is getting paid. Designs change, scripts change, new costumes may be required, and additional budget meetings may be held. The work is never-ending for the associate.

Once the costumes are ready for transport to the theatre, the associate works with the team to assemble the costumes and oversees their delivery to the theatre. Sometimes the wardrobe supervisor and their assistants are hired a bit early in the pre-production period. They work with the design team to prepare undergarments, make labels, and even attend fittings so they can begin being exposed to the designer's process. The associate consults with the wardrobe supervisor to discuss any special rigging needed for the costumes, or if there are any costume details not farmed out to a shop that need to be done in-house.

Wardrobe is a vital part of the costume department, and the costume team strives to make sure everyone is included and up to date with necessary information. In essence, the wardrobe supervisor is tasked with managing the show when the design team is off contract, so it benefits everyone to have inclusiveness. Collaboration among team members is a must.

Rehearsals

While the actors rehearse offsite, there can be special clothes elements that affect their movement, such as long skirts or choreography in high heels. The associate and assistants pull together stand-in costumes so the actors can rehearse in items that resemble what they will ultimately be wearing. With a new musical, there are a myriad of changes for each department and the stage management team, choreographer, and costume team stay in communication about changes or hints of changes. If it is rumored a dance number will be using raincoats, the costume team looks for rehearsal raincoats so when the decision is confirmed two days later, they are prepared.

The designer and the associate might visit rehearsals frequently, especially with a new musical, and the designer is in constant discussions with the other creatives to make sure any changes are handled appropriately. Then the associate's job is to make sure the changes are implemented seamlessly into the workflow. Also the management office must be informed of any additional costs anticipated for the changes and approval must be obtained.

For a musical, the changes could be the clothes need more flexibility to execute revised choreography (i.e., lightweight fabrics or adding extra room under the arms). Singers might need more space in the chest area to allow for deep breathing. A play usually does not have many adjustments for active body movement, unless it is a very physical play or there are lots of tricks and/or effects. *Harry Potter* is an example where there were magic effects, water effects, etc.

When asked regarding the difference of costumes for a musical or a play, the consensus is that design work is design work, grounded in research, truth, and support of the storytelling. Costume designers are special in that they approach their design work with a deep understanding of how clothes need to function under a very specific set of circumstances. The designer, costume makers, associates, and assistants all operate under the knowledge of these requirements, and while their strength may vary from show to show, there is an element of each that will always be present when it comes to theatre.

Costume designer Gregg Barnes is quoted elsewhere in this book that creating costumes on Broadway is an old-world craft. Associate designer, David Kaley, said something similar:

> Someone says, "Oh this isn't working. Couldn't you just find something different?" My reply is "I'm happy to go to the 1840s' Dancing Norway Store and find the perfect dress to match everything else on stage. I'll be back in a few hours." Ultimately, the thing for us on a show like this [*Frozen*] is we're making couture. The clothes are custom made, they literally start from scratch, and that is why it costs so much.

When anyone in the costume department says they are making couture, it is because costumes are constructed to withstand a brutal eight shows a week regimen and each costume is given the same detail finishing as a Paris runway creation. Costumes are a long-lasting investment for a Broadway production.

Out-of-Town Tryouts

A new musical is like an untamed animal. No one, including the creators, knows what it will be until it is on its feet in front of a paying audience. With a big show the financial stakes are so high that no one wants to open cold in New York anymore. When a production goes out of town, the completed costumes are assumed destined for the Broadway production; however, costume issues can develop. If there are a number of changes that happen out of town, an extension could be discussed with management, but the costume team has to wait until the Broadway transfer is confirmed before they can resume work. Approval for such changes is highly rare after the out-of-town opening.

Normally during an out-of-town tryout, the costume department leaves one team member in New York to troubleshoot problems, find needed items, and ship them to the venue. Sometimes everything goes smoothly and sometimes not.

The associate's job can extend a few weeks after opening primarily to complete administrative work, finish up with understudies and swings, show documentation, and perform budget reconciliation.

On more successful, long-running shows, the associate can be placed on a retainer to facilitate any type of cast change. In that instance, the associate would converse with the designer and the wardrobe supervisor to discuss the best course of action with the current costumes. Can they be refitted for the new actor or, if there is no time for alterations, does the designer need to design a new track or adjust the proportions of the design for a new actor? Whatever the situation is, the process for the associate remains the same. They meet with the designer, contact the shops, make a budget, get it approved with management, place the orders, either purchase the same fabrics or swatch new fabrics and have them approved by the designer, have all the necessary fittings, and manage the build so that the put-in dress rehearsal can happen on schedule. In some cases where the designs have been established, where the designer would not attend the fittings, the associate would remain in constant communication with the designer throughout the process. With a replacement star, the process remains the same.

Every costume is vital to the overall design of the show and every costume is treated with the same attention and care. It is all about making sure every actor is confident and comfortable in the designs and looks their best.

Computers

Computers and technology have changed how the costume department communicates information, tracks expenses, builds bibles, and takes fitting photos. Computers are an enormous asset to the costume management process, and all the new advancements really make it easier to outline the designers' specific requests and create consistency among multiples of the same costume or across multiple productions.

Although younger designers are more computer savvy, they may start with a pencil and paper, scan the sketch into the computer and finish painting it on the computer. David Kaley said, "There is a big push to go digital, but there's something tactile about the design work and I think most people enjoy getting their hands dirty, literally, and just sketching in longhand." The creative process is slow and sketching with pencil and paper is a slow, deliberate process, which allows the artist to think about the design, just as longhand makes the writer focus on the word.

Three-Dimensional Printing

As mentioned throughout this book, the influence of technology is having an impact on almost every facet of theatre production. The dawn of three-dimensional printing for costumes and accessories is an exciting frontier, but it is still in early stages of development. It is possible to take a piece of antique fabric, scan it into a computer and if you have a large enough printer, print enough yardage to create authentic period costumes. That possibility is still in the future. The cost is still relatively high and turnaround slow, but eventually it will become less expensive and faster. Presently, it is very useful in creating accessories and sculpted items, for example jewelry, crowns, belt buckles, and shoulder pieces. It is even possible to create chainmail through three-dimensional printing. These developments influence how theatrical designers work and contributes to hitherto unimagined designs.

Load-Out

The wardrobe supervisor is the person who handles the costume load-out. Generally, load-out is mostly a managerial process for the costume department. The costume associate can be needed if there are specific pieces the production wants to use on the tour to determine where those pieces go and how best the tour can access them. The associate also determines what assets are reusable, how they are to be distributed, and whether they should be donated, stored, or discarded. The general management office may request specific paperwork they want the associate to put together.

Associate designer David Kaley said, "If I had known then what I know now, I would have gotten an MBA instead of an MFA." Associate Alexander Gottlieb concurred: "I agree 100%. As someone who thinks of math as a second language, I have spent many years refining practical business skills to perform this job to the expected standard. Associates are first and foremost facilitators of the design, project managers, and money managers."

Full-Service Shops

Once in New York City when musicals were not so complex and rents were not so exorbitant, there were many full-service costume shops. Two of the busiest were Barbara Matera and Parsons-Meares. They had multiple departments under one roof and could execute the costumes for an entire show. Those full-service theatrical costume workrooms were the go-to one-stop shops to build costumes from the initial draping phase to the finished product. The advantage of that was the draper, stitcher, milliner, tailor, and other artisans could coordinate the fittings for the entire show which saved money by not having the actors come in four different times for four different fittings at four different shops. It was like having a built-in assistant. Today Matera's shop produced several alumni who have their own shops, and only a handful of full-service shops like Tricorne, John Kristiansen, and Parsons-Meares are still in New York City.

With rents soaring, many full-service shops broke up into specialty shops, such as beading, fabric painting, millinery, and tailoring. Many shops moved out of the city entirely. Today, no one shop makes *all* the costumes for one show, even a full-service shop. A production's costumes are distributed throughout a network of full-service and independent businesses. Often one shop is working on one costume or costume part (a hat) for up to twenty-five different productions (and other venues like film and television) with different deadlines rather than working on a whole show. Now it is more likely a full-service costume shop can bid on a specific character or a single page in the bid book, meaning they would produce the entire costume for the character from head to foot for that one page.

This change is partially due to the compressed timeline of a production and budgets. Whereas in the 1970s and 1980s there would be twelve weeks of rehearsals for a musical and fittings built into that timeline, now it can be four to six weeks of rehearsal. Also, no single company can typically handle fabrication of an entire show due to the sheer volume of costumes. Consequently, the work is distributed across several shops, sometimes according to their strengths. For example, one workshop can be contracted to make only the chorus costumes for one dance number in a musical, while another will be contracted to make all the military coats for one number.

The structure of a full-service shop can vary. John Kristiansen has a design background and does some hands-on work, but as his shop grew and he was able to add more departments, like millinery, crafts, and tailoring, his role expanded to include more oversight and administration. He handles the bidding and negotiating process, supervises the various teams, makes artistic suggestions, and makes sure the designer's vision is accomplished.

Usually, the leader of a full-service shop is a draper or a person who has a background and experience in pattern making. The structure of a shop depends on the owner and the shop's needs. Katherine Marshall is a draper who runs her own full-service costume shop, Tricorne Costumes. Ms. Marshall is primarily a draper who worked for Barbara Matera's full-service costume shop for over twenty years. Tricorne is not a huge shop, but it has in-house drapers and a staff, and engages individual shops for specific services that are not in-house.

Essentially, a costume shop team interprets what the designer envisions and works directly with the designer and/or the design associate. As they construct the costume, the costume fabrication team considers how the garment must function onstage, how the actor feels wearing it, and how the actor can move in it.

Another change in costume accessibility in New York City is rental shops. In the 1970s, there were costume rental shops in New York City where regional productions could send measurements for a production and find the costumes they needed. There still is the Theatre Development Fund costume collection, Western Costume in Los Angeles, and some vintage rental places in New York City. That sort of shop has mostly disappeared. Renting a large open space filled with costume inventory and little staff in New York City has become financially unsustainable.

There are so many other elements and decisions other than sewing that cause headaches. Metal closures, zippers, hooks, or bars should not be used because they can rust; if they are used, they have to be painted to protect against rusting. Plastic zippers in clothes should be used because metal zippers rust and the closure will not work. Costumes, unlike street clothes, are built to last and endure. Of course, the Broadway community, like the entire nation, has been confounded by COVID-19. John Kristiansen's shop had built costumes for the English show, *Six*, that was coming to Broadway just as it shut down. He explains how the costumes had been constructed in layers of plastic:

> By the time the show got ready to open, the costumes had medical mesh base (cefar), a layer of holographic vinyl over that, a layer of clear plastic on that to keep the vinyl intact, and a layer of vacuform (a vinyl that was cut into pieces with metal studs on it). Now these costumes were very technical, very sleek, very Ariana Grande/Beyoncé. Once they were left unattended for a long period of time, moisture got in between the [plastic] layers. In order to reopen, we had to reconfigure the fabrication of the costumes.

Some costume challenges only become apparent during tech. How to make the closures better, make quick changes better, and make everything work smoother. The unexpected costume problems of *Six* is a large additional expense for the producer. Many of these issues are fixed with the understudy costumes after the trial and error of the originals.

Shoes are another critical costume component. Costume shops do not build shoes, but they work on them. For the show *Dickenson*, the shoes needed gaiters, which were common in the nineteenth and early twentieth centuries. Gaiters are protective shoe coverings and can be made out of leather or fabric, like spats. Shoes can need distressing for a scene or have to be adapted for stunt/stud shoes, which need cleats like a football shoe. There are quick change shoes that need a trick to accomplish the quick change. Essentially, when a shoe needs a trick, the costume shop does that.

Costume Industry Coalition

Although reduced in number, the majority of costume shops used on Broadway are located in New York City, whether they

Costumes / 97

are full-service or independent entities. Many of them service television, film, cruise ships, concerts, opera, dance, and regional theatre as well. When COVID-19 hit, everything in the entertainment industry shut down resulting with all shops and auxiliary businesses closed.

In June 2020, the Costume Industry Coalition (CIC) was founded to respond to the global pandemic, which shuttered the entertainment industry. CIC members include fifty-five small businesses employing over five hundred specialty artisans, who create, supply, and care for costumes for stage and screen. At the end of 2020, CIC members calculated an economic loss of $26.6 million in gross revenue and faced millions of dollars in collective debt. The mission of the CIC was to advocate for the survival of their members, so all the employees would have an artistic home to which to return once everything reopened.

By coalescing, CIC members raised their profile; for many in the industry, it was the first time they gained some industry awareness of what these members do and what they contribute to the theatre business even in the industry they serve. Producers know designers, but few fully comprehend how their show costumes are created. Brian Blythe, the business manager of John Kristiansen, who organized and is the founding member of the CIC relates an aha moment for a producer:

> One Broadway producer balked at the price of a gown and did not understand why it cost so much. The designer [on the production] offered to design an opening night look for the producer. This required going through the entire design process—fabric meetings, a fitting for the mock-up, with people bustling around taking notes, tucking here and there, sending it back for adjustments, and returning for the final fitting. In the end, she said, "I get it. I get it. I understand now."

The CIC raised money through a variety of initiatives to aid their members and developed a grant program through a nonprofit fiscal sponsor, the Artisans Guild of America.

There are several other positive outcomes from the formation of the CIC, as the members now shift their focus to recovery. It opened communication among colleagues who are dealing with the significant losses aside from work. There is a community effort to rebuild their depleted workforce after losing a large number of employees due to early retirement and the loss of young talent who left because they could not sustain living in New York City.

The CIC also empowered many of the shop owners who have confronted the misogyny of one sort or another for years. Costumes, in general, are viewed as feminized labor, and often do not receive the same respect and budgeting as other design elements. There is now more willingness to say no if the costume timeline is unrealistic or the budget for the costume fabrication is not robust enough.

Costume Draper

Costumes for a Broadway production are a very complex process. As previously stated, numerous artists contribute to each garment. A costume shop is normally contacted by the costume designer regarding a new project and an initial conversation follows.

In the past there were full-service theatrical costume shops that were one-stop shops to build costumes that took the costume process from shopping for fabric swatches through to the finished product. Today Broadway costume making is a mix of full-service and specialized independent shops.

At the head of the costume-making process is the draper, whether it is a full-service or individual shop. A draper is the person who takes the designer's sketch and translates it into a three-dimensional fabric mock-up of the costume, from which a pattern is made. They have knowledge and experience in pattern making. Most New York shops are run by drapers or a person with a design background. Rarely is one run by an administrator. It is more efficient to have a draper with the experience and knowledge of how to make a pattern and put a costume together.

Each shop submits an estimate for their work. If several independent shops are involved aside from the draper, such as beading or fabric painting, their estimate is submitted to the draper or shop owner. Then the draper or shop owner calculates the cost of the assigned costume and submits the overall estimate to the designer or the associate. Sometimes a formal bidding session is required similar to the set design bids, but this does not happen as often as it did twenty years ago. The costume associate integrates all that information into the costume budget, which is submitted to the general manager for approval. Any cost issues are negotiated and once the budget and shops are approved by the general manager/producer, the shop(s) is hired.

The next step is the draper. The costume draper technically drapes the fabric onto a dress form, supervises the actor's fitting, makes the physical dress pattern, and oversees the costume fabrication. Costume construction flows from the pattern.

Katherine Marshall worked in Barbara Matera's shop until 2000, when she opened her own full-service costume shop Tricorne Costumes. She is the lead draper with a staff of several drapers organized into groups. Each group is led by a draper and is responsible for a garment from beginning to end. By monitoring the costume build, the draper knows the problems encountered and adjustments necessary for that specific costume. Each shop has its own modus operandi, but Katherine Marshall tries to attend every fitting with her drapers, so the designer or the design associate has one designated contact to handle queries.

Scheduling and organizing the many specialty components (i.e., draping, pattern making, first cutters, padding, beading, fabric painting, stitchers) takes precision planning to coordinate all those elements in the fabrication process to meet the deadline. The draper oversees all of it while the design associate monitors the progress.

A draper is brought into a production about four to six weeks before rehearsals start. This is prep time during which the shops obtain swatches of fabrics (possible fabric samples), if this has not been done by the designer or the design staff. The samples are shared with the designer who makes the final decision for each costume.

Generally, the commercial clothing industry uses computers, because it is mass manufacturing of clothing. Certainly, fashion designers make finely built garments with a theatrical flare for their runway shows, but theatrical costume making is not mass production. Theatrical costume makers construct garments that are reinforced to withstand immense wear and tear being worn eight times a week for possibly three to five years and survive. The costume is specific to a character in a production. Much of theatrical costume making is done by hand.

Some designers use computers for their costume sketches, but many still do hand-painted watercolors. Often at the initial draping of the mock-up on the dress form, the designer or associate is present to answer any questions the draper has. Whether hand drawn or computer drawn, the draper needs the full picture of the design, including the front and back, because the mock-up draping goes completely around the body. If the draper did not have a drawing of the garment back, the designer can explain what they want for the back of the garment.

This is all done in the draper's prep time, because fittings require actors and cannot be scheduled until the actors are in rehearsal. All of the design issues must be settled because there is no backtracking or major changing once the costume work moves forward.

The draper makes a rough mock-up (a test version of the garment), referred to as a *toile*, using a dress form. The toile is usually in muslin or a draping crepe. The choice of toile fabric must correspond to the qualities of the real costume fabric, because a muslin mock-up for what will be a jersey dress does not look the same or drape properly. A mock-up is created for most costumes in a show. If it is a giant musical and has three hundred costumes, it is possible three hundred mock-ups are created.

When rehearsals begin, actors' fittings are scheduled around their rehearsal schedule. The draper and their team take the mock-up to the first fitting to try it on the actor. With the reality of a specific actor and more knowledge of what the staging or choreography is, adjustments are made to the mock-up. Occasionally, though not often, a director attends an early costume fitting, especially if it is a star or a replacement star.

Once the mock-up is accepted, either the draper or the first-hand takes apart the mock-up and corrects the flat paper pattern, which is a feat of engineering. Next the first-hands, who are the fabric cutters, place the pattern on the fabric and cut it into pieces. Sometimes the fabric stays whole and is sent to a dyer or a fabric painter. When the fabric has been treated by those skills, it goes back to the first-hand who cuts the costume pattern. If there is beading for the entire yardage, the beader is given the cut pattern pieces to bead. For small beaded pieces, the beader is given that fabric piece, which later will be sewn onto the costume.

The pattern pieces are given to the stitchers who use the sewing machine to stitch the garment together. Finally, the garment is passed on to the hand-finishers who sew on all the buttons, closures (i.e., zippers, hooks, snaps), and hems. This is all fine hand-finishing; no machines are used in this stage.

The draper's team is finished when the costumes are completed, leave the workroom, and go to the theatre. However, when the production is in tech, the team is available if any issues arise that the wardrobe team cannot handle. During the run if there are cast changes, especially a star lead, the shop can be called in to create an entirely new set of costumes for the replacement star. It depends on the finances of the production. Sometimes for other cast members, the choice of whether to alter the costumes can depend on how long the costumes have been worn and what condition they are in. Now with the existence of COVID-19, how costumes are managed may have new rules. Actors' Equity rules are that any garment worn next to the skin must be new or newly built.

If there is an out-of-town tryout, a shop might send two or three people to the location to manage adjustments while keeping a staff member in New York. With a new production, things are always in flux. Suddenly a dance number requires an alteration. If it is a tour of a show that has already opened, the costumes are shipped to the venue and the wardrobe supervisor handles the changes.

A play has a smaller cast and fewer costume changes. The difference between a musical and a play is the sheer volume of costumes. A musical has a chorus, more people, more costumes, more physical movement, and definitely more wear and tear. Changes are inevitable even during tech, so to work in the costume department one cannot be married to an idea that no longer serves the purpose of show. Anyone working on a new theatre production must have tremendous flexibility in thinking, execution, and good blood pressure.

Disney is a very large organization and for their Disneyland walkarounds they sometimes ask for a digital file for the pattern, but as Katherine Marshall said, "We're pencil and paper people. We rarely use computers for our patterns."

Beading

Another fascinating "old-world craft" that some designers use with frequency is beading. Beading is exactly what it says. It is creating beaded pieces or beading fabric for a costume by hand. It is a highly specialized skill that is beginning to get lost due to cost increases, easier methods (which have great limitations), and a shrinking talent pool. There are many people who do beading as a hobby. There are not many professional beaders working today, and most in New York work in a traditional costume shop. On Broadway, the beader, in the shop, works primarily with the draper or shop owner. The freelance beading designer works with the costume designer.

There is a teacher in Kentucky who teaches beading, and there is École Lesage in Paris that offers classes in embroidery and beading. As a profession, beading is *very* detailed work and can be physically tedious. There are a couple of costume shops in New York and one in California that have in-house beaders, and there are several companies in India. When a Broadway show has a large beading requirement, the overflow is dispersed to California and India.

Tambour beading is a French style of hand beading and has a very specific technique. The French use this technique to embellish couture gowns, interiors, and accessories. It is also a technique used on costumes. Bob Mackie made beading quite popular when creating costumes for Cher's television show in the 1970s. There is a great difference between beading a costume for a television show that will be worn maybe three or four times and a Broadway show where the costume is worn eight shows a week for as long as the show runs. It requires durability and maintenance once a show opens.

If it is a heavily beaded show, like the musical *Aladdín*, the costumes endure a lot of wear and tear. In that situation, a beader can be hired to work in the theatre a couple of days a week just for maintenance and repairs of the beading. Although beaders in the costume shops do not belong to a union, if a beader works in the theatre they must belong to Theatrical Wardrobe Union,

Local 764, under the IATSE umbrella. Then the beader works through the wardrobe department.

On Broadway, the costume designer can spend up to a year doing sketches, meeting with the director, and finalizing the designs. By the time a costume shop is engaged, the decision to use beading has been made. There are always deadlines in theatre, and opening night is going to happen. Depending on how much beading a show is using determines when the beader's work begins. Beading is an extremely slow, deliberate process, and it is only one step in building a costume. The beader must be proactive in scheduling their work because a small beading project can take five days and a large project can take months.

Once the costume design and shops are approved, the draper makes a mock-up of the costume for the actor's first fitting. From that fitting, the pattern is adjusted and the corrected pattern for whatever section is to be beaded goes to the assigned bead designer. In most cases, the bead designer cannot plan their schedule until they have a finalized pattern for the garment from the draper.

The next step is to design the beading and draw it on the draper's pattern. The costume designer and beading designer work in tandem, each contributing ideas. By now in the process, the costume designer's designs and color palette have been approved by the production. Next a sample of the beading assignment is made using the suggested beads for approval.

It is most likely that the bead designer will choose the beads, as they will be most familiar with what is available. The bead designer estimates the quantity and what kind of beads are required. The amount of beading for a costume can vary widely on Broadway. A costume beader can be hired for a specific part, such as the back of a jacket, or it can involve the entire costume. The basic process of beading is the same.

A beading project can use a variety of bead types and colors. There is a vast cost difference between Swarovski crystal or Chinese crystal. If the production is planning to use Swarovski crystal, it could cost five times the Chinese crystals. There is also a vast difference between using crystals and sequins (both of which can use the Tambour technique).

The bead designer is responsible for purchasing the beads and is reimbursed by the production. The receipts are accumulated and turned into the production company after the design and sample have been approved.

The bead designer then draws the beading design on the chosen costume fabric. This can be done using tracing paper or a stamping system. For Tambour beading, the design is marked on the wrong side of the fabric. Next the bead designer makes a *key* for the beading, which means painting that design pattern with color markers corresponding to the placement and color of each bead to be used, and providing the bead selection which corresponds to the colors used on the pattern, turning the process into a sort of "paint by number."

The piece of fabric is stretched on a wooden frame, which can be set on two sawhorses. The beads are strung on a thread, which is wrapped around a spool that is held up often with a nail tacked onto one of the sawhorses. This is a rather primitive frame setup, but there are fancier frames.

The beader works facing the backside of the fabric using a small hook, somewhat like a crochet hook. With the left hand underneath the fabric (assuming one is right-handed) the bead is moved to the front side of the fabric where it is to go. With the hook in the beader's right hand, the hook is inserted into the fabric, catches the thread, and pulls it through, tightening the bead flush with the front side of the fabric. The beader repeats this by moving another bead to the fabric and hooking it. It is an extremely old technique that is actually similar to crocheting.

In India, the beaders are mostly men and they work on the right side of the fabric. They put the beads directly on the hook, but the stitch is the same. As mentioned, in Tambour beading all beads/sequins must be strung on a spool of thread. The spool gives the beader a continuous length of thread with which to work. This is made easier if the beads/sequins that are purchased are already available on strings. Then the beader simply ties the string of beads/sequins to the spool and moves the beads/sequins onto the spool.

When crochet or Tambour beading, only the shape of the pattern pieces of the costume are beaded. The beading is close to but not on the seam line and the costume is stitched together with a zipper foot. Purchased beaded fabric is beaded from selvage to selvage top to bottom, so there is no seam allowance. To make the garment, the pattern pieces are marked on the fabric and the beads are cracked off in the seam allowance space. The thread is not cut because it is a crochet stitch and if the thread is cut, a dot of fabric glue is applied to stabilize the stitch. Either way it is very labor intensive.

Once the beading is finished, the beader puts a light covering of fabric glue on the wrong side to secure the threads. The work is then sent either to the bead designer or directly to the draper, who, with their team, will cut and sew the costume.

If the beader needs a line of beads comprising different beads, those beads have to be hand-strung on the thread. Sequins purchased on strings are called "worms." However, they all have to be transferred to a spool for Tambour beading. If a combination of beads is required, they can be set up on one-yard lengths of thread and then transferred to the spool as needed. This combination of beads is called a "mix." The mix stringing can be done by anyone in the shop. At Barbara Matera's shop, a sample would be made and members of the housekeeping staff would do the stringing. Finding beads or sequins already strung for sale is basically available only from a few wholesale companies.

Aladdin went on tour in Japan and the costume beading was essentially the same. However, between the time of the original production in New York and the Japanese tour, five bead sources had closed. So finding sources and material is getting more difficult in many facets of costume making.

When ordering costumes for a new production, there will typically be a costume for the first cast, each of the understudies, and swings. If there are cast changes, much depends on whether the replacement actor is close in size to the original actor. The original costumes can be altered, but a new beaded costume would be made for a major star.

Disney uses beading frequently for their theme park walkabout characters. There were plans for re-creating costumes from *The Black Panther* for ten walkabout actors. A lot of sections of the costumes are beaded. The beader made a prototype and once Disney approved, the beading was duplicated for ten costumes originally and more later.

Hand beading is an exquisite art that has a special quality as opposed to glued on beads or sequins; show lighting can enhance or detract the effect. As with many artistic pursuits, economics enters the equation and the bead maker Swarovski has developed a method called hot fix, where a lay person can buy rhinestones or gems with glue on the back that melts when it gets hot. Hot fix comes in various shapes and colors. One does not need any skill or knowledge of beading to do it.

Although there is a distance between the stage and the theatre audience, the combination of beads and colors using hand beading gives a richness and sumptuousness under the lights that glued on beads cannot. Even the untrained eye can discern the difference of the luxurious distinctive look of hand beading. More importantly, glued beads/sequins certainly are not as sturdy as hand beading for a Broadway show.

Polly Kinney, an exquisite professional beader, said, "For just one costume for one actor it's 80 people. All the stitchers, dyers, painters, beaders, drapers, etc., etc."

Fabric Painter

Painting has been used in theatrical productions for centuries. It was used to create illusions onstage such as backdrops, room interiors, balustrades, and costumes. It embellished costumes to make the fabric look more opulent and to give historical detail to a garment. Sometimes fabric painting today is used when the designer cannot find the right fabric or color for their design or when a character has a particular look, for example, the cats in *Cats*, Pinocchio's wooden look in *Shrek*, or the scales on the Little Mermaid. Although this book focuses on Broadway, fabric painting is widely used in rock shows, ballet, opera, film, television, and fashion.

The process takes time and is expensive in today's overall production costs. When big musicals like *Cats* and *Will Rogers Follies* came more into vogue in the 1980s and 1990s, some production costs were not quite as expensive as they are today, costume scenes were bigger, and producers were more willing to allocate money for a costume specialty like costume painting.

Fabric painting is painting with dyes, not paint, and there has been a tremendous improvement in those dyes. In addition to being a fine artist, the painter must be fully knowledgeable regarding the science in using the dyes on fabric. On Broadway the work must be durable to withstand eight shows a week, especially a long run. Also the improved dyes allow flexibility for dancer movement and durable laundering. Painting with dyes is mostly done on silk, wool, spandex, or nylon. Cotton can be painted as well, but it is a different process. The painter must know what works on which fabrics and how the dyes react under theatrical lighting.

Once the costume designer has completed their drawings, the designer and costume associate start to compile costs for the costume building budget and prepare for a bid process, similar to sets. The designer may indicate the need for fabric painting in their sketches, or it can be a shop owner while accumulating pricing for the bid who thinks fabric painting might be needed. There are full-service shops who may have in-house painters and then there are painters who work independently and have their own shops. In either case, the fabric painter can be hired for a specific costume or a group of costumes. If the painter works independently, their approval is by the designer and the general manager/producer. If the work is coming from a full-service shop, the owner chooses the in-house painter which is part of the shop's contract. Sometimes a designer may prefer a specific painter.

The fabric painter works primarily with the designer and the draper. The fabric painter meets with the costume designer, discusses the designer's vision, and reviews the sketches. The painter then tests samples of the selected costume fabric with dyes to make sure the dyes work on that fabric. Those tests are shown to the designer for approval.

Fabric painting for a costume, like beading, is totally determined by the costume designer's drawings. The uses of fabric painting are quite varied. It can be a border, a single design pattern to be appliquéd, the entire costume, or the entire costume yardage. Sometimes they paint on the finished costume. The need depends on the design.

Once there is a cast, the painter attends the actors' first fitting to see where their work is actually to go on the costume and how the design drapes on the actor's body. A painter uses a pencil to draw the design on the white muslin mock-up at the first fitting with the sketch in hand and the designer present. The pencil might describe where color flows from place to place on the costume mock-up, or the performer's anatomy (muscle highlights on a flesh unitard, for example) is sometimes marked. Those pencil marks from the mock-up are transferred to the paper pattern the draper has created along with any fitting corrections the draper has encountered. The draper then has the costume paper pattern laid out on the "real" fabric and all those paint marks, including seam allowances and/or relevant anatomy marks from the fitting, are transferred to the fabric.

The painter is given the fabric to be painted with the paper pattern outline and paint marks transferred to it, and using the marks as a guide stretches the fabric out on a table to paint. After the painted fabric is steamed to set the dye and washed, it is returned to the draper to cut and put together for the second fitting. At this time adjustments can be implemented such as deepening a color or making seams match perfectly.

If the design is a border, the draper marks the fabric where the border goes and sends the fabric to the painter to work on. When finished, the painter returns the completed painted fabric to the costume shop, where the stitchers sew the pieces together.

If it is a piece that is to be an appliqué, the draper gives the fabric piece to the painter with the paint marks transferred to it. Those pieces are returned to the shop where they are appliquéd to the costume.

Fabric has grain directions and sheen components, so the draper tells the painter exactly the grain direction the painting should follow or which way the sheen of the fabric works. These are critical details for how the finished costume will look onstage and under lights.

The painter attends rehearsals in the theatre to check how the lighting affects the costumes. Changes that occur during rehearsals on the finished costume are crucial, as fabric painter Jeff Fender said, "It is easier to *put something in*, but *hard to take anything out*." There is no time or budget to rebuild a costume at that stage of the production.

There are some unique styles for a fabric painter in their arsenal. One is ombre painting, which is a dying technique where the color grades from dark to light or blends one color to another in a gradual manner. This is frequently used in ballet or dance costumes. For Broadway more often ombre is marked during the fitting and painted on the pattern pieces to avoid fabric waste. Ombre has become a popular fashion style in some commercial clothing.

A fabric painter may be commissioned to paint a costume that is already put together. For *Movin' Out*, the dancers' costumes had custom flowers on the bodice and a design that went down and across the hem of a skirt. In this case, the costume pieces were partially basted together, so the fabric could lie flat for the painter to paint flowers across seams.

Some fabric painting, but not all, is done *after* the costume is made, which makes the whole process very intense. There was a set of white chorus costumes in *Frozen* that were painted after they were made. They were shaded, air-brushed, and spattered with white paint, just to make them look less solid white. Then there is something called "fantasy aging" where the costume is made to look richer and more sumptuous. Fabric painter Margaret Peot recalled a production of a classic play where beautifully tailored suits had brocade patterns painted on them with metallic paint, which caught the light and made them appear more elegant.

Distressing or aging a costume is another instance where the fabric painting is done on a completed costume. Distressing usually refers to making it look old, bloody, or muddy, but can also mean making a costume look a little less new or simply dirty. When aging costumes, the painter often attends the tech rehearsal with the designer to see how the costume is used and what happens to it onstage. The designer may want adjustments such as making it a bit dirtier or grayer. Tech is late in the production process, so there is no room for error. Despite all the detailed work, the very best costume aging is when the audience does not see the details of the mud splatter or the darkening into a seam but accepts the visual reality as part of the storytelling.

A musical or drama is not that different for the fabric painter, but each form has its own challenges. For both genres, distressing is the same for a homeless character, but in one they are dancing and in the other they are standing still. It has more to do with lighting, sets, movement, and what it looks like as a whole piece. Distance in the theatre also affects the painter. How big the theatre is and how close the audience is to the stage affects how the illusion of the painting is received.

Today's stage lighting is a very critical element of theatrical fabric painting. The painter needs to know what lighting colors or power are being used on the sets, whether the lighting is warm or cool, and what kind of overall effect is wanted on the production. Today's LED lights can sometimes wash out costume painting subtleties. Also a lot of choices are character driven, such as is the character mean or nice. All of these issues affect the painter's use of dyes. As fabric painter, Jeff Fender, recalled:

> I remember doing *110 in the Shade* designed by Santo Loquasto. It was tricky because a lot of the actors had the same costume for two Acts and everybody had to be sweaty and hot. The whole first Act was bright yellow lights, hot; then it was night, and the atmosphere was lavender and cool. I had to almost paint the costumes twice so they would show up in hot lights as well as cool. Sometimes you just have to experiment to solve that kind of problem.

Theatre is finding more applications for digital printing even with its limitations and expense. It can be especially useful in certain costume circumstances. It does not have the depth or quality of hand-painting and can appear a little mechanical. However, digital printing can be a cheaper process if costumes for an entire chorus number are needed. The dyes are printed on the fabric and the dye does not soak through as much as hand-painting. If the design is all-over polka dots (again because the fabric or color could not be found), digital printing is cheaper than hand-painting, and it certainly is less monotonous, as one painter would have had to paint all the polka dots in the past. For the original *42nd Street*, there was a set of Hawaiian shirts that were all hand-painted because the designer wanted specific colors. Now they would print them. In the current production of *Aladdin*, the Genie wore Hawaiian shirts. The first one was hand-painted, and the rest were digitally printed. It was cheaper.

On a long run, how well fabric painting holds up varies on the type of show and the use. In a show like *Cats*, three unitards at a time per character were ordered because it was such a physical production. If someone simply walks out onstage and sings a song, the wear and tear is much less and maintaining a supply of the costume is less demanding. If a new cast member joins a long run, anything worn close to the skin is made new. Anything not worn near the skin (i.e., a jacket) can be altered if the replacement actor is near the same size as the original actor. If painted costumes get worn out or damaged, they are repaired or replaced. And finally, and perhaps most importantly, it is possible to touch up a painted costume.

The circle of fabric painters in New York City is relatively small. As mentioned at the beginning of the chapter, they work in many venues. Jeff Fender has his own studio with one assistant who is a painter and handles administrative details. He also has two in-house painters and hires more as work demands. Margaret Peot is an in-house fabric painter at Parsons-Meares, LTD, a full-service shop mentioned earlier.

Milliner

Millinery is another very specialized skill, and there is a huge difference between fashion millinery and theatrical millinery. Fashion millinery is primarily designed and manufactured to be worn by a general public, so the construction and sizing is more uniform, limited in size, and more mass-produced. For a fashion milliner, it is often making the same thing with variations over and over again.

Theatrical millinery is an entirely different product and is used in opera, Las Vegas, circuses, cruise ship theatrical productions, and theatre. Millinery in theatre is part of a character in a story in a specific time period. On Broadway, the hat is created, worn by, and constructed for a specific person or persons in dramatic or comedic situations. The problem-solving issues of taking a designer's sketch and turning it into a wearable piece of headgear contribute to making theatrical millinery more creative and providing infinite possibilities. There are not many skilled milliners in general and not all Broadway shows have hats, so the work is limited. Most active milliners work in multiple venues at the same time to sustain a living.

There are frequent cast changes on cruise ships, so the millinery process is not quite as specific as the other venues.

There are various general instruction online sites for millinery, but few in-person programs. Some college theatre departments have millinery classes. The milliner Taylor Green recalled:

> The theatre department [Boston University] was based out of the Huntington Theatre at that time, which is a LORT B regional theatre in Boston, so I worked with their milliner, Denise Wallace-Spriggs, for a while. It was like an internship and I was sort of her assistant. It's like a regional theatre that's in-house. but one show at a time. Usually, the designer would come to the theatre as the designer in residence while the show was being built. There was a lot more interaction with the designer.

For Broadway, the costume designer submits the millinery work for bids. Whether it is an independent millinery shop or part of a full-service costume shop, the bidding process is the same. It is the shop owner who negotiates the contract. It is the milliner who calculates the number of labor hours and the cost of the materials it will take to produce the job. Then there is a negotiation period with the general manager and producer. Once the bid is accepted the process commences. An individually owned millinery shop usually has a small staff of three or four milliners and only produces hats or headgear.

A full-service shop might be lucky enough to rent space to a wig designer, so when bidding on a job if that wigmaker is already hired for the show, that shop can offer multiple services in-house. The advantage for the milliner of having a wig designer in the building is that they can work directly with the wig designer and there can be one fitting for both wig and hat for the actor. Economically, this saves the production expense because an actor must be paid for additional fittings after the initial four fittings allowed by the Actors' Equity. An example is John Kristiansen's shop was awarded the job for all of Diana's looks in the musical *Diana: The Musical*, which saved the production money. The actor could go in once to fit every costume and hat.

With hats, there is often the lead milliner and an associate who is equally skilled as a milliner. However, many milliners work alone. Hat making starts with a hat block, which is a wooden block carved into the basic shape of a particular hat style. A commercial hat-making company has hundreds of blocks to fit all sizes, head shapes, and hat styles, but there are not blocks for everything.

A theatrical milliner does not have that sort of inventory, so it requires experience, problem-solving, and creativity to materialize a designer's vision. Each type of hat has its own configurations, and every human head is different. One example is a top hat.

Top hats are *very* hard to make, require a lot of experience, and are used infrequently onstage, so theatrical milliners do not usually keep a block in inventory. It is also not built the same way a fashion house would. Taylor Green reflected, "For something like a top hat we don't have a 100 million blocks to choose from, so a lot of it is done by hand. That is when I usually take over because it is more consistent and quicker for me to do it myself."

Fitting the head is extremely important because it can become uncomfortable very quickly. If an actor is wearing it in multiple scenes eight shows a week, the top hat must endure strenuous wear and tear, especially in a musical. It involves the circumference of the head, the shape of the head, and how long the head is from front to back. The milliner must consider wigs and hairstyles, which affect the fit. All of that affects the pitch of the top hat or the shape of a hat.

Some designers are more hands on, and others delegate a lot of responsibilities to their associates. On a large musical, the milliner consults with the wig designer, the costume designer, and the design associate. If a microphone pack is to be hidden in the wig, the sound designer is also involved.

British designers do both sets and costumes, so their associates are extremely important. They speak for the designer who may be in England, but they are in constant communication for any developments or questions that crop up regarding sets or costumes. The British designer's costume associate is often an American who works with the New York shops and has a relationship with the makers.

Hats in a musical are especially troublesome because of the additional element of choreography. There is much more vigorous physicality, so if it is a number that requires a hat to come off and on during a dance, how do you keep the hat on the head of a dancer? Taylor Green recounts working on a production of *Guys and Dolls*:

> The only difference is the element of choreography. You might think about how to bond the hat a little more aggressively. When I was working with Lynne Mackey on *Guys and Dolls*, there is the "Take Back Your Mink" number. The dancers had little teeny, weeny perky hats with feathers. The choreography required them to take off the hat, throw it on the ground, then put it back on. How do you make the hats stay on? Normally you would pin them and do all sorts of tricks to make the hats stay on during their number. What we did was have magnets in their hats and we sewed magnets into their wigs. So their hats would just go "ponk" and connect with the magnet to

their heads. The wigs were pinned to their hair and solid, so the magnets disengaged without pulling the wigs off.

Theatrical hats are very different from street hats. Special material is used to construct them to make the hats strong enough to survive eight shows a week and the choreography. The milliner uses a variety of gusseting, stretch panels, and plastic sheeting versus buckrum in the hats. These are techniques to make the hats sturdier. Plastic sheeting is a stitchable plastic that is much sturdier than buckrum (coarse linen/cotton cloth stiffened with gum or paste), and it does not break down. The hats are finished with coatings, lacquers, and different painted surfaces to aid their strength and longevity. Double seals (which are doubled sprung steel wires) versus a single wire (softer traditional millinery wire in fashion hats) in the brims helps maintain the shape. Multiple pieces or extra seaming is used to make sure the hat shape stays consistent.

If a show goes on tour, the hats are packaged into road boxes, put in trucks, shipped, unloaded, and reloaded at the next venue. There is a lot of manhandling. Another tour contingency is if it is going on cruise ships, not just being shipped overseas. It will be exposed to sea air, which causes metal to rust and break. Consequently, plastic rods, plastic nylon rods, or cord, which are not affected by salt air are used in the hats.

During the run, the hats are repaired by the wardrobe team. If the hats are not working, they can be changed or remade up to dress rehearsal. If something breaks, a wire snaps, or a problem needs solving, the milliner works with the wardrobe crew. Hopefully, there are duplicates. Ideally the leads get two of everything and the understudies get one. If there is a cast change later in the run, an entirely new hat must be made.

If a hat is damaged after the show has opened, then the millinery shop has to charge when the item is brought back for repairs. That is mostly avoided because it is a new expense, which productions want to avoid.

Actors' Equity has specific costume rules for Broadway. The exterior of a costume can be altered, but if a costume touches an actor's skin, it cannot be reused. The same goes for a hat. With

Frozen, there were cast changes which required reordering a whole set of costumes for a new actor, including fittings.

Every department on Broadway is tasked with problem-solving. The creativity for the talent is figuring out how to make a design work. Taylor Green relates a story about the *Beauty and the Beast* character Cogsworth for the Disneyland in China:

> The original Broadway Cogsworth character designed by Ann Hould-Ward was a clock, which was stiff, could not sit, and stood the entire show. The Chinese Disneyland, which Ms. Hould-Ward was also designing, wanted him to be able to sit down, stand up, move all the way around, *and* have a door to open in the front for his pendulums to come out. It was a *huge* problem. How can you have a hard door, have a guy that could sit, *and* look like a clock. I think that is so fascinating and you really have to work closely with the designer to figure it out. That's pretty much fun. Every show is different. Every designer is different. Every associate is different. The more you work in the business, you realize what each designer wants.

Body Padding

There are very few milliners in the Broadway community and since it is a limited need, milliners often diversify their skills. Another costume component is body padding, which is adding variously constructed padding for an actor to wear for a specific character. A lot of milliners, like Taylor Green, learn how to do it. Some have more experience than others, but it can be an asset on a tour to have multiple skills. There are videos on YouTube and other internet sites, but learning body padding is mostly from observing other people doing it and then figuring it out. It is a skill handed down from one person to another. As Taylor Green said, "It's like sculpting, art, and anatomy combined!"

The first thing is the padding creator must discuss with the designer what is supposed to be accomplished. Body padding can range from subtle to massive. Is the character fat or pudgy, or does the character have a middle age paunch? Although the costume designer provides a character sketch of the look they want, in the end it is the actor's body that ultimately determines the proportion of padding to the body.

The first step is to cast an actor and then make drawings of the performer's shape and figure. A visual balance is worked out with the designer before any costume discussions. Proportion is crucial. The body cannot be so big that the actor's head looks small.

Marketing a show is another issue, especially if it is a star. Pre-press begins about three months in advance of a Broadway opening, so building a star's costumes must start another three months before that. At least one look for the star must be ready for press photos and advertising to generate ticket sales. This is added pressure because the general body suit shape needs to be completed before the costume team can even begin. The costume team needs accurate padding measurements to make shirts, pants, and whatever else goes with it.

Fat padding is tricky, so often on Broadway it is helpful if the fat padding and outer garments can be built together at a full-service costume shop because there can be more in-house coordination, which results in a better garment. Once the base fat pads are done, the suit is given to the tailoring or dressmaking department where it is put on a dress form to drape the pattern.

There is a specific process in building body padding. First, an undersuit fitting close to the body sort of like a sleeveless leotard or 1920s bathing suit is made. Everything else is built out from that undersuit. Open-weave or reticulated foam is often used (like what is used in air-conditioning filters) because it can be cut and shaped with a razor blade, and it is washable and breathable. Hooping (steel or nylon boning like what is used for a hoop skirt), gel beads (like those used in stuffed animals), and pellets are sewn in bags to resemble a saggy fat roll. Sometimes the designer wants the fat padding to move and squish realistically as the performer moves, which is where the pellets or beads come in. (It resembles a less exaggerated version of Carol Burnett's rice bag breasts.) The choice is a matter of addressing the needs of the design, the character, and the weight of the padding, which is important for the performer who wears the padding eight shows a week.

Depending on the goal, in addition to the undersuit, there can be a few spots of fat that are fabric covered and stitched over the undersuit. If it is a whole-body suit, there are three layers—the undersuit that touches the body, the muscles/fat patches, and the cloth outer layer covering everything—and all the layers get stitched together like a sandwich.

There are tricks to make the body padding sturdier and last longer. Nylon rods can be used as well as quilting to help keep the shape. Everything can be encased with a sports jersey or athletic cloth so that moisture from perspiration can escape out of the foam, so it does not break down. The athletic cloth also helps the padding keep its shape. The trickiest part of body padding is figuring out how to get it on the actor and zipped up without leaving a big zipper line. The surface must appear smooth.

Aside from the labor cost of making body padding, the most expensive part is the foam itself. It only comes from the West Coast in enormous sheets and is quite expensive, so there must be a long lead time to order the materials for shipping. The other financial consideration is limited New York City space for storing materials, so costume shops do not like to overstock. All of these criteria are factored into the bidding process.

Padding is actually more common on a tour or arena show because that casting is more focused on someone with a particular skill like ice skating rather than whether they look right for a part. Then the need for the padding is more intent on making the ice skater resemble the fat character in the story. Broadway can just cast the body they need.

Again, like everything in a Broadway production, body padding must be durable, built properly, and especially maintained properly. That responsibility falls on the show's wardrobe team, which is highly professional. The wardrobe team works in an unbelievably small, hot, steamy space, especially in the winter and the team is scrunched together.

There are certain procedures for body padding followed in a production. Actors perspire profusely performing eight shows a week under hot lights. Body padding cannot be thrown into the dryer. It must be hand-washed and aired out, with enough time to dry completely. Frequently, two identical body paddings are made so the actor can alternate.

Sometimes the costume is really complicated with lights, battery packs, and other gear. Since during the run the wardrobe supervisor maintains the padding, the padding maker brings the supervisor to fittings to explain how the padding is constructed and show the best way to maintain it. Taylor Green recalls one of the costumes for *Cats*.

> We did the Magical Mr. Mistoffelees who lights up. He had little LEDs lights all over his jacket with wires going all the way through his jacket. The lights were plugged into a battery pack and they were also plugged into a remote control box managed by the light board. The wardrobe team was responsible for making sure the batteries were changed and replaced every night, as well as making sure all were working every show.

With body padding that intricate, the padding maker must make all the equipment accessible for the wardrobe team to do their job. Sometimes they make a lining with a zipper, so a team member can reach in and grab everything. To house the equipment, they create little Velcro bags to hold the boxes, wire containers, buttons, and any other technical items that can be put into the padding in such a way so the costume does not look too bulky. In addition, to protect from perspiration shorting out the wires, little fabric tubes are made to cover the wires.

It is all very detailed work.

6

Wardrobe

Wardrobe Supervisor

Once the costumes are constructed and the cast moves to the theatre, the next essential costume component is the wardrobe supervisor. A wardrobe supervisor recommends their team, which is an indispensable unit of a show. The supervisor is the liaison between the wardrobe team, the costume designer, the design associates, the production manager, and sometimes the producer.

The supervisor can be recommended by the costume designer or the producer and requires approval from both, but they are ultimately hired by the producer. The supervisor preserves the designer's creative vision from opening night throughout the run. The producer wants someone who can determine the most cost-effective way to have a team who maintains the costumes and works in harmony.

The first thing the supervisor does is read the script. The supervisor needs to know the cast size, the number of scenes, the style of costumes, how many costume changes are planned, what workspace the wardrobe team will have, the estimated number of people needed for the department, the estimated number of work hours a week *outside the show* are needed to tend the costumes, and how much and what kind of equipment is anticipated. The budget must include everything from cleaning, repairing, and repurchasing replacement items, including how many ironing boards, irons, sewing machines, threads, and scissors are required. A supervisor is responsible for understanding the designer's vision and how each costume is constructed. From this preliminary research, the wardrobe supervisor prepares a budget, which is submitted to the producer for approval.

A wardrobe supervisor can be hired early in the production, but more often it is just before the cast moves to the theatre. Often when the supervisor comes on board, the costumes have been designed and are in the construction stage. Sometimes the prep time for a supervisor can be part-time, but it is pro-rated as part of their salary. It depends on the show.

If the show is big, the process of designing and producing the costumes can be a year or more before the supervisor is hired. Once hired, the supervisor attends fittings to learn the process of building the costumes, how they are to be used in the production, and what special requirements for use or care each costume may have.

A wardrobe supervisor, like a carpenter, has a kit of the tools of their trade. Kits can include ironing boards, irons, bins, threads, needles, plastic drawers—anything that a wardrobe department uses. Sometimes the production company has equipment from past productions that are stored and revised. When a new show opens, using recycled or upcycled goods is part of building a wardrobe kit. In developing the budget, the wardrobe supervisor checks what equipment they have, and what the production company has, to determine whether additional equipment is needed. The only two things a Broadway theatre has in-house is a washing machine and a dryer. Everything else, the wardrobe department brings in.

Over the years, a supervisor may have worked with the same team, so the supervisor knows what equipment the team prefers. If fifty-five shirts are going to be ironed every day, the ironer prefers a specific iron. It is a repetitive job, and carpel tunnel syndrome can occur. If the iron is too heavy, the grip does not feel comfortable, or the pitch is not quite right, it makes that job much harder.

Sometimes a garment was designed just to be worn but evolves into requiring a specialty function. For example, a tuxedo that originally was simply to be worn now needs to break away in thirty seconds for a quick change. The street jeans now need to be distressed or have blood splattered on them. The supervisor and the team find solutions to accomplish these changes. Distressing can be done by the fabric painter earlier in the costume development, but design changes can occur late or need to be maintained. A wardrobe supervisor executes these tasks.

It is an asset if the supervisor has some background in a performance art. That experience helps the supervisor understand and advocate for a performer's needs, while keeping the designer's vision intact. Issues present themselves when the actor executes stage business in a costume, or a dancer needs more flexibility in their costume to execute the choreography. A singer's stage business is more demanding, and they need more space in the costume to breathe.

A wardrobe supervisor must learn the overall details of each costume in the show. Every button, thread, and fabric are specific to a particular garment. If the garment is a historical replica, knowing how it was made, what the fabric is, who made it, and why it was made that way is beneficial. This is *before* any garment is put on a body.

Broadway tickets are expensive because there is a lot of detail when producing a Broadway show, especially with costumes. If the designer says the hem of a particular garment must be 7.5 inches off the floor, the supervisor must be sure that no matter who wears the costume, what body type, or what age, that particular dress always stays at 7.5 inches off the floor. That exactitude applies to all the costumes and everything that goes with it and on it. Every piece of trim needs to be exact. If the trim is no longer made on this earth, it is the supervisor's job to try to replace it as close to the designer's initial creative vision as of opening night, no matter how long the show runs.

Although the wardrobe department is fairly self-sufficient, wardrobe interacts with all aspects of a production. The supervisor's job encompasses more than costume maintenance. The department must be prepared for pretty much any mishap at any given moment. If wardrobe equipment breaks down, a costume gets damaged during the show, the production manager has a curtain hem problem, or the head of props needs help in adapting a prop, the wardrobe department comes to their aid. The wardrobe department also builds all the packs and belts that hold the microphones on actors' bodies or on instruments. They work with the sound team to find the best placement on the actors for those microphones and packs for quick removal if the microphone or pack need repairs during the show.

Team

How many people are on the wardrobe department team depends on the size and complexity of the show. For a play, there can be the supervisor, two dressers, a star dresser, a laundry person, and a stitcher. For a musical with three hundred costumes, there can be the supervisor, one assistant supervisor, eight to ten ensemble dressers, two or three principal dressers, a star dresser or two, a laundry person, a full-time stitcher, and a team of day workers. The space they all work in is inhabited by the staff, ironing boards, sewing tables, and equipment.

Most Broadway theatres are a hundred years old or near that. The front of the house has been refurbished, but the stage and backstage areas of Broadway theatres are the same dimensions they were a hundred years ago. The wardrobe staff are usually the first people in and the last people out of the building. The space the wardrobe department works in is incredibly small, not temperature controlled, and a lot of hours are spent in that space. Having a congenial team and a pleasant environment is especially important when there is an inherent stress factor during a show run.

Since the theatres do have washing machines and dryers, the wardrobe department is established near that space. Because Broadway backstage is so limited and depending on the number of costumes in a show, every piece of air- and ground-level real estate is used to store costumes, set pieces, and props. Costumes that are not going to be used are hung in the air.

Union

On Broadway the wardrobe supervisor and the team belong to the Theatre Wardrobe Union, Local 764, which is a sister component of the stagehands' union (Local One). It is a stand-alone organization within International Alliance of Theatrical Stage Employees (IATSE), is fully self-funded, and is largely unique to New York and Los Angeles. Members handle costumes only. In New York and Los Angeles, there is a separate union for hair and wigs. On Broadway, there are very specific rules regarding costumes and hair/wigs. With touring companies and regional theatres, the rules differ. In those jurisdictions, the wardrobe supervisor can be responsible for costumes *and* hair and wigs.

The supervisor acts as the union representative and is responsible for protecting the team and upholding union rules. Sometimes there are disputes about not being paid properly, overtime, and questions governing contractual rights and meanings. As contracts get renegotiated, there are more gray areas. With so many different unions in play on a Broadway show, the supervisor tries to seek mutual ground with a common goal. Obviously, it requires diplomacy.

In recent years, there have been bigger disputes about film usage. The union has very specific rules governing usage in commercials, news, and B-roll.[1] If they shoot a B-roll to be used only for news coverage, you get X amount of dollars. If they shoot a commercial for the show that is intended to play on television, you get Y amount of dollars. Sometimes a member turns on the television and sees that the B-roll is being used for a commercial and they were not paid for the commercial rate. Then the complainant goes to arbitration between The League of Producers or Disney and the union.

If the play is a revival, like *The Crucible*, the starting reference point is a known. The characters, the costumes, and the scene changes are established so it is easier to estimate the show's needs. If the show is new, like *Natasha, Pierre & the Great Comet of 1812*, where only nine characters have names but there are thirty people and ten costumed musicians, and everybody has

---

1. A B-roll of video is used as a complement to perhaps an interview or a news review.

their own look, it is obviously more difficult for the supervisor to evaluate the budget and the team for the show. If it is a non-traditional structure and the script changes from day to day or hour to hour (e.g., Larry David's *Fish in the Dark*, which was treated like an episodic television show), it is even more of a challenge. Jessica Dermody recalls:

> It was like twenty people on stage every day. What was interesting about it, we were kind of doing a two-and-a-half-hour episode of "Curb Your Enthusiasm." He [Larry David] would make changes all the time. Because of that, it was structured like a TV sitcom, so you had cast members who were only in the show for a minute one day and seventy-five seconds the next.

For most musicals, the aim is for everyone to have two of everything, so if something rips, there is a backup. Also, costumes must rotate so everything is clean all the time, especially for dancers. At the beginning of a new show run, understudy costumes and costume duplicates are being completed. All of this means there is a full-time laundry person, which is an entire operation unto itself. On a musical, that person can be doing laundry for upwards of forty people. The wardrobe supervisor is overseeing all of that work.

When it comes to working onstage during a performance, a supervisor is limited in participation. They are not allowed to dress the show. They assist in one costume change; however, they are not allowed to have a track of changes (following one actor throughout the show). The reason is simple. The supervisor's job is to understand what everybody does in the building during a performance, so in the event someone gets injured or something goes wrong, they can step in or get help. With musicals, dancers invariably have injuries.

The wardrobe department, above all other theatre departments, is the most personal and sensitive department because of its close contact with the performers. The actor is greeted, introduced to the costumer, pleasantries are exchanged, then the actor is asked to take off their clothes so they can be measured. It's an incredibly personal situation. Costumers learn to read personalities and try to make a vulnerable environment as comfortable as possible.

Understudies

The costume designer often leaves after opening and the associate designer remains. With a large show there can be several understudies or swings. How the understudy/swing costumes are dealt with depends on the producer. Building those costumes is costly, so often the producer will delay that decision until after the show opens allowing the producer to gauge how long the show might run. If the producer estimates that the show has a good run, they will budget that expense. This presents a different issue. The design associate remains on the job and is the surrogate for the costume designer.

Usually at this point nothing has been prepared for the understudy or swing costumes. Extra fabric and trim have not been purchased. Experience during tech can reveal costume problems to consider, which can result in slight alterations from the originals. The design associate stays on until all understudy and swing costumes are completed. With really big shows that have national touring companies, the associate designers often stay with the show indefinitely. It just depends on the show.

Dressers

Dressers are discussed separately in this book, but they are hired by the supervisor and are part of the wardrobe team. If it is a big star-driven show, there will be a specific personal dresser who is totally dedicated to taking care of that star and their costumes. For the supporting cast and supporting principal roles, the normal breakdown would be two to four people per dresser. For the ensemble, there is the male ensemble and the female ensemble, and usually four to five people are assigned to one dresser. All of these dressers are overseen by the wardrobe supervisor.

People who work in live theatre are a unique group of people. The curtain goes up at eight o'clock, not 8:15 because you did not feel like getting there at half-hour. People who get the opportunity to work as a professional in theatre have a kind of dedication.

Dressers have to deal with people who are sick in the middle of the show. Before the show begins, the wardrobe department plots and plans all the places this person can potentially throw up onstage without anybody noticing. Wardrobe also figures out how to help a person who is experiencing stomach problems wearing a complex costume who may need access to a bathroom, but it is far away. There are times where there really are no boundaries. It becomes very personal, and everyone must lean on each other. This may all sound too sensitive, but live theatre is composed of real humans with vulnerabilities that need addressing. The old school mentality of the show must go on no matter what still exists. It helps to have a team that can function efficiently under such duress.

The wardrobe supervisor is a troubleshooter and problem-solver. To a lay person if someone has preset the wrong costume or the wrong shoes or someone else's shoes, it may not seem like a big deal. But if the supervisor needs to put two people with an actor in a small space to do a quick change in fifteen seconds because a big set piece is coming in, it feels like life or death. Theatre people are taught that it is life or death, but at the end of the day they are not curing cancer.

As Jessica Dermody described backstage for dressers changing an actor on *The Producers* set:

> There were six tons of set pieces hanging on both sides of the stage and it was like a river in motion. One piece moved, another descended from above, and something else would happen, so the deck space you had to stand on was constantly in flux. If you were standing in the wrong place you could get crushed and you wouldn't even know. Or there are shows on turntables, the stage itself is moving, and very dangerous. You have to have people who understand and respect what the production manager does. Understanding other people's jobs is really important and doesn't always happen. We all have to work hand-in-hand and rely on each other.

It also helps to have some concept of the stresses the performer is under, plus how the time constraints as well as the fatigue factor can affect them.

Hair and Wigs

On Broadway there are a lot of jurisdictional decisions that need to be decided among hair, makeup, and wardrobe during a performance. If the teams have worked together on other shows, there is a collegial relationship already established. Wardrobe people do not touch hair, and hair people do not touch costumes. A lot of time is spent in determining who handles a hat or pair of gloves that falls onstage. If a wig falls onstage or needs touching up, wardrobe does not touch it. Hair does not touch a costume if it falls onstage. However, if the arm is falling off a costume, then the protocol is to bring it to the wardrobe department. These departments must know if an item is a prop or a costume, which affects jurisdiction.

Hats are particularly tricky. The costume designer designs the hats, the milliner constructs the hats, which go to wardrobe, but hats go on top of wigs. The hat has to be put on and taken off by a hair person. This specificity is important because if a wig worn in one scene is worn in the next scene, there are tricks to how hats are kept on people's heads. The wig must be checked so when taking the hat off, it does not cause the hair to fly away and look crazy.

To a non-theatre person, this may seem rather extreme, but backstage there is low light, confined space, and time is expedient. The crews are working under immediate pressure, so each person needs to know their job. When there is a thirty-second change into a ball gown, there is no time for mistakes.

Shoes

A lot of craft and artistry in the costume industry is vanishing, specifically, the art of making shoes, a critical component for any performer, especially for dancers. At one time there were many shoe companies who produced hand-crafted shoes.

As those craftsmen have aged, the craft is disappearing. Today there are only a few primary shoe suppliers for Broadway.

T.O. Dey in New York City makes most of the Broadway shoes. They produce a last and a foot mold, and make the shoes specifically for those feet. For a dancer who is dancing eight shows a week, this is vital to their health and longevity. There are many people who wear LaDuca shoes, which are manufactured in Italy, but the maker has a shop in New York City. The shoes come from a specific vendor and are not totally custom made to the person's foot. There is also Capezio which is very popular with dancers. It should be noted that most shoes worn by actors on Broadway are given rubber soles to protect against slipping.

Recycling Costumes

The supervisor stays for load-out. The wardrobe department must inventory everything that is left in the department. When a show closes, the supervisor oversees where the inventory will go. If the producer has bought their own inventory, they will have a storage facility to store items either for a possible tour or new productions. Sometimes the supervisor manages that storage facility. If the kit belongs to the supervisor, they may have their own storage facility where everything is moved.

In the last couple of decades, there has developed a very conscious effort to recycle as much as possible because there is an incredible amount of waste in the commercial theatre industry. The Broadway Green Alliance has developed and is managed by members of the Broadway community. The Theatre Development Fund (the same organization affiliated with TKTS) is one company that will help facilitate the disbursement of reusable things. If a closing musical has four hundred pairs of tap shoes that will never be used again in a production, the Theatre Development Fund helps locate a school to donate the shoes to.

Dresser

A dresser working a Broadway show is exactly what the title says. A dresser is the person who facilitates costume changes for the principals and ensemble members during the performance of a show. A dresser is hired by the wardrobe supervisor. Although it can be viewed as merely a servitude position since service is part of the dresser's responsibilities, the paradox is they are everything to an actor during a performance.

Backstage is a fraught and very dangerous place during a performance. There can be fifty to seventy-five people executing various jobs, but everyone knows their job and they work together. In a way, everyone backstage is in a support position furthering the story.

A dresser belongs to the Wardrobe Union Local 764 under the umbrella of IATSE and joining the union (and several unions including the Actors' Union) is a Catch 22. You cannot work on a union show if you are not a union member, and you cannot become a union member without working on a union show. Often getting a dresser job on a Broadway production is through someone. You can register with the union once you get a union job. You pay your union fee, dues, and then start accruing hours to achieve the required thirty days of employment to become a full member.

On a big musical, there can be ten to twelve dressers, two supervisors, and a full-time laundry person. This staff is hired by the wardrobe supervisor and is part of their budget. Smaller musicals and plays do not need as many dressers. The dresser Katherine Chick said: "Our work is invisible. I mean literally. We come to work and we wear all black all the time. Our job is to blend into the scenery. If you don't know what we do, that means we're good at our job."

The set load-in has been occurring for a month or two before the dressers join the wardrobe supervisor in setting up the wardrobe department's workspace. Once the wardrobe department location backstage is determined (which is where the washer and dryer are), the costume load-in begins, usually a week or two before the actors enter the theatre. The team starts receiving the costumes and unpacking boxes of equipment. The next job is labeling each costume with the show title, the identity of the actor, and in which scene the costume is worn. While this is happening, the costume associate and costume assistants are buying underwear, tights, and socks (anything worn close to the skin) which also needs labeling. By this time the dressing rooms have been assigned, so the dressers distribute the close-to-skin items at each actor's station. When the actors arrive at the theatre, the dressers put the costumes on the actors to make sure all the closures work and check how they function for the scene changes. Most importantly, all shoes must have rubber soles applied to them for safety reasons and union rules to protect against slippage.

During the run of the show, the dressers arrive an hour before the actors to gather all their freshly laundered underwear and place it at their dressing room station. The dressers check to see if there are any cast changes (if someone has called in sick) for every performance to make sure they set up the correct underwear and tights at the correct makeup station. They prep the costumes by ironing or steaming, and check the shoes, hats, and jewelry. They make small repairs if they are able to do that. Dressers always want to know if something is going to fall apart before it happens in the middle of a quick change during the show. The stitcher comes in the hour before the show, so if a repair is too big for the dresser, the stitcher does it. The dressers fill the water bottles for the principals and leads. The ensemble members are responsible for their own water bottles. The star's dresser is responsible for their star.

The bare bones process for every show, whether a musical or a play, whether it is street clothes or seventeenth-century ball gowns, is the same. Dresser Katherine Chick said:

> Once I have set everything up, I just wait for the actors to arrive and see what they need. Whenever the show starts, you get them dressed and just kind of run around with them backstage. That's how I describe my job. I run around backstage following the actors and help them change their costumes during the show.

In a musical, dressers are assigned to ensemble members and principals. A star's dresser is responsible for that one person. However, any dresser can be called to help a star with changes if needed and must be available at any moment. The first and foremost priority is the star. Some stars have their own personal dresser who is not part of the wardrobe supervisor's team. That dresser works with the department but is solely obligated to the star. There are fewer dressers on a play.

Depending on the size of the show, six to ten dressers are hired for a musical ensemble. There are male ensemble dressers and female ensemble dressers. The assignment of ensemble members is divided up, but there are at least two dressers for an ensemble, never just one. It takes a lot to chase one girl, much less two or three to whom the dresser is assigned. According to Ms. Chick, "The thing about chorus girls is that they all tend to change at the same time, so you kind of line them up and just go zip zip zip right down the line."

For the principals, again it depends on the show. On *Frozen*, the male principal dresser was assigned to three or four principal men. Some of them changed costumes multiple times and some did not. The dresser needed to make sure the principal who was not changing had his water bottle, everything he needed, and gave him a quick look over. When necessary, the dresser presets the costume changes where the change will happen and either follows the actor or chases them down.

Dressers work very closely with their assigned actor, and the primary purpose is to meet the needs of that actor. It is important that a dresser understands their charge, and it is equally important the actor treats the dresser with respect. The dresser is not the servant of the actor, but they facilitate the actor's ease in focusing on their performance and not worrying whether the next costume change will be ready. Theatre is so collaborative there is just no time for personality issues.

Every Broadway show has actors who are "swings," whose job is to wait in the theatre just in case someone gets sick. Usually there are two male and two female actors who cover multiple roles in the show, whether a principal or a lead. Before each show, the dressers check with stage management to see if anyone has called in sick. A swing can also be brought into the performance if an actor is injured during a performance. They have their own separate costumes, which are also maintained by the dressers. This triggers what is called a "switch out." Whether it is before or during the show, the dresser assigned to the sick or injured actor switches all the costumes in the dressing room, so the swing actor has all their costumes in position. They also usually sit at the dressing room location of the actor they are replacing. A switch out also happens in the middle of the show. Then the dresser grabs everything they can as fast as they can. This happens frequently in musicals with dancers who are often prone to injury. It can also happen with a star and if it happens at the beginning of the show; the curtain can be held a little bit to give the dressers and the swing more time. If need be, the dresser goes to the supervisor and everyone pitches in.

Technical difficulties can stop a show. As mentioned, during the show wardrobe people are following their actors backstage. If there is a technical crisis during the show, the best thing the wardrobe people can do is get off the stage and stay out of everyone's way. Usually, the dresser gathers all the actors and they retreat back to their dressing rooms while the stage crew resolves the problem.

Often if there is a major wardrobe malfunction, that is on the wardrobe department but it does not stop the show. Katherine Chick mused:

> Things might look weird. Somebody might be in the wrong costume or it might not be fully fastened, but actors can get into trouble from the stage management team if they miss an entrance. So even if the quick change goes badly, often actors can be bold, just go out, and do whatever they need to do because that is their job. That's the magic of Broadway.

Dressers can get attached to their actor and if the show goes on tour, the dresser has an option to follow their actor. Tours are a little less money, and there is a smaller dressing crew. Most often dressers are hired locally.

When the show ends, most dressers are supposed to leave fifteen minutes after the show comes down. First and foremost, the dresser gets the actors off the stage and out of their costumes. The hair people get them out of their wigs. The dressers hang up the costumes, put away the shoes, and collect the washables (underwear). The ensemble is expected to exit quickly. A star dresser may have to stay to help with the star's guests and sometimes escort them on a backstage tour.

Every show is different but most often there is a laundry person for the show and typically once the dressers have collected the washable items, they sort their actors' laundry (darks and lights) in preparation for the full-time laundry person. The show launderer usually arrives at 9 AM the next morning to start the laundry and have it ready for that day's performance. Actors are given at least two sets of their laundry pieces (underwear, bras, tights) because sometimes the laundry load is so large the laundry cannot be turned around fast enough if it is a two-show day, especially with a large musical.

When a show ends, the dressers help load-out the supplies. They pack everything and either send it to a storage facility or if the show is going on tour, they help ship the costumes to the next venue. This process can take one or two weeks, depending on the size of the show.

Not everyone is cut out to be a dresser. There's a certain degree of hand-holding, depending on who you are actually working with, especially under fire during a performance when a costume malfunctions.

Stitcher

There are so many hands that a single costume goes through from design, construction, and maintenance on a Broadway show that it is dizzying. Another member of the maintenance team is the production stitcher, who is separate from the costume draper's stitcher. Costumes worn for eight shows a week undergo a tremendous amount of deterioration. A stitcher is a person who repairs a costume either during the day or during the performance of a show.

A stitcher belongs to the Wardrobe Union under IATSE, Local 764. Under the union rules, they can either work as a day worker or during the show. Either way they work in four-hour shifts. They are incorporated into the wardrobe supervisor's budget and their fee is a union standard under agreement with the Broadway League or Disney. There are subtle differences between the two entities, but the rules are not widely different.

Joining the union is an awkward affair. One registers with the union, pays an entrance fee, submits three letters of recommendation, and must accrue thirty four-hour union calls that fall under the union agreement before becoming a full union member. The difficulty is in acquiring those thirty work segments. A lot of the union work is through word of mouth or who the stitcher knows. It can be a lot of luck.

A stitcher is paid as an hourly employee. As long as they have the available hours, they can work on multiple productions simultaneously. Thus, a stitcher can work during the day on one show and at night on another show. The two four-hour segments could have different hourly rates depending on the two different agreements. To clarify, the night four-hour segment actually covers the night's show performance. Being able to work multiple shows at the same time enables a stitcher to have what would be a full-time schedule. Sometimes a stitcher can only work two days on a performance and then someone else works the other days. Some shows can have two stitchers who can alternate depending on their schedule. That allows the wardrobe supervisor to be assured of having at least one stitcher for their show, especially if it is a big musical. Some stitchers on a show can fill in as a dresser, which is another rate. No matter what their position is, they come under the wardrobe department budget but are paid by the production.

Working as a day work stitcher once the show is up and running can be fairly low key. It's mostly making small repairs or alterations to the costumes for the evening performance. The job requirements for a musical or a play are the same, but a play usually has fewer costumes and a slower pace.

The job is very different when the stitcher is working the show itself. It requires a certain flexibility and temperament. Sam Brooks thrives on the versatility of the job and actually finds an element of fun in what some people could find stressful:

> What I think is really fun is if you're a stitcher during tech, because it's super-fast paced. Someone comes running down to the basement, throws a shirt and zipper at you, and says, "I need this in ten minutes" then goes running away. Then he'll come back in five minutes and say "the entire scene just got cut. Get rid of it. Here's something else I need you to do." And off they go again. I think it could be very stressful, but to me there's an element of fun, because interest keeps moving. There's always something changing and happening.

The stitcher has an unusual position in that although they belong to the wardrobe union, they are not really contracted to any Broadway show. They work more or less under a verbal agreement. They also can accept non-union work. As one stitcher told me, "It's like freelancing within your own union."

A stitcher can be hired while the show is in rehearsal, maybe the week or two before the actors enter the theatre. During that time, they are working with the wardrobe department labeling costumes, making tags, and labeling laundry bags.

If they are brought on to the regular show staff, they have a mini setup—a sewing table, ironing board, etc.—to facilitate their work. Because the wardrobe rooms in a Broadway theatre are like closets, affability in a stitcher's personality is a necessity. Everyone is under pressure and on top of each other. There is really no room for egos or tempers.

Currently, there has been an evolution in that there are more contemporary musicals and a lot of those costumes are street clothes. Department store purchases are not made to last like traditional theatrical costumes, but they still need to be maintained to look a certain way.

A stitcher seldom goes with the show on tour. Stitchers are usually hired locally wherever the show is playing.

A tour is ostensibly the same show on Broadway, but it has been edited down a bit. Tours are a little shorter, some production elements are changed, and it is streamlined for ease of transport. Although it is not a standard, there often is one less person in each ensemble, so a track of clothing from the men's and women's ensemble members has been eliminated.

The most obvious talent for a stitcher is that they are accomplished sewers. Several people I interviewed said they learned sewing from either their grandmother or mother or both. They did not start out thinking of stitching as a career, but came to it sort of sideways.

Sam Brooks related that he had a fundamental knowledge of sewing when he went to college to study design, but like several people mentioned to me, he had a professor who was very formative.

> I got an incredible trial by fire education, particularly of sewing. In my costumes department my main professor's angle on that facet of the industry was basically, "I don't care if you can draw a pretty picture as a designer. You need to understand how these things are made because it will inform your work as a designer. It will enable you to communicate with the people who eventually make your work. You need to know *how* to make these costumes because if there's no one else around, you're going to be your own costume shop and have to make it."

Theoretically if a male ensemble member is replaced, the stitcher works with the wardrobe department to fit a new costume track for that replacement. Anything that touches the skin is purchased new, such as shirts, socks, shoes, and underwear. Hats may have to be made anew. Outer garments such as slacks, vests, and jackets are refitted if possible. Often with overcoats and similar garments there is kind of a gray scale, in that the new person fits costume X, but costume X has been worn for two years. Replacing it with a new costume is considered. If someone is replaced quickly there is no time, so the wardrobe department researches what is already in the theatre to see if they can make it work.

7

Stage Management

Production Stage Manager

> To be a stage manager, you just have to juggle everybody. You can't really be a volatile person. I don't think it would really be effective. I think definitely being able to be a problem solver, think on your feet, be even tempered, and enjoy the process. You have to enjoy the process.
>
> –Gwendolyn M. Gilliam
> Production Stage Manager

The production stage manager (PSM) position is crucial in any theatrical production. By the time they join the production, various departments have already been working independently for some time. A PSM can set the pulse, tone, and mood of the production. There are only thirty Broadway theatres, so there are only thirty PSMs working at any given time. Those thirty people do the same tasks, but how they do them and the atmosphere they create depends on their individual personalities.

Today a person can learn the rudimentary craft of stage managing in college, but entering the professional world is an entirely new environment. Experience in all areas of theatre is a deep resource for a stage manager, whether it is performing, sewing costumes, or building sets. Once the show is up and running, the PSM is managing at least seventy-five people every night on a big musical. The more knowledge and understanding of the stresses of each department provides a PSM with the ability to effectively communicate with all the departments to solve problems as they arise.

The PSM is usually recommended by the director or the general manager, but they are hired by the general manager/producer. Stage managers are members of the Actors' Equity Association, and there are a couple ways of joining Actors' Equity Association. If the stage manager is working in an Equity theatre (i.e., regional theatres) and accrues a certain number of weeks of work, they can apply for membership. Some stage managers were performers, so they already are members of Actors' Equity Association and just change their designation.

A PSM's job on Broadway is colossal with a multitude of tasks and responsibilities. On a play, a Broadway PSM usually has one or two assistant stage managers (ASMs). If it is a large production, there could also be a production assistant, which is a non-union position or a union person working non-union as a production assistant. Depending on the size of a musical, there can be four, five, or more ASMs. The PSM recommends the ASMs for their team, but sometimes the general manager or producer has a preference. However, most PSMs will strongly fight for their first ASM, because the first ASM is the PSM's right-hand person and covers the PSM position. The first assistant learns the cues for running the show and can call the cues after the transition to the theatre if the PSM is working with other departments. Eventually, all of the ASMs learn to call the show, especially during a long run. The first ASM joins the company the week before the cast.

One could say there are five different stages to a production: pre-production, rehearsal, dry tech, tech, and the preview-run. As each phase changes and morphs into the next, so does the PSM's role.

Pre-Production

Before anything or anyone enters the theatre, the Broadway producer has already expended an enormous amount of money which they are gambling on the new show. Months before there is a cast, several departments are already at work. The costume designer, the set designer, choreographer, the general manager, and the company manager have been working, and a general vision of the show has been reached.

A PSM can be approached early in a production and have a verbal agreement with the general manager/producer, which is binding. According to union rules, the PSM contract includes two paid weeks before the Broadway cast goes into rehearsal. This becomes the pre-production period. A PSM might attend production meetings before being on contract to learn how the show is shaping up, which informs them once rehearsals begin. These ad hoc meetings might involve a couple of days, which can be applied to the two-week paid period.

When the PSM formally joins the production, those first two weeks are full of preparatory tasks. Paperwork setting up forms for use during the run are created and completed so everything is ready to use when cast rehearsals begin. There are contact sheets for the actors, crew, designers, and staff, essentially the entire production. There are forms for the calendars, daily rehearsal reports, daily rehearsal call sheets, and more. PSM Nevin Hedley opined:

> You come in and lists from everyone are thrown at you. The director wants to set a rehearsal schedule. The PR people want so-and-so for interviews. The cast dressing rooms need to be assigned. The design teams have needs. The producing team wants your attention. You take *all* the different aspects of a production and organize it so there is comity, which is important. You have to communicate with and be the conduit for communication between all the desperate aspects of a show, otherwise you might as well be in Timbuktu.

The PSM works closely with the director, because when the director leaves, the PSM is responsible for maintaining the director's vision of the show. They confer to work out rehearsal schedules and how the director wants the rehearsals to function.

Before rehearsals begin, the PSM sets up the rehearsal rooms and is responsible for running the rehearsals. A musical requires multiple rehearsal spaces for dancers, musicians, and book scenes. The script for a musical is broken down into scenes or songs, which is important for the production crew. The PSM makes sure the scripts and piano/vocal scores are set for the cast. All that work is accomplished before the cast walks in for the first day of rehearsal.

The PSM gets the ground plan from the set designer and re-creates the ground plan coordinates onto the floor of the rehearsal rooms with tape. Then everyone understands where the set walls are, where the doors are, where a window is, etc. As the rehearsal process proceeds, the tape markers change, and they change again with the move to the theatre. Adaptation is necessary because what was staged in the rehearsal room may not function on the actual stage space.

The PSM works with the props supervisor and the production manager who are directly responsible for supplying the props and needs for the rehearsals. From the props supervisor, the PSM gets a list of props for each scene, so they are ready for the rehearsal and on the scene list. The PSM confers with the production manager to acquire the odd props like a spinning bed, because the production manager handles the nuts and bolts needed for the show and has knowledge of the budget. The PSM deals with the creative process in the rehearsal hall.

Before the first day of rehearsal, the PSM meets with the general manager and producer to learn who is expected to be present. Does the production want a welcome or a meet and greet?

The third week of the PSM's job is when the cast arrives, and the rehearsal rooms, rehearsal props, and contact sheets must be ready for distribution.

Offsite Rehearsal

Once in rehearsal, the PSM must secure the daily script changes, update the script, and make copies for the cast. A lot of this work is done by the first ASM. The same procedure occurs with the music. The songs are split for the principals and the ensemble and are kept updated, copied, and distributed. The music intern/assistant feeds the music updates to the PSM.

Since the early 1990s, computers have become invaluable with keeping up with script changes, script cue changes, and production cue changes. There are several computer programs available, but they keep changing. An ASM does most of the computer input, because the PSM's attention is involved with running the rehearsal.

Before the company moves to the theatre, the PSM goes to the theatre site to assess the dressing room assignments. The PSM is informed by general management of an actor's contractual requirements such as requiring a single room or a bathroom. Having run the rehearsal, the PSM knows the cast personalities and who will mesh with whom, which helps in assigning dressing rooms, especially those with multiple actors. Also, a critical factor is whether an actor can run up three flights of stairs to change between scenes and if there is time for the change. Remember, the backstage area is relatively small. Generally, it is the stage management team, the general management, and the company management who approve the final distribution.

With the dressing room assignments completed, it is the props department that sets them up. Working with the props supervisor or head of props, the PSM chronicles what each dressing room needs, such as a cot, a chair, a refrigerator, or a table, which the props team locates and loads in. Only a crew person (at this point usually the head of props or the props crew) can load items into a dressing room; stage management is not allowed to touch anything.

Also before moving to the theatre, the PSM, props, and wardrobe teams determine how many quick changing stations are needed and where they can be placed backstage. It is the props people who construct them.

Paperwork continues throughout the rehearsal process. The PSM writes a daily rehearsal report detailing the activities and problems of the day, costume issues, prop issues, and anything that is relevant, and that report is distributed to the appropriate departments. The first ASM creates and maintains the call board listing daily rehearsal schedules and call sheets for cast and crew, for which days, what time, and who is required. While all of this is going on, there are constant script rewrites and songs being thrown out and new songs introduced.

In a union theatre, you cannot have a rehearsal without a stage manager present. Rehearsal is a time of discovery for the actors as well as the director, and changes are inevitable. The PSM becomes the eyes and ears for the other departments during the rehearsal period, which are busy building scenery, creating costumes, and preparing lighting and sound. The PSM notes every change, much like a script supervisor on a movie shoot. If an actor improvises sipping a cup of tea although it was not in the director's directions or if something new is placed on a table, that must be noted for props, so a teacup is available for the next rehearsal.

The PSM tracks cast entrances and exits for every scene, which is given to the production manager and is important for the movement of stage scenery. Wardrobe also needs to know those entrances and exits to facilitate quick changes, if there are any. Those quick changes can be affected by scenery coming on or offstage. Simultaneously before moving to the theatre, the ASM creates detailed run sheets for each crew department during rehearsal. An initial run sheet is a cue sheet for each department's actions during the show and is handed out on the first day of tech. Of course, all the cues will change.

Often there is a designer run the last week of rehearsals in the rehearsal studio, so the designers and tech departments can come in, see how the show runs, and where people are. Until that time, the designers and tech people have been occupied in the theatre preparing scenery, wardrobe, lighting, sound, and other production elements of the show. They are not current with the progress of the script. Although the PSM or ASM do blocking notes (the actors' movements onstage) during rehearsal, the designers come in and do their own blocking notes. In addition to the entrances and exits sheet, the stage management team tries to provide a semblance of scene running time so people estimate how the time can affect their department during the tech run. All of this work is necessary to give the design and technical departments advanced knowledge of what the show looks like in the rehearsal room before going into tech rehearsal in the theatre with the cast.

At the end of each rehearsal day after directorial notes have been given, the director and PSM meet to discuss the day's rehearsal and the next day's rehearsal schedule. Sometimes a director is concentrating on one piece of business and misses something the PSM noticed.

To eventually run the show, the PSM acquires the director's "voice," which is achieved by listening to and writing down the director's directions throughout the rehearsal process and through the final run-through notes session. The PSM is responsible for rehearsing the understudies and swings, so assimilating the director's approach to the characters, knowing all the blocking, and maintaining an accurate and current account of evolving stage directions is essential.

Dry Tech

The next stage of the production is what is called "dry tech." It happens before the cast is in the theatre and involves the PSM, ASM(s), production manager, all the technical people, designers, and crews. The entire technical staff basically runs through the show without the cast to practice the timing of all technical elements, the scenery movement, its placement, and how it looks. If it is a musical, the PSM has taped music of the show so moving scenery on and off the stage can be timed with the music. The dry tech is to ensure everything technical works and, if not, to correct it before the cast joins them in the theatre.

Before the cast arrives, the production manager supervises setting up tables in the orchestra section for the director, the PSM, the designers, and choreographer. That is where they can watch the tech and communicate with their individual departments and with each other.

The Tech

When the company moves to the theatre, the period of tech begins and continues until the company is able to run the show smoothly, hopefully before previews. As mentioned, prior to the company transition, the stage crew has already been working in the theatre, so the move to the theatre affects the cast and crew work schedules. The PSM and production manager meet (sometimes also the director) to determine those work schedules.

With this move, a producer can purchase a number of ten out of twelve-hour days, which allows the cast to work ten hours with an hour for lunch and an hour for dinner. The PSM and production management company work together to figure out how many ten out of twelve-hour days the producer may need. The type of production (musical or drama) and the cast size determines the producer's decision. The current union contract allows for seven ten out of twelve-hour rehearsals prior to the first paid public performance, but more can be purchased if needed.

The crew continues its work while the actors rehearse in the theatre, but they must work around the actors' rehearsal schedule. If the crew comes in at 8 AM to work, they lunch between 12 PM and 1 PM. The cast half-hour call cannot be at 12 PM because the crew is on lunch, but the half-hour call can be at 12:30, which allows the cast time to get into costumes and be ready to work by 1 PM. In other words, the PSM and the production manager organize the time schedule for the cast and crew to accommodate union rules.

Typically, on the first day in the theatre, the cast gets acclimated to where their dressing rooms are located and the layout of the building. They set up their dressing room and learn where to sign in and out for each performance.

As mentioned in the production management company chapter, the PSM and the production manager work on parallel tracks. The production manager is the supervisor in the theatre as the set is being built, assembled, and installed. Concurrently, the PSM is the supervisor for all the offsite rehearsals before the production moves to the theatre. Those dual tracks change once the production moves to the theatre. The PSM then runs the entire show while the production manager reverts to a support position supervising the stage crew and handling technical issues.

The reason for this transposition is because the PSM is coming in with knowledge the production manager does not have. The PSM has gone through the rehearsal process and has first-hand knowledge of cast entrances and exits, which affects where things need to be positioned onstage and backstage. The production manager attended some rehearsals, but not consistently; their primary focus was in the theatre.

Now all the departments that have been working in their separate lanes come together to see if what they were creating works. The tech is the first time the entire crew and cast are together on the same stage trying to work through the show. Now it is no longer an idea of what is supposed to happen, but a reality. The taped set space in the rehearsal room is what is imagined it will be onstage, but now the company gets to the real set and things change. Sometimes the issue is as simple as sightlines (can the audience see the action), so the staging and cues change.

Tech is slow and methodical as the production starts at the top and works through the show. This is a stop and start experience. As the PSM Gwendolyn M. Gilliam related:

> It's tech the whole time until you can run it, because at that point you are unable to run it. So that's why the director will often say to the cast, "OK this is where we're at. When we leave the rehearsal room don't lose what we've worked on because we're not going to be doing any of that for the next few weeks because you have to get through the show moment by moment, bit by bit." It's a long tedious period of standing and waiting, standing and waiting. They'll do something and the lighting designer will say, "Stop there." He'll change the lights, refocus them, and we move on.

Again, it is important to remember there are still script rewrites and songs in and out, and scenes are moved around to make the story work better. While everything is evolving, the paperwork load continues. Script, songs, cues, and blocking updates are incorporated in the various run sheets and scripts, which are copied and distributed daily to the appropriate people and departments.

The PSM works with the sound and music departments to keep track of who is singing what, whether it is principals or chorus ensembles. If dialogue in the script says Male 1, Male 2, and Male 3, those actors and their understudies need to be named for the sound mixer. Sometimes during the rehearsal process a dialogue line or solo song line is reassigned on the spot. That information is given to the sound people so they can reprogram their cues. The PSM works with the conductor and composer to determine how many orchestra read-throughs are needed and when the orchestra should join the cast.

At times during rehearsal in the theatre, the PSM is out in the house gathering cues from lighting, carpentry, automation, a fly person, and sound. They keep updating the call script, which is organizing all the cues into the PSM's call script to run the show, which the ASM inputs into the computer. When the PSM is in the house, the first ASM calls the show.

Separately, the music director rehearses the orchestra before it joins the production, which is usually late in tech. There is allotted time for rehearsing with certain cast members (usually soloists), which the PSM organizes in conjunction with the music director and the director. In the meantime, a rehearsal pianist has been accompanying rehearsals.

During tech, there will be what is called a *sitzprobe*, which is where the orchestra and cast are brought together for the first time for a run-through of the entire show. Everyone is hearing the full orchestra and the orchestra is hearing the entire cast for the first time. It is a totally different experience from hearing a solo piano. There can be microphones and a list of the order of the numbers. The entire cast is present as well as the PSM and the mixer.

For the PSM, this is important because many of their cues are integrated with the music. Although the ability to read music is not required, it is helpful if the PSM has enough ability to know when cues happen with the music and on what beat. If they sit in on musical rehearsals, hearing the musical phrases repeated often helps solidify where a cue might be.

As with everything that is new, once everyone learns where everyone and everything belongs, through repetition, the organism starts to function as a unit and run-throughs of the show from top to bottom are possible. There are *still* rewrites occurring, but hopefully nothing major. A production tries to accomplish as many run-throughs of the show as possible before previews begin.

Previews

After tech comes the preview phase where the show finally has a live audience. Although most of the production kinks have been worked out, previews provide the production the opportunity to fine tune everything. Since the PSM runs the show cueing the entire cast and crew, they are the first person contacted to problem-solve.

PSMs have individual preferences in how they run a show. Some use an iPad to call the show and others use a call script. In either case, the PSM wears headphones to communicate with various departments during the show, to call the cues, and to alert everyone of a problem.

There is a set of television screens in front of the PSM that show different views of the stage area, for example, a shot of the full stage, an overhead shot of the stage, or the conductor in a musical. There is night vision so when the stage goes to blackout, the PSM can observe the activity onstage. There is a warning light and then the PSM says "Go" for the cue to be executed.

Run

During the run, the PSM sits out in the audience during one or two performances a week to monitor the performance, the audience reaction, and take notes. In the beginning, the first ASM calls the cues and runs the show.

Even during the run, there is a mountain of daily paperwork. The calendar, call sheets, and rehearsal calls are updated daily. The PSM is responsible for writing the nightly performance report. The PSM gathers notes from the ASMs who have been working the deck (backstage) and all departments who have notes that are relevant to that night's performance. A cast member may have fallen, someone cannot hear their music cue, or someone has a complaint. It gives the timings for the show, discusses what happened during the show, audience reactions, how curtain calls were received, and any notes listing something that needs repairs. It relays who was in and out of the show that day, and why they were out.

That report is submitted nightly and is distributed to a list of people and departments who receive that report, including the general manager, the producer, and the director. It is an extremely important backup document for legal, medical, or union issues. Hard copies of the reports are kept in volumes. The PSM also oversees medical and insurance forms submissions.

Understudies and Swings

Although it is the PSM who schedules the understudy rehearsals, the entire stage management team is involved. Some PSMs try to start that process as early as possible, even while the company is in the rehearsal hall. An actor can become ill at any time and if it is before an understudy is rehearsed, it can be a fraught situation for the understudy as well as the production. All the note taking of character and blocking is useful to quickly prep the actor who is stepping in.

Once the show is up and running, understudy rehearsals are held weekly. With a play, often not all of the other actors are present for the understudy rehearsals, so as the PSM conducts the rehearsal the ASMs act the parts that are absent. With a musical, it is usually the stage manager, musical director, and the dance captain who are conducting the understudy rehearsals. There are more people than a play because of the musical components, but not everyone is present. The dancers work with the piano, and the dance captain usually guides them.

The stage management team also rehearses the swings. There are swing actors and swing dancers. A swing actor can cover four or five roles in a musical to cover an actor who gets sick during a performance. There are usually a few male and a female swing dancers who cover all the female and male ensemble dance roles in a show. Having several is insurance there is always someone to cover the dancers as dancers are prone to injuries.

Being a swing is a very specialized talent, whether an actor or a dancer. The first time performing a cover role is, of course, terrifying. A swing is rehearsed but has not performed the role until they are called upon in the middle of a show. Those who are successful swings are able to compartmentalize the roles and use a cheat sheet to remind themselves of the role before they go on. This position is not for everyone.

Cast Changes

In musicals there are frequent cast changes, especially dancers who frequently suffer injuries. Depending on which cast member is leaving, the PSM talks with the general manager, the dance captain, the musical director, and the casting people to determine how much rehearsal time is needed for the incoming cast member. The PSM learns when the cast member is leaving, when the replacement needs to be ready, and determines when the replacement rehearsals should start. The company tries to adjust the wigs and costumes, but if the new person cannot fit either, there are discussions with wardrobe and hair as to how much time they need to make new costumes and wigs. All those departments are consulted to formulate a timeline for when that person joins the show. If it is not an emergency and the PSM is notified a few weeks or at least a month ahead of the change, the stress is eased.

Children

Working with children and their parents on a Broadway production has its own issues. A Broadway production is required to hire a child guardian or chaperone who is the person who attends the children in the theatre during the run. That person should be comfortable and be able to work with the children *and* the parents.

The Equity rules governing children on Broadway have tightened over time. Movie sets have had rules in place for decades, but theatre was a little loose until more children became a production component. Now the parents bring the child to the stage door and hand them over to the chaperone and leave.

The rules are stricter, and the children's time is more regimented. They are required to attend school a certain number of hours per day per week. There is a tutor hired for that purpose who works with the PSM for the teaching schedule. Between rehearsal and school requirements, the children's scheduling becomes an ordeal. Although the major scheduling is done by the PSM, because they are setting the schedule every day for rehearsals, the ASMs also contribute to the schedule organizing. The number of hours of work and school per day are spelled out by the actors' union and state law.

The children's roles are double cast and although one cast could be considered primary and the second cast considered understudy, they more often split performances. So, while the daily rehearsal and daily school schedules are planned, both casts have to be incorporated into those schedules.

The PSM meets with the director daily to learn what the director wants to accomplish the next day and how much time the director wants for each scene. Once the PSM has that information, they start to figure out how to make that schedule work within the day. Knowing the rehearsal schedule, the PSM works in conjunction with the tutor to make certain the required school time is achieved. If the director wants to rehearse a specific scene that includes Joey, but Joey is in school until 11 AM, setting up the next day's rehearsal, the director knows they will not have Joey until after 11 AM.

It is important for the atmosphere of the run that the children get along. Unless they are rehearsing or in school, they spend most of their time together. Some children have done shows before and others are new to the experience. Children are certainly influenced by their parents' attitudes, so it is helpful if the parents have a positive disposition toward the situation.

Animals

As one PSM said, animals are sweethearts. They do not have temperaments and they follow directions. They do have a trainer and also an understudy.

Plays versus Musicals

Throughout this book it has been stated the difference between a play or a musical is size and simplicity. A play can have only one or two set moves where a wall comes in and out or something comes on or off from the side. If there is music in a play it is usually prerecorded. If it is live music, there could be a pianist onstage or a guitar player in the corner. For a PSM a play can be more static with fewer cues, fewer set changes, and less to do. Also, the subject matter can be very serious and weigh heavily on one's psyche with eight performances a week.

A musical has a larger cast and maybe eighteen to twenty set changes. The music component is an enormous layer with an orchestra, a musical director, a choreographer, associate choreographer, dancers, as well as a rehearsal pianist. There are fifteen or twenty people other than the cast to manage. For a PSM there are many more cues to call for a musical which keeps the PSM constantly occupied. According to Gwendolyn M. Gilliam, an added perk is "You can hum along!"

Tours

When the producer decides the show is a success and wants to have a tour, the PSM rehearses and prepares the new tour cast. While they are busy rehearsing the tour cast, the first ASM subs for the PSM, runs the show, writes the reports, and reports back to the PSM.

The Job Ends, Closing, Load-Out

The PSM's job usually ends when either they leave the show or on closing night. If the show ends, the team can still be on contract for a week after a show closes, during which time the team packs up their office, finishes the paperwork, and prepares a production book in case the show revives as a tour. The PSM is responsible for maintaining and keeping current the prop list and inventory of the show, especially since things change during a year or two run. About a week before the show closing, the PSM starts sending emails reminding the cast of the closing date, that the dressing rooms have to be cleared of all personal possessions, and any other pertinent information prior to closing.

For load-out, the production management company comes in and supervises load-out (the dismantling of the entire production).

Troubleshooting

In any theatre production whether on Broadway or regional theatre, if anyone has a complaint or problem, the protocol is to go to the stage manager. The PSM acts as a firewall for day-to-day family squabbles in a production. A production comprises many people so there can be personality issues or sometimes substance abuse issues. Some annoyances eventually vanish. However, some situations are absolutely black and white, are taken very seriously, and can implode a production.

Long before the #MeToo movement, sexual harassment and harassing fellow cast members was and is taken seriously and is cause for dismissal. Actors' Equity, the actors' union, has very strict rules governing behavior. Complaints relayed to the PSM are included in the nightly performance report. Those complaints are placed in a member's union file and remain a blight on an actor's reputation forever. If there are too many complaints filed against an actor, the union can take the action of removing that actor from the union.

Summary for Production Stage Manager

The PSM helps keep order and coordinate technical, legal, artistic, safety, union rules, and personality issues. They conduct the entire performance—everything that happens from the moment a person steps through the doors of the theatre to the time they leave. The doors do not open to seat people, the overture does not begin, the curtain does not go up, the sets do not move, the cast is not in place until the stage manager gives a warning and then says, "Go." The PSM uses a headset with channels to every department (light, sound, carpenters, props, dressers, dressing rooms). They use a walkie-talkie to talk to the front of the house (i.e., the mixer, house manager, and ushers). In addition, they oversee the quality of the show, so if you see the fiftieth performance or the 150th performance, it must have the same quality as it was opening night.

Assistant Stage Managers

An ASM has been mentioned throughout this segment because the stage management team's work meshes together as they collaboratively manage a show. Whereas the PSM calls the show at the monitors, the ASMs are on the deck (backstage) facilitating the PSM's cues. The ASMs make sure the actors are in place for their entrances. They generally handle the majority of the paperwork; they take notes of everything that happens during the show which is given to the PSM for inclusion in the nightly performance report.

The first ASM substitutes for the PSM whenever needed. Eventually all the ASMs learn to call the show, so if anyone is out, the show will go on.

One central difference between the PSM and an ASM is that it is the PSM who receives the call that an actor is out of the show. That call triggers a set of actions involving the ASMs. Once informed by the PSM of someone being out of the show, an ASM works on paperwork informing other people and departments that so-and-so is out. The actor's understudy has to be called if the PSM has not made that call yet. An insert for the program needs to be produced. The cast board in the lobby needs changing.

Essentially, all the stage managers work as a team, no matter their position.

8

Choreography

Choreographer

A choreographer tells a story through a sequence of steps and body movements to create an emotional response in pure dance form. Unlike a ballet where the narrative is told only through dance, on Broadway dance design fits into an emotional narrative that combines words (song and acting), music, *and* dance. The primary job of the choreographer in a musical is to contribute and push the story forward through dance.

Of all the theatrical disciplines, dance is an early career, because it takes such a serious toll on the body. There are dancers who know how to protect their instrument, their body, and dance into their seventies or later, like Chita Rivera. Some dancers remain dancers their entire career and expand their artistic life into acting or choreography as they age. Other dancers recognize the storytelling aspect of dance and start choreographing very early in their career.

A dancer can learn the art of choreography from teachers with whom they study or choreographers with whom they work through observing how a dance number is constructed. Like every creative pursuit, choreographers have different strengths that are reflected in their work. Christopher Gattelli, a prolific Broadway choreographer, recalls two choreographers who profoundly influenced him, Scott Salmon and Christopher Chadman:

> Scott and Chris inspired me to choreograph. My first two jobs were with these two gentlemen. I did the Radio City Music Hall Christmas Spectacular with Scott, and *Guys and Dolls* National Tour with Chris. Scott was a showman and I loved watching him direct, put the show together, and his overall vision with the Rockettes. His eye was incredible with all the stage craft, touches of surprise, and the showmanship. It was beautiful. Then when I worked with Chris, he did all of those things as well in his own way, but he also was very adamant about the storytelling given *Guys and Dolls* was a book musical, about every step having a meaning and a purpose. That *really* stuck with me.

For a choreographer it is not only about dance, but also under-standing stagecraft. How the technical aspects of theatre work can enhance and support dance movement in the storytelling. How lighting, for example, can embrace a body in motion.

Some choreographers are defined by a specific style they develop, for example Bob Fosse, Michael Bennett, or Agnes de Mille. When you see certain hand movements you know it is Bob Fosse. Other choreographers like Jerome Robbins, who was basically grounded in ballet, could morph his style into many dance forms to tell the story. One quality for all artists is they keep learning and expanding their skills.

Choreographers first begin as dancers studying all types of dance styles, which eventually they use in their creative arsenal. Christopher Gattelli finds learning new dance forms fascinating:

> In general, I think all choreographic styles have somewhat the same root. I've never studied flamenco or ballroom and they look very different and technical from other forms I've studied, and would think, "I could never do that." But every instructor I have ever collaborated with said, "At the end of the day, you learn the basics then throw them away. It's all about the feeling." So as different as they all look and as for-eign as they seem to be, the instructors/teachers all said the

same thing. "You break the rules, dance from the heart, and do whatever you need to do to tell the story."

The director usually recommends the choreographer, but the producer has a say as well. The choreographer is hired early in the production, often soon after the director. The choreographer works very closely with and supports the director's vision; however, choreographic ideas can influence other production departments.

Initially the director meets with the choreographer to discuss the overview of their vision and how to proceed. This is all during the pre-production phase where much design work (sets and costumes) is unfolding. Every director's work method is unique as is a choreographer's work style. Sometimes a director likes to be in the room to observe, some want the choreographer to do research and bring it in, and yet others want to see the completed dance. Whatever the method, the director has suggestions and works with the choreographer.

A choreographer constructs a dance much like a songwriter constructs a song. In a Broadway musical, the choreographer is helping push the story along. They build a dance with a beginning, a middle, and an end depending on where it fits into the storytelling. Through body movement, the choreographer creates an emotion that suits the story and reveals the character's emotions. The visual element helps convey intimacy of a love scene or conflict in a fight scene. Directors are primarily focused on the acting scenes, but choreographers know how to move people onstage, especially in a large ensemble number.

Although this chapter is predominantly about Broadway musicals, plays often need choreographers. Depending on the era and play content, some plays require movement. An example is *Dancing at Lughnasa*, where authentic movement/dance is part of the story, but it does not necessarily require singing. Another example is *The Ritz*, where a cabaret performer is doing a funny song with movement/dance but it is still a play because she is singing and dancing in the reality of the play. It is not a heightened reality as with a musical.

The choreographer receives a fee for choreographing the show. On bigger productions, there can be a separate allowance for a pre-production period, which gives the choreographer an opportunity to work out ideas and develop a dance vocabulary for the production. For this pre-production period, the choreographer hires a small group of dancers with whom the choreographer has worked who understand their shorthand, allowing the choreographer to get a sense of the style of the show, the basic construction of the numbers, and what suits the show's storytelling. If it is not a big dance show, the choreographer works on their own. During this early dance pre-production work, the choreographer works with the director who may be in and out of rehearsals. It also gives the producers and production team an opportunity to observe things that can affect their concept of cast size, sets, and costume needs.

During this pre-production phase, the choreographer might work with a dance music arranger, who is the liaison between the choreographer and the eventual production music team. As dances evolve, the arranger writes, adds, subtracts, and edits music for the dances, which will go through transformations until the production is Broadway bound. Frequently with dance rehearsals there can be a drummer for rhythm.

Often a choreographer does not read music, so the arranger writes down the arrangement in a way the choreographer, the rehearsal pianist, and the drummer (if there is one) can understand if the dance music arranger is not available to play the rehearsal. Eventually, all the dance music arrangements are given to the orchestrator to incorporate into the orchestrations.

Pre-production is well before there are any preliminary readings. Once a production is firmly in view, there are elemental readings with just some actors reading the script from music stands, which the choreographer attends to observe. After several such readings there are semi-staged readings where dancers are included. Now the choreographer starts to apply their pre-production ideas to the current script and music.

Once a full tryout is planned, the principal creatives (the composer, lyricist, book writer, director, choreographer, among others) are present at the cast auditions, which usually becomes the Broadway cast. These auditions give the choreographer the opportunity to see how the potential cast moves, assess if they suit the show's dance style, and have some say in the casting.

The pre-production phase was somewhat in the abstract, but now a cast is assembled, an opening date is set, and the abstract becomes reality. The original ideas change, steps are reset, adjustments are made. Excitement is high in early rehearsals, and a dancer executes a difficult step with enthusiasm, but when repeated daily it becomes harmful to the body. Having been a dancer, a choreographer is fully aware of the hazards for dancers performing eight shows a week and tries to ensure the dancers' physical safety and comfort when choreographing. Despite all the precautions taken, dancers are the most frequently injured members of a Broadway cast.

In every show there is also a dance captain, a person whose job, in addition to performing, is to maintain the quality of the dance numbers during the run. If it is possible, the choreographer can advocate for one of the dancers during casting to fill this position, because the choreographer knows the person has the requisite skills and may have experience being a dance captain. Once the show is up and running, the dance captain teaches the understudies, swings, and new cast members the choreography and those rehearsals are joined by the music director, the associate music director, or a rehearsal pianist.

There are a few male and female swing dancers who cover all the female and male ensemble dance roles in a show. Having more than one male and one female swing is for insurance so that if someone is ill or cannot be at the performance, there is always someone to cover the roles. They stand-by during a performance in the event anyone is injured.

A choreographer usually has an associate for a show who is their right-hand person. The associate keeps notes, tracks all of the dance steps and patterns, and notates all the information. If the choreographer cannot be present for rehearsal, the associate steps in, has all the documentation, and conducts the rehearsal. The dance captain will get a copy of the documentation as well.

When the show is in full production, the cast is in rehearsal for about four weeks before moving to the theatre. During that time, the music director can be present to work with the director and choreographer to discern musical needs as changes occur, such as the balance of sound for a chorus number. If a chorus soprano sings a line that needs to be more prominent, but because of height is staged in the back, she needs to be brought downstage to be heard. People need to be nearer each other to hear each other with a difficult harmony. All of one type of voice (i.e., tenors) are staged on one side of the stage causing an imbalance in sound.

All this work unfolds during offsite rehearsals. Once the company moves to the theatre, other issues manifest themselves. In the rehearsal room everyone was relatively safe, but once onstage choreographic details need adjustments to maintain safety. Suddenly the stage space differs from the rehearsal room, so dance movements need alteration. A set step is higher or lower than was expected, affecting a dance step. Lights from the side of the stage are shining directly in dancers' eyes. Set pieces are moving on and off the stage. Eventually, the cast is in costume and makeup, and suddenly a costume restricts a dance movement.

Technically the choreographer's job is over opening night, but in reality it is never finished. After opening night, a choreographer can return to the show to assist in putting in new cast members, clean up the choreography, or make sure the dancers are not injuring themselves.

Like composers who notate their compositions on paper, choreographers keep track of their choreography by using a form of dance notation. It is primarily tracking the stage blocking of the dancers. Dance notation began in the late 1600s and has evolved through the centuries. In 1976 there was a sweeping revision of the copyright law in the United States and in that law the word "choreography" was finally formally used. Copyrighting a dance is still very fluid. According to the law it has to be a fixed or tangible thing, not an idea in a choreographer's head. In 1948, the choreographer Hanya Holm became the first Broadway choreographer to have her dances copyrighted for her work on *Kiss Me Kate*. However, copyrighting choreography is still a developing concept.

There are many different methods of dance notation from graphic symbols to figures, numbers, letters, and words. Today a choreographer can use a magnetic board with little pins to indicate the dancers' blocking as they move around the stage. Notating a dance helps the choreographer codify their creation and serves as a reference for someone re-creating that dance. Today of course there is video to record a completed dance, but dance notation helps the choreographer remember where they were in the choreographic process. Not all choreographers notate their work in a traditional sense. Christopher Gattelli does not write out the steps of the dance but writes out the emotion of a particular dance and where it occurs in the storytelling of the production.

As mentioned, years of intense physical dance are hard on the human body, but a dancer's longevity is individual. Some careers are shortened by youthful excitement, injuries, or not pacing themselves. Others have a certain intellectual discipline and last a long run. They take care of their instrument (their body), do the ballet bar daily to warm up before the show, take class, and do physical therapy.

As a dancer, the choreographer was a member of Actors' Equity, but as a director they are a member of the Society of Directors and Choreographers. Joining the Society of Directors and Choreographers requires a choreographer to work in a venue like regional theatre or Off Broadway. According to Society of Directors and Choreographers guidelines, a choreographer receives a royalty for their work for the original Broadway production. This royalty ends once the production closes. However, each show and contract are different. It is possible for a choreographer to receive payment for their work if they choose to use and acknowledge it in another production. Also, if they leave a profound choreographic imprint on a show, they can receive a certain fee or percentage with regards to the show being licensed out.

For someone who began as a dancer, the fascination of creating a dance can be an overpowering draw. As Christopher Gattelli recalled, "I would have been happy to keep going [dancing] but there was such a pull I couldn't even focus on stage anymore. I just wanted to create. The storytelling is different every time, so it always feels like a new experience."

9

Music

Music Director

The music director (MD) of a Broadway musical is in charge of the entire music department and all musical aspects of the production. It is a multifaceted job with a multitude of responsibilities.

In addition, the position of music supervisor has been incorporated in certain circumstances. If the musical has multiple national or international tours, the supervisor oversees the music departments for *all* the productions to ensure the same quality and choices as the Broadway production are being observed. Often the music supervisor of subsequent productions is the MD of the original Broadway production. The term music supervisor is still in a transitory phase even though some people I interviewed used the term to refer to the MD of a single production. For the purposes of this section, the term music director will be used.

For young people hoping to have a career on Broadway, it is noteworthy to point out that whereas in the past MDs were predominantly men, female MDs, associate MDs (AMDs), and conductors abound in today's Broadway productions. Even the classical world is changing, and there is an increase in female symphony conductors.

In the beginning, a Broadway music department consists of the MD, the associate music director (AMD), and sometimes an assistant/intern. From the initial development of a new Broadway musical to opening night, the music department is very fluid with several jobs overlapping.

Although the MD is a work for hire position, once they join the production in the early development stage, they are intimately involved in the creative process. Working with the composer, lyricist, book writer, choreographer, and director, ideas, songs, music, lyrics, and dialogue are tried and discarded boldly and constantly. It is a time of discovering how best to tell the story, and the process can take several years with everyone's input.

By the time the show is destined for Broadway, there are several other additions to the music department that are discussed in the music section of this book. Each of these individuals have specific tasks that complete the music department overseen by the MD.

Most United States university musical theatre programs are for actors, not musicians. There are a few institutions that do have a degree program for a theatre MD, but music degrees are predominantly issued through university music departments where the focus is classical music. So most musical theatre musicians are exposed to some level of classical music training. Thus, a theatre MD can come from a variety of backgrounds and, interestingly enough, not all are music majors.

There is a strong interaction between music and science and some MDs majored in science. Music has a universal structure and language based on what is generally referred to as classical music fundamentals. Music is part of our aural scape, and sound has a strong science and math component. That soundscape involves sound waves, sound frequencies, pitch, rhythm, and tempo. For a Broadway show, the human element in performance (onstage or in the pit) adds emotion and sensitivity to the soundscape.

MDs are hired by the general manager at the suggestion of the composer, director, or producer. Some MDs negotiate their own contract or work with an agent. A Broadway MD belongs to the American Federation of Musicians (AFM) New York Local

802, which is not difficult to join. A musician pays the initiation fee, the annual membership fee, and then work dues on each job.

There are, of course, revivals of traditional musicals, but today there is a great variety in musical theatre styles, which reflect the sensibility of the composer and the story for which they are composing. It helps, but is not required, if the MD has experience and knowledge in the specific genre for the show such as country or pop.

The AMD is recommended by the MD and approved by the general manager/producer. The AMD is a crucial part of the music team, as they perform many of the same tasks as the MD and substitute for the MD if they are not present in the room. The MD and AMD work very closely together, so compatibility is of the utmost importance.

As with most aspects of a Broadway show, there is no one path to becoming an MD. The composer, lyricist, and book writer (the originators) work on a project together. When they need to hear what they have written, they sometimes gather friends to read through a script or make demos of the music or even try songs out in a concert. It gives them a chance to evaluate their work and monitor their progress. Sometimes the MD is involved in the project this early.

There is a certain mayhem in bringing a musical to the Broadway stage, whether it is a revival or a new work. However, a new work can be more challenging because it is an unknown quantity. There is no one method for doing anything in theatre, nor is there a straight throughline to success. The miracle is that it all eventually comes together.

A piano/vocal score is used throughout the development process of a musical even after the orchestrator joins the production. An orchestrator creates a score and instrumental parts for the musicians starting from the piano/vocal. However, actors use a piano/vocal even after the show opens for understudy rehearsals, new cast members, and subsequent productions. If a show is to be conducted from the keyboard, a piano/conductor score is created, which incorporates the orchestrator's work, so the conductor can successfully lead the ensemble of musicians. If the show is to be conducted from the podium, sometimes a full score is used or a piano/conductor score is used, depending on the conductor's preference or what is available.

Once a producer is formally involved and a production planned, they can structure a course of action. There can be simple readings with a cast standing at music stands using the current script and songs or it can be a staged reading with minimal movement. The MD and AMD teach the cast and rehearse the current show version with them.

As discussed a little later in this music section, composers today use computer software programs for their work. At some point in the reading stage or earlier, an intern/assistant is hired and their primary task is to digitally keep track of and input to a computer all of the continually changing dialogue and music, print the sheet music, and distribute the material to everyone promptly in the rehearsal. Their unofficial title is "keeper of the score." Until there is an intern, that task can be executed by the AMD or a dedicated hired transcriber. It depends on the size of the show and the producer.

As the show progresses the next step is workshops, which are modestly staged presentations with some or no set dressing, props, and minimal costumes or no costumes. Now a full cast with dancers work with the choreographer and usually a small combo of musicians. This is an opportunity for the sound designer to work with the composer, the director, the orchestrator, and the MD to explore the sonic goals desired for the show (e.g., the instrumentation colors). Throughout, the MD, assisted by the AMD, rehearses and leads the proceedings. The size of the workshop depends on the budget, the producer, the composer, and the ideas to be explored. Workshops can be for two to four weeks, and sometimes even six weeks. The workshop cast is not necessarily the Broadway cast, because at this stage everything is still evolving.

Whether it is a reading or a workshop, there can be a limited invited audience. The purpose is two-fold, to get a human response to the show and to whet the appetite for possible investors to help move the show forward. Although during COVID-19, the number of invitees was smaller, they still easily exceeded twenty.

Throughout the various permutations, the composer, lyricist, and book writer are in and out of rehearsals rewriting constantly as new ideas are explored. Material is tried, thrown out, rewritten, and tried again. What was rehearsed the previous day is revised. The MD needs to be agile, adaptable, and imaginative, in addition to being an excellent musician.

During the early development when songs and song assignments are in constant flux, the MD or composer can write a quick simple vocal arrangement if necessary so the rehearsal can continue. There are musicians who specialize in vocal arranging and dance music arranging and they join the production a bit later in the process.

When the production has Broadway in sight, there are tryouts which are full productions. In the past, tryouts were standardized and there were tryout circuits (i.e., a variation of Boston, Philadelphia, and Washington, DC). Today there are usually tryouts mounted at a regional theatre like The Globe or the La Jolla Playhouse, both in California, or Off Broadway. On occasion, a Broadway production may decide not to have a tryout and open directly on Broadway, but that can be financially risky.

Once the show is at the tryout stage, the cast can be set for the Broadway production and the orchestrator can be hired. If there are tryouts, the orchestrator enters the production during rehearsals just before the actors move to a theatre. As soon as songs are set, they are released to the orchestrator by the director/ choreographer and MD, and the orchestrator begins their work.

Throughout all these stages, the MD is working with their team, as well as interacting with all the other principals, teaching, consulting, discussing voice issues (if there are any), and contributing to the decision-making.

By the time the production moves to the theatre, the size and instrumental composition of the music ensemble has been determined. The orchestrator needs this information before they can begin their work. After conferring with the composer and lyricist, the orchestrator goes off and works on their own. The MD and sound designer start discussing sound concepts. The MD's knowledge about the cast's vocal capabilities can impact the sound designer's reinforcement work, so this collaboration is essential.

Later, when the show is well on its way to finalization, changes and tweaks continue until the show is frozen which, though rarely, can be as late as opening night. One thing is certain, and that is musicals are not for the fainthearted. Few new musicals arrive fully formed.

In the past, singers were trained to project their voices to the back of the orchestra section. There might have been foot mics but not sophisticated amplification. Today, all musical actors wear microphones. Once in tech when the cast begins to wear microphones, the MD, sound designer, and sound mixer confer regarding sound issues, such as balance, volume, and instrumental color that arise with the cast members and the orchestra. Eventually the sound designer designs the sound reinforcement and the mixer coordinates all the sound equipment used in the production adhering to the wishes of the sound designer.

The next step is assembling the orchestra. Now a music coordinator enters the picture and works with the MD. The objective is to have a group of musicians who serve the composer's creation best. Music is an international language and musicians can play any score, but experience with a specific genre, such as country, jazz, rock, or traditional musical theatre, enhances the subtleties of that style.

The coordinator contracts the musicians. An MD can have a first-choice list of musicians with whom they have previously worked, having established a line of communication. If the first choice is not available, the music coordinator gathers information about the show from the MD and chooses people they think would meet the MD's wishes. An interview is arranged, and hopefully the hire works out. If it does not, there is a limited time frame for dismissal governed by AFM union Local 802. The music coordinator makes the offers to the players, handles any ensuing negotiations, and the union dictates salaries. The MD is not involved with musician negotiations.

The MD rehearses ten to twelve hours with the orchestra alone before it joins the production. Then there is the *sitzprobe*, which is the first time the orchestra and the entire cast are brought together for a music run-through of the entire show. Everyone hears each other for the first time; the cast hears the full orchestra, which is quite different from a solo piano. The orchestra hears the full cast, the stage manager hears the full show, and the sound mixer attends to learn the show.

It is not unusual today for the orchestra to be distributed throughout the theatre, from the balcony to an unused dressing room to the basement. Where and how the orchestra is located today depends on the director and producer, and several other factors. The orchestra pits are the same size as when they were built in the nineteenth and early twentieth centuries, so they are limited spaces jammed with people and instruments. Reducing costs is always a consideration and technology has enhanced the ability to have smaller ensembles that sound like a full orchestra (thanks to the digital synthesizer). By this kind of distribution, the producer might be able to have two extra rows of seats for paying audience members. Sometimes musicians are onstage as part of the story. Sometimes it is simply because all the instruments do not fit in the pit.

Sound design has become a huge component of modern Broadway productions partially brought on by modern music styles, sound technology, and the remote locations of musicians. Once the decision is made, the MD and the sound designer work closely together to achieve the best sound reinforcement possible for the production while preserving the music integrity. Decisions on how to group the musicians for a particular show are critical. Electronics that were used only in recording studios and rock arenas have been incorporated into theatre and make this instrument disbursement possible.

If the musicians are disbursed to multiple locations, the MD and musicians use headphones and video monitors to see each other, communicate, and play together. There is no sound delay, but there can be a video delay. Wherever the MD is located, they are visible via monitors and able to communicate with the cast and the musicians. Headphones and monitors are not always necessary, especially if the MD and musicians are traditionally placed in the pit, where the visual with the cast and musicians is more direct. The beauty of a production is the creativity and versatility.

It is interesting to note that sometimes the MD is not the conductor for the show, even though they oversee the entire music department. Conducting a show is more than keeping the ensemble together and is an inherently complex job. A conductor not only leads the cast and the musicians through a performance; they shape and accentuate the drama or comedy through the sound and color drawn from the musicians and the cast. To that end, the musicians add their individual musical skills and experience. Once that curtain goes up, the conductor manages the onstage performance, along with the production stage manager who is calling the show.

Things do go awry in any live performance. When an actor jumps lyrics or measures of music, standing on a podium in front of the musicians and cast allows the conductor to communicate more directly with everyone and have more control over the performance. It is a bit more complicated when the musicians are distributed throughout the theatre.

Today the MD/conductor's job can be more intense with additional duties. They can conduct a show and also be incorporated into the show onstage as a performer. This is a gray area between AFM Local 802 and Actors' Equity Association if the MD becomes a performer in the show. Furthermore, the conductor may be required to play multiple instruments, like any other musician in the ensemble. This is called doubling and is quite common.

The ensemble musicians are only required to play 50 percent of the shows to keep their chair. If a musician is out of a performance, it is the player's responsibility to find a sub for that performance. Most show musicians have at least four or five approved subs to call upon in any situation, including an emergency. The subs usually observe several performances and have some time to prepare before playing a show.

The stage manager is in charge of the entire production every night, so in emergencies the MD has a handset to communicate with the stage manager. There is also a monitor on the MD all the time, so the stage manager can tell whether the

MD is aware of a backstage problem and is adjusting for it. On the handset is a light that flashes if the stage manager needs to talk with the MD. Sometimes the technical problem onstage is obvious and the MD can listen on the handset as the crew finds a resolution to the problem.

No matter what problems arise during a performance, everyone's goal running the show is to make sure the storytelling continues, and the audience is not aware of any interruption—unless of course the show comes to a complete technical halt!

Associate Music Director

Everyone in the music department on a Broadway production wears many hats. The principal job of the AMD is to be a partner to and supporter of the MD, a role that varies with each MD. Essentially, the AMD is an excellent musician and executes many of the same tasks as the MD, but is not a decision-maker in terms of the production. Even though their work intersects during the process of a show, the MD leads the music team and is responsible for all musical aspects of the show.

Most often the MD recommends an AMD with whom they have previously worked. It can also be word of mouth or by reputation. Final approval is from the general manager/producer. When the AMD is hired can vary widely, depending on the show size, budget, and producer, but certainly when more than one person is required to manage the music responsibilities.

Aside from having obvious musical qualifications, a person can become an AMD in a roundabout manner. They can initially be hired as the rehearsal pianist or even a transcriber and later be offered the AMD position. Again, each situation and production is unique.

The MD relies heavily on the AMD when the MD is not present in the room or interacting with other departments. Both the MD and the AMD are usually accomplished pianists and share rehearsal duties, which include teaching the cast the current show version and playing rehearsals. If the cast is large, the MD and AMD split rehearsals into separate rooms and the AMD apprises the MD of any changes that might have occurred in the other rehearsal room.

The early readings can be very rudimentary with actors at music stands, but they are an opportunity to explore and develop the show. The songs and characters change, solos morph into ensemble numbers, dialogue changes, lyrics change. Everything is in motion. When the production reaches the workshop stage, dancers working with the choreographer are added.

As mentioned in the MD section, updating the score is primarily an intern/assistant's job, but until one is hired, that task is the AMD's. In the past, dialogue and score changes were done with that old-fashioned tool, the pencil, and xeroxed, which took time and slowed the rehearsals. With computers and multiple software programs, in which most musicians are proficient, the new technology has altered how rewrites are produced accelerating the pace and method(s) of transmitting score changes to the music team and cast.

During rehearsal, if a composer plays a change on the piano, the AMD or intern transcribes it into the computer, prints out the sheet music, and distributes the copies so the rehearsal can continue. Sometimes the changes are done by hand and the scores are updated at a later date. It all depends on where in the process the show is. Any method that keeps the production moving forward is valid. The urgency is to not lose time and keep the rehearsal flowing.

Maintaining the score today has an added detail. Whereas in the past the script and music score were separate entities, now frequently the music style is sung-through like an opera, where a lot of the dialogue is written within the music score with music accompaniment underneath. This is referred to as an *integrated score*. With this style as the music is updated, the dialogue changes must also be inserted into the score. Basically, the AMD or intern continues this piano/vocal updating process even after an orchestrator enters the picture when the cast moves to the theatre.

When the show is in the full production phase, the AMD's musical tasks from rehearsals continue, plus some administrative responsibilities. The associate maintains a "change sheet," which keeps track of music edits. If music bars are cut, added, or lyrics are changed, the AMD is responsible for tracking those edits, delivering the document to the stage management team each day, and clearly communicating all those changes to the entire company. After each rehearsal, the director has a notes session, and the creative team decides when those new changes go into the show. The AMD relays all of that information to the stage management team.

The AMD's day does not end after the notes session. Some work is done at night as homework. The AMD practices the score for the next day's rehearsal and waits for more rewrites from the creative team. During rehearsal if a song or dialogue is not working, then the composer, lyricist, and book writer go home, rewrite songs or dialogue, and digitally send the rewrites to the AMD or intern as an audio file. However long it takes for those rewrites, upon receipt those changes are transcribed and input into the computer and the rewrites are sent to the appropriate people before the next morning's rehearsal. If it is a new song overnight, it is transcribed the next day.

The AMD arrives early for rehearsal to confirm the previous day's music changes have been completed and inserted into the scores. The day's activities include playing rehearsal piano, teaching the cast music, and conducting rehearsals if the MD is occupied with other departments.

The MD rehearses with the orchestra for ten to twelve hours, during which the AMD observes the rehearsals, unless they are a member of the orchestra, which is often the case. The AMD does not actually rehearse with the orchestra, but steps in when needed, even during rehearsals, where music tweaking is still occurring. Once a show opens, the AMD is the first substitute for the MD, often conducting two performances a week, usually the matinees. The AMD's preparation is to practice the score and monitor the MD during performances.

The AMD is a member of the AFM, New York Local 802. Most AMDs negotiate their salary above the union scale to cover all their duties. With their negotiated base weekly salary, there are salary bumps for conducting a performance, being onstage playing the keyboard, or being in costume. Musicians in an ensemble frequently do what is called doubling—playing two different instruments—which the union allows under the basic salary. If there are several additional instruments, there can be added salary bumps.

Music ensembles are reduced from traditional orchestras, and whether it is the MD, the AMD (the first sub), or the sub-sub after the AMD, all the conductors play the same instruments, because everyone plays the same show. If there is a specialty instrument in the orchestration, the production tries to hire musicians who already know how to play that instrument or express an interest in learning it. For *Jagged Little Pill*, they had to play the keyboard and the harmonica; for *SpongeBob*, they played the keyboard and the accordion.

Two or three days a week during a run, the AMD is responsible for rehearsing understudies, swings, and new ensemble members. The AMD teaches the music and can play the piano for those rehearsals, or there can be a rehearsal pianist. Again, it depends on the production as duties vary. A replacement star is usually the domain of the MD, depending on their preference.

For the music department on a Broadway production, technology has enhanced the skill of transcribing music immeasurably, but it also influences generally what and how a composer can create today. Recently Ben Moss, the MD for an Off Broadway show (he has been a Broadway AMD), received audio files from the composer. The audio files had twelve singers singing twelve different lines, but some singers were singing the same notes on their line. Formerly, a transcriber had to listen and try to separate out each line being sung. Now there is a computer software program where each line can be separated out and eleven lines muted, so one line can be transcribed individually into the computer. It would be virtually impossible to deal with twelve voices in this manner without the composer writing or notating the music out. Technology is a great asset to support composers in this way. As mentioned previously, the technology enables music transcription, key changes, printing, and distributing altered material in rehearsal considerably quicker than in the past.

Intern

An intern on a Broadway musical is recommended by the music team or through word of mouth and hired by the production. The intern can be non-union or union, but they are usually labeled intern/assistant, which technically is a non-union position.

There is not a specific method for how an intern is approached for a Broadway production, but frequently the company management reaches out to the intern with the amount of money being offered and not necessarily with a contract. When an intern/assistant is hired, their formal job is "the keeper of the score." An intern position is a wonderful opportunity for a young person to get their foot in the door of the Broadway community, to make contacts, and to develop a reputation.

Dance Music Arranger

A dance music arranger is a person who does exactly as the title suggests. The choreographer is the *dance* arranger. The dance *music* arranger arranges the *dance music*. They work primarily with the choreographer and function as the go-between for the choreographer and the music team on a Broadway show. The dance music arranger interacts infrequently with the actors or director as they rehearse. They write music, arrange music to suit the choreography, edit the music as a dance evolves, and write it down so the choreographer, the associate choreographer, or an accompanist understands what is needed.

The dance music arranger is a musician, a member of the musicians' union, Local 802, and usually proficient on the piano. How a musician becomes a dance music arranger can vary widely, but basic music knowledge, music notation, familiarity with a variety of dance forms and music styles, and happenstance all contribute to the journey.

A dance music arranger may never have danced but they may have accompanied dance classes or been around dance. It is someone well-versed in a vast number of musical styles and understands choreographers. On Broadway, the dance music arranger's job is to take whatever song they are given and help the choreographer push the story along through the music.

Accompanying a dance class or rehearsal requires more than just playing the music on the page. Dance music arranger Zane Mark describes his first encounters with playing dance rehearsals for the Broadway production of *Bubbling Brown Sugar* under the music supervisor Danny Holgate:

> I remember being fresh out of high school when he called needing someone to play dance rehearsals for the show. The music section they were going to rehearse couldn't have been more than 16 bars and only four chords, so I started playing one chord per measure (no other rhythm). This was supposed to be the big swing section of the number and here I was playing like a robot.
>
> Danny yelled, "Stop! What are you doing? You need to be the entire band at the piano. You need to emulate the bass,

the horns, etc." Swing music has to have a walking bass and I needed to play the "horn hits," because that's what the dancers were looking for. "Bigger, bigger, bigger!"

Dance music arranging is used in many venues other than Broadway, such as film, television, arena concerts, and videos. Whereas on Broadway the music is arranged *for* the choreography as the show evolves, in television or videos, for example, the arrangements are usually established before the dancers rehearse. The choreography is created *to* the written music arrangement and there are usually no musical edits.

Each choreographer has a particular method of working. Some choreographers hear a song and want to dance to that song without adding anything to it. Depending on the moment, an entirely different piece of music needs to be added. Zane Mark recalled:

> When I did *The Full Monty* with the choreographer Jerry Mitchell, he waited until he was in the production rehearsal room to create his dance. So to be prepared, I had to know the song, how the song went, and be ready to improvise something that was going to further that part of the story often departing completely from the original song.

On Broadway, the dance music arranger is usually requested by the choreographer or the music director. Often, depending on the production budget, the choreographer is given a pre-production time where they work out the choreographic vocabulary (ideas) before a show goes into full cast rehearsal. A dance music arranger can be included in that pre-production period to aid the choreographer.

In that pre-production phase of a Broadway show, the choreographer starts with knowing how many dance numbers they are expected to choreograph for the show, which can change as the production develops. In addition, the choreographer has a sense of the spirit wanted for each number. During the pre-production period, the choreographer often hires a skeleton crew of dancers, usually friends or dancers with whom they have worked. With the dancers, the arranger, and often a drummer, the choreographer explores dance ideas so on day one of production rehearsal with the Broadway cast, the choreographer is ready to begin in earnest. The dancers in the skeleton crew may not necessarily be cast in the show. Depending on the ability of the hired cast members, the choreographer makes changes, edits, and moves forward having already worked out the principal language of the choreography.

When formally joining the Broadway production, the dance music arranger needs to know the size and instrumentation of the band, as this influences their arrangements. It is hard to write for a "Count Basie–style big band" with only a trio! Initially, the dance music arranger is given a piano/vocal score or full-blown demos that tells them what the songs in the show are. The goal of incorporating dance music sections into a song is that it should make sense and flow together with the rest of the song, not disrupt the mood with something disconnected like kazoos in the middle of or after a string ballad.

Once production rehearsals begin, there will be a rehearsal pianist provided for the dancers (often someone who will go on to play in the show's orchestra). The arranger does not necessarily play rehearsals; they are there to create the dance music arrangements. The arranger's job is to figure out what the choreographer needs and write it down in a way that the rehearsal pianist understands, if the arranger is unavailable to play the rehearsals. When the creatives involved in the production are watching and learning, things will change. The dance music arranger creates something new only when requested.

Since the choreographer essentially does not read music, the dance music arranger figures out what the choreographer wants and translates it into musical terms for the MD/supervisor or orchestrator. Today, most dance music arrangers use software programs such as Finale and Sibelius to write the music arrangements. The complexities of the arrangements submitted to the orchestrator or MD/supervisor vary depending on the situation. Sometimes it is a simple piano/vocal chart with just chord changes. Sometimes it is a very detailed chart spelling out exactly what the arranger envisions each instrument playing. This is where the relationship with the orchestrator comes in.

If it is a swing arrangement with a walking bass line, the arranger can just write "walking bass" and the pianist or orchestrator will know what that means without having to write each individual note. Frequently for the drummer, it is hits/accents tied to a choreographed arm or leg movement. Once the basic groove (the sense or feeling of the rhythm) and style of the song is set, edits are easier.

Dance music arranging can be quite descriptive. For example, when Zane Mark joined the production of *Mrs. Doubtfire*, he was asked to create music that supported the choreographic storytelling. In one scene, Mrs. Doubtfire is cooking dinner. While cooking dinner, the lyrics read, "First we add the salt and pepper." Zane Mark decided to support that with various musical shakers. When Mrs. Doubtfire starts to tenderize the chicken with a hammer, he used drum hits to coincide with the movements. Each sound was chosen to support the onstage storytelling.

Change seems to be the operative word on Broadway, and with a dance music arranger it is the same. Once on the stage, a section of music might need to be lengthened or shortened to support offstage happenings, such as costume changes or scenery movement. The arranger needs to make the edit sound seamless and musical.

One through line from everyone who contributed to this book is the commitment to the storytelling. Zane Mark said:

> My thing always is the music, the whole entire show. If we're not invoking some kind of feeling, then we've messed up. I'm supposed to make you feel a certain way. Happy. Sad. Agitated. Whatever the *it* is, something is supposed to happen. If the song is not doing that, get the song out of the show. With the good shows, you have a song that's pushing the story along, and the choreography and the dance does that as well.

If the dance music arranger is finished with the arrangements and nothing major is changing, they stop going to the theatre daily. The show continues and everyone's attention is on the big picture. If the dance music arranger does drop by after a brief absence, they might hear subtle changes, which would be helpful to mention to the music team, which is focused on other problems, for example, perhaps the drum accents have gotten a little softer and need to be a bit more pronounced.

When the show is in previews, the dance music arranger is still on call for any last-minute edits. Once the show opens, depending on the production, the dance music arranger job ends. Usually they receive a weekly royalty, which ends when the production ends.

Each production is its own identity. Although the royalty ends with that production, if there is a road company (depending on the contract), additional royalties are paid per company. All contracts are unique.

Vocal Arranger

As mentioned previously, when a Broadway show is in development, the music and song assignments are in flux and any vocal arrangement at that stage can be done by the composer or the MD. It is unusual for a production in the early development phases to hire a professional vocal arranger. On occasion a professional vocal arranger can be brought in to consult with the composer and MD, but most often they join a production before rehearsals with the cast begin. The arranger works alone and once the arranger listens to the music, the kernels of ideas begin to live in their head.

A vocal arranger can have multiple musical talents, but the show's needs determine when the arranger is hired and what the arranger's tasks are. When joining the production, the arranger consults with the creative team (composer, lyricist, and director) and music teams to learn what their expectations are. Early on, the creative team often articulates certain artistic wishes ahead of time so the arranger understands their goals. For example, if the composer or director want a fuller sound for a particular number.

A vocal arranger is just what it describes. The vocal arranger in a Broadway musical is the person who takes the composer's melody and the lyricist's words and creates the vocal lines and harmony for the singers to sing (i.e., the soprano, alto, tenor, and bass lines in an ensemble number). All the songs in a musical have an emotional journey to further the storytelling, and how those songs are voiced is dictated by the music style. The vocal arranger's objective is to complement the composer's and lyricist's creations and to allow the vocals to ride above, but not compete with, what music exists already. Vocal arranger Michael McElroy explains:

> The role of the vocal arranger, as is the entire creative team, is to ensure that the storytelling is centered. I need to know the plot, why and what the character(s) need to express musically in this particular moment, and most importantly, the musical arc of the song. Then my imagination begins to work out how

to support all those factors. In the beginning I keep in mind
each vocal part, where each part sits in the singer's range, and
how each part supports the song's emotional journey.

Having a broad knowledge of music genres and an understanding of the human voice, its capabilities, and boundaries
is an enormous asset for a vocal arranger. By the time the vocal arranger is hired, the cast is set. So depending on the voice
composition of a song (e.g., a musical number is all women,
all men, SSA [soprano, soprano, alto], or SATB [soprano, alto,
tenor, bass]), the vocal arranger creates the harmony and decides
where the power for each range should sit for dramatic effect.
This is important because each vocal range should sit in a place
to give the production the sound it wants and keep stimulating
the audience's ears.

At the beginning of their assignment, the vocal arranger goes
to the production once or twice a week to observe run-throughs,
which is beneficial as it gives the arranger an opportunity to hear
the cast's voices, which can inspire a vocal arrangement.

The process for a vocal arranger can vary according to the
production and where in the process they join the production.
The arranger can start work from a piano/vocal chart, a sketch
of a song, an audio track, or with an orchestration that is still in
flux. Sometimes the vocal arrangement can evolve as the instrumentation is built. Sometimes the vocal arrangement can inspire
where the orchestration goes. During previews songs are still being cut, new songs added, songs assigned to different characters.
Michael McElroy explains:

> It happens in different ways, but the vocal arranger's role is
> always the same. Serve the story and collaborate with what
> is happening orchestrally. Whether starting from a piano
> arrangement or listening to a full orchestration, the work is
> the same: integrate into the existing musical landscape and
> through the vocal arrangements propel the story forward.

If it is a traditional musical, the quality of sound is structured with
certain confines and parameters that are mostly preordained. For
example, with a musical like *Oklahoma!*, the placement of the

soprano, alto, tenor, baritone, and bass voices are standard. That music is established, the voicing is more conventional, and the dramatic arc of the songs is built into the musical line.

Contemporary musicals, such as rock and pop, require a certain kind of vocal quality that suits that music style. With the variety of musical genres on Broadway today, it is important that the performer can produce the sound quality required to bring that specific story to life.

Every singer's voice has its own characteristics and limitations. Good singers who have a strong technique and craft know how to protect their instrument and not push it where it is not meant to go. Likewise, a good vocal arranger understands the human voice and writes arrangements that support the voice and not work against it.

With contemporary musicals, there is an explosion in the parameters for how voices are placed, creating more variety and experimental harmony. A vocal arranger's assignment is to craft a vocal line to tell the story and to take the audience along that journey. According to Mr. McElroy:

> Having been a singer in musicals as well as a composer and arranger, the musical style of the show determines the vocal quality needed from the singer. The vocal arranger's role is to ensure that the show's musical style is supported through the vocal arrangement. More contemporary shows (i.e., pop, rock, R&B, or folk genres) require different vocal sounds. The vocal arranger tries to craft arrangements with knowledge of each voice range, marrying the song's emotional arc with the emotional qualities inherent in each vocal part. It is important to avoid sitting in one vocal place for too long as it desensitizes the audience's ear, so a vocal arrangement must ebb and flow with the character's journey thereby enhancing the audience investment in the story.

A vocal arranger is a member of the musicians' union Local 802. The union sets an arranger's fee by the page or by measure. The arrangement varies with each production according to when the arranger joins the production or what the arranger's task is. Working on a new musical, a vocal arranger can share in the weekly royalty percentage the creative team receives. There are various union stipulations depending on the situation (e.g., if an arranger ceases to work on a show but the arrangements are integral to and retained in the show or if there is a reason for a buyout).

Vocal arrangers use the software programs Finale and Sibelius, to write their arrangements. It allows a composer or arranger to sit at the piano, write music, input that into the computer with a keyboard connected to the computer, and notate it at the same time. The composer or arranger can add different instruments, play it back, and change the tempo. It has streamlined the music processes for a Broadway show.

The job of a Broadway vocal arranger ends on opening night. If a tour is being considered, they can be hired again if the production wants to make some changes based on what was learned from the original show. Also, with a tour there can be one less male and female ensemble member, which can require the vocal arrangements to be adjusted. Smaller shows for touring or student versions might require a vocal arranger to return to make adjustments.

Orchestrator

One of the last positions to join a Broadway musical production is the orchestrator. They are usually hired by the composer but are paid by the producer. Their job does not actually start work until the production reaches the tryout phase as a full production or is about to move to a Broadway theatre.

The element that sets a musical theatre piece apart from other live music genres (except opera) is that the songs and music support a long narrative. The composer creates a melody line with harmony and rhythm and the lyricist writes words to illuminate the story. The composer writes for the piano or guitar, not an orchestra. What enhances and underscores the drama or comedy and the audience's theatrical experience is the accompaniment an ensemble plays filling the entire theatre and touching our senses. That is the work of an orchestrator.

Often an orchestrator started out as an instrumentalist. They usually studied music in college, sometimes classical music, sometimes jazz. During that time, they studied orchestral scores and learned how to notate a score (putting music symbols on a page). Orchestration can be defined as adding instruments to a piece of music, usually to an existing piano accompaniment.

In the American musical theatre, composers have traditionally had other musicians orchestrate their music. During the Tin Pan Alley era, songwriters like Berlin, Kern, or Richard Rodgers always had someone else orchestrate their compositions for everything from small combos to large orchestras. Sometimes a classically trained composer like George Gershwin or Leonard Bernstein bridged classical music and musical theatre, was classically trained, and could orchestrate their own compositions. Today, a few Broadway composers like Jason Robert Brown and Adam Guettel orchestrate their work, but most contemporary Broadway composers do not. According to orchestrator Michael Starobin:

> The actual writing for the instruments has traditionally been someone other than the composer. Stephen Sondheim was someone who was capable of learning to orchestrate. But he

valued the collaboration of another creative voice bringing orchestral colors to his music.

There is a difference between the use of music in a musical and in a nonmusical play. Music is an *integral element* of a musical, unlike the incidental accompaniment of a nonmusical drama. In a musical the score is integrated into the actual writing of the drama in a more direct manner and is not incidental. The use of music in a play is more indirect. It underscores the action and the mood of the play and is mostly used as a device for transitions.

An orchestrator can be approached by the composer or producer anywhere from a year or two before the show goes into a full production. There is often a long pre-production phase for an orchestrator during which no work takes place. The orchestrator will attend multiple readings and workshops. As the show keeps changing in this period, the orchestrator will attend rehearsals, observe the actors' performances, get familiar with the story and characters, and follow the changes made during development.

Finally, there is a fully staged production where an orchestra is engaged and orchestrations are needed. This can be an out-of-town tryout or the actual Broadway production (if the producers are confident enough they do not need a tryout out of town or Off Broadway). The orchestrator starts their work as the cast starts rehearsals for the production, four to six weeks before the first preview. Songs are still being added, dropped, and sometimes assigned to different characters. Because the score keeps changing as the orchestrations are being written, this work becomes highly pressured in a limited time frame.

By the time the orchestrator is hired, management has already approved the size and type of orchestra, so they understand the instruments they will be writing for.

The orchestrator is given a notated piano/vocal score (the melody line with lyrics and piano accompaniment). The work of the dance music arranger and vocal arranger have been added to the composer's piano/vocal score during rehearsals. This is the musical skeleton of the score. The orchestrator then dresses that musical skeleton with the instruments of the orchestra using such skills as counterpoint, polyphony, color, mood (drama or comedy), sound textures, and momentum. The orchestration is continually refreshing and engaging the audience's ears. The orchestrator does not rewrite the music. Their work is an extension of the composer's, the lyricist's, and the writer's creation through orchestral sound.

As the production rehearses prior to previews, troublesome songs are often held back from the orchestrator by the MD. Orchestrator Michael Starobin clarifies:

> As the company starts to actually stage the show in the rehearsal room, they may discover that they need more measures to get people to a different place onstage . . . or that the singer who was able to sing the song in one key for a single reading or workshop now finds it difficult to sing day after day and needs it a half step lower. All sorts of decisions come along during those four weeks of rehearsal. Therefore the music is given to the orchestrator song by song over those four weeks as decisions are finalized. You end up having a very short time to get a lot done.

It cannot be emphasized enough that a new musical is a moving target until it is frozen. This continues even in the previews when the audience's response is also taken into account.

The orchestrator has a thorough knowledge of instruments, their individual sounds, and their technical characteristics. A composer focuses on wonderful melodies and a lyricist focuses on words for a character. But like the work of the authors, the orchestrator's work should further the story being told. Michael Starobin muses:

> One of the reasons a lot of designers and musicians enjoy their work in the theatre is the collaborative mission of telling a story. We all work at being mini-playwrights helping to interpret the play. For me, I present the story and what each character is experiencing through orchestral sound. I am simply continuing the process of the musical storytelling the composer started.

There are still musicals being written that are based on original ideas. However, for many decades a source for adaptation to musicals has been films and nonmusical plays. Recently, recording companies have been cashing in on their old catalogues and the fame of the original performers. Movie studios like Disney have been adapting their own products into Broadway musicals. This type of musical has a built-in audience and has become very successful for media companies. Then these staged musicals (made from films) can be remade yet again into movie musicals. It is very lucrative.

The process of creating a new musical involves different personalities, egos, and methods of working. Collaboration in many ways defines the nature of what a musical can be. While the central creative team of a new musical is a small group (i.e., composer, lyricist, book writer, director), once they reach a preproduction phase, they can find further inspiration through the give and take of working with others and sharing their ideas. Michael Starobin orchestrated two Stephen Sondheim musicals (*Sunday in the Park with George* and *Assassins*) and recalls:

> The amazing thing about him [Stephen Sondheim] was how he always listened carefully and worked closely with his collaborators. Despite his years of experience, he never treated his collaborators as anything but equals. He developed a close working relationship with his book writers and they deeply influenced each other's work. The success of how well his songs are integrated into the play's structure is due to that close collaboration.

After some initial consultation with the composer about what the composer is looking for, the orchestrator works on their own. Orchestrators often do not work with an assistant. Later when the work is presented to the composer, there will be more consultation and revision.

As the orchestrator creates the orchestration, their eye moves up and down the page to make sure the chords, harmony, and notes for each instrument are correct. All of these lines will eventually be separated out and proofed by the music copyist to create individual parts to be distributed to each instrumentalist.

After the orchestration is completed and individual parts created by the copyist, the music is rehearsed by the orchestra led by the MD with the orchestrator and composer present. The composer has been hearing the music on just a piano for many years and now it is being played in full instrumental color for the first time. It can take a bit of an adjustment because it may differ from what the composer anticipated. The orchestrator may also have written things that the composer does not feel are right for the score, so changes will be made.

After the orchestra rehearsals, a *sitzprobe* is held (German for "seated rehearsal"). This is where the cast first hears the accompaniment to the music they will be singing and the composer first hears the vocals and orchestra together. This is the first opportunity for a choreographer to hear the orchestrated version of the dance music.

After orchestra rehearsals and the *sitzprobe*, the orchestrator is present for tech rehearsals and previews.

A preview audience further influences the creative team: for the first time there is an audience reaction to songs, jokes, and scenes. The creative team discovers what works for an audience and what does not. A play or musical starts with an idea on paper but until it is assembled and presented to an audience, no one really knows how it will be received. Thus, revisions can happen very late in a production during previews. Michael Starobin says revisions for an orchestrator are easier than the first draft because the boundaries are already there:

> Even if you made a mistake in writing the orchestration, the mistake taught you so much about what the piece is that writing the revision is easier. Sometimes revisions are not written they are literally dictated. I'll stand at the side of the orchestra pit and dictate a whole change over a few measures for what people should play and not play.

Once a show opens the orchestrator's work is essentially done (unless there is a recording of a cast album). Occasionally during the run of the show, a new actor is cast to replace the original actor and will need their song to be transposed to a different key. This may require adjustments from the orchestrator.

An orchestrator is a member of the AFM, Local 802, in New York. It is not a difficult union to join. There are no requirements for joining except to be a musician and pay an initiation fee. However, the union has very specific rules governing various musical jobs under its jurisdiction such as instrumentalists, arrangers, orchestrators, and venues (i.e., jazz clubs, small theatres, concert halls, Off Broadway, as well as Broadway). It also has very specific fees for an orchestrator on Broadway, which makes it easy for the orchestrator and the producer to determine the cost for a show.

The work of an orchestrator on Broadway is considered a "work for hire." While they receive remuneration for their work, they do not have copyright over their product. Ownership of the orchestration is held by the composer. The AFM states the orchestrator gets an initial payment for Broadway, then another payment when the work is recorded, another payment for a first-time video, and another payment if it goes to rental for stock and amateur productions.

If a revival of an older Broadway production uses a newly written orchestration, the original orchestrator does not get paid nor do they receive a royalty (unless the original orchestrator is hired to write the new orchestration). When making a film of a musical, new orchestrations are often written to take advantage of the larger number of musicians who can play in a recording studio as opposed to the limited space of a Broadway pit.

Payment for an orchestration is based on a set amount (page rate) for each four-measure page of an orchestrated score. The cost of an orchestration can always be estimated by multiplying the page rate by the number of four-measure pages in a show. For example, seven hundred pages (or twenty-eight hundred measures) times fifty dollars equals thirty-five thousand dollars. The union scale page rate is determined by the number of and nature of instruments in the orchestra. An established orchestrator is usually paid a negotiated rate higher than the union scale rate.

The use of a page rate protects both the employer (the producer) and the employee (the orchestrator). The orchestrator is paid for exactly the amount of music they orchestrate, no more. But if the production keeps making changes to the show and requires the orchestrator to keep making those changes, the page rate ensures that the orchestrator will be paid for their additional work.

A theme that runs through several chapters in this book is the influence of technology on Broadway. Today music is written in digital notation programs like Finale or Sibelius. A few seasoned orchestrators still notate by hand, but most have moved to digital notation. Technology is also affecting the sound of the orchestra with the use of synthesizers.

Since musicals have such a long incubation period, an orchestrator can be involved with several shows in development at the same time. But occasionally two shows become active at the same time for an orchestrator. In such cases an orchestrator will often call on their colleagues to help orchestrate a few numbers. While these same colleagues are competing for the same jobs, the professional camaraderie wins out and the favor giving of assistance is often returned later.

Some shows are easier to share work between different orchestrators. A show with an established sound (a revival or a juke box show) makes it simpler for the different orchestrators to match sound. But a new show that is trying to sound different than anything that came before it should usually be left to a single orchestrator.

Music Copyist

The most important goal for a composer or orchestrator, no matter what area they are writing for (concert, symphonies, recording session, opera, theatre, jazz), is to get their musical ideas down on paper as quickly as possible. In doing so, they use a system of music symbols (notes) to represent what an instrumentalist or singer is to perform. This is the act of musical notation. In the act of composing, they are more concerned with capturing the accuracy of their musical ideas, not necessarily with the visual aspects of the notated page. This is when the professional music copyist enters the process.

There are several professional music preparation companies for Broadway in New York City, but one of the busiest is Emily Grishman Music Preparation. The company works with Broadway, Off Broadway, and regional theatre productions, among other entities, and employs music copyists who essentially take the composer's or orchestrator's work and create a complete and accurate instrumental part for a musician to perform.

Music copying is the art of creating a clean, legible, musically accurate, and visually organized piece of music for a musician to read/play. Music copyists do not create music. They are more like copy editors, fixing spelling, syntax, and layout for each instrumental part (and often for the full score). A music manuscript must have a consistency in format, a visual clarity, and a certain finesse to the finished product.

There are different degrees of music copying, such as music engraving, where the work is being done for publication and requires a slightly more rigorous set of standards. Another is transcription, which is often required during the development of a Broadway musical, where a person writes down or digitally notates music that is heard from an audio source. The source can be a composer dictating a change during rehearsal or a new song sent digitally for transcribing for the rehearsal the next morning.

In the past, composers and orchestrators wrote their scores by hand using pen and ink. The music copyist did the same work they do today but also used pen and ink. It was very careful, precise work, and it still is. However, today most composers, orchestrators, and music copyists are well-versed in using one of several computer software programs (Finale, Sibelius, Dorico) to complete their work.

On commercial assignments (i.e., theatre productions, film scoring), a time deadline is a primary factor that precludes a composer or orchestrator from refining their manuscripts for players to read in rehearsal or performance. They do not have the time, interest, or expertise to make that music notationally perfect or visually well-laid out on the page, which is essential for a musician to read/play. Pen and ink has been replaced by the notation software, which is a wonderful aid for keeping up with the rapid changes on a Broadway musical.

The focus of this book is Broadway, and there is definitely a time deadline for opening night. Whereas in the past a music copyist might have had six weeks to two months to work on a score, today the timeline is compressed and could be as little as two weeks. Most often there is a team of music copyists required in order to complete the job within the given time frame.

There is a constant flow of email communications between the production and the music preparation team as changes occur during rehearsals and previews. Each music preparation supervisor develops their own method of keeping track of those changes, informing their music copying team of the change requests, and confirming the changes have been made.

The standard Broadway orchestrator's score has four measures on the page and as many lines as needed for the given number of musicians who will be playing the score. In preparing the score, the copyist separates out each music line and generates an individual part for each instrument. Music editing is a large component of the job as copyists check for spelling and poor notation, and validate that the music chords are accurate and labeled correctly.

The page layout for each instrument is unique because each instrument plays a distinct musical line, requiring the music copyist to make adjustments for spacing, bars of rest, and to facilitate page turning for the musician, ideally while the player has rests in the part.

Once the scores have been finalized, everything is proofread, copied, printed, and bound into individual instrumental parts. The final parts and scores are then delivered to the theatre and distributed to the music team, the orchestra, the creative team, and the production team.

When a show is in full production mode, music copyists' hours are long and the pressure is intense. As opening night approaches, any small last-minute music changes may be dictated by the orchestrator to the individual musician affected, but ultimately, all changes are updated in the copyist's files so that they reflect the final version of a score.

There are practical reasons for working with a well-prepared score. Time and money are serious considerations for an MD and a producer. Rehearsal and recording time are always limited (because it is expensive), and a well-presented score saves time because there need be no discussion of notation errors or missing parts. It allows the musicians to give their best performance without struggling to figure out what they are supposed to be playing.

Music Coordinator

Perhaps thirty years ago, the music coordinator was called the music contractor on Broadway. The truth is most musicians at some point in their career act as contractors. They call a friend to play a gig at a club, a recording session, a church job, or accompany a singer for a concert. A contractor finds musicians to fill a position in a group or for a solo performance.

When the British transfers of the 1980s like *Cats* arrived on Broadway, the English production brought personnel who may have been the British conductors but were not going to be conducting the Broadway transfer. Instead, they possessed extremely valuable information about the show's overall musical vision, which was essential to the success of the American production. From that point, the music contractor term on Broadway morphed into music coordinator. The contractor's job evolved into more of a music consultant and was no longer only hiring musicians for a production.

The music coordinator can be contacted a year in advance of the show coming to Broadway or three weeks if a theatre suddenly becomes available. The initial call can come from the general manager/producer, MD, the music supervisor, or the orchestrator.

In the beginning of the production, there can be an exploration of whether the company should buy or rent the music equipment. What would be economically feasible? The music coordinator's knowledge is helpful to give the producers every option. How much does an instrument cost, what is the cost to rent it, and who is going to repair it? A coordinator likes to supply every contingency plan, answer all questions, and suggest some things that were not considered because those issues will crop up down the road.

It is inevitable that processes change over time, and that is true for a music coordinator. Music coordinator John Miller relates the procedural changes on a Broadway show:

> Many years ago, I remember doing a show with Cy Coleman and Billy Byers. In those days, they would call a couple

of months before opening and say, "Here's the music style; here's the instrumentation." I might ask what instruments are doubled and what instruments for the reeds? They would give me that information and say, "We'll see you in six weeks at the first rehearsal." There were no suggestions of who they would like. The choice was mine as the coordinator.

Today the coordinator's job starts in earnest when they hear from the MD or the orchestrator that the production is in motion. The coordinator is told the size of the orchestra and the instruments to be used. An in-person or online meeting is held to hash out a list of musicians, consisting of whoever in the production has an interest in assembling the ensemble. It will mainly be the MD, music supervisor, orchestrator, possibly the dance arranger, and general manager/producer.

Each participant will have musicians they want for specific chairs, but music teams differ. Some say exactly who they want, some say who they are thinking about, and some are not sure because they are new to New York. So the coordinator adjusts to the request. The ultimate goal is the same: to have an outstanding group of musicians for the show.

All the musicians are members of the musicians' union AFM Local 802, and there is a collective bargaining agreement that has been approved by both the musicians and the Broadway League of Producers and Disney. The union has specific nonnegotiable terms and salaries for rehearsals, performances, and overtime. It is very cut and dried.

Most audience members understand that performers gain their roles through the audition process. According to union rules, the musicians are not auditioned unless the producer pays a fee for the musician's time to audition. Part of the coordinator's job is to assemble an ensemble that will work stylistically and personality-wise for the production. Consequently, the caliber of musicians on Broadway is very high.

It is very unusual for a contracted musician to be dismissed from a production, but there is a limited time period for dismissal if the musician does not work out. The real goal for the coordinator and the music team is to hire an ensemble of musicians who are congenial, professional, and talented. Playing a Broadway show is a collaborative undertaking that, for a large musical, involves seventy or eighty people who work together to execute a live performance every night. There is really no room for personality issues. A difficult personality playing a recording session that will last only a few hours is one thing, but a Broadway show can last years. There is an art to delivering such an ensemble.

Another responsibility for the coordinator is to suggest musicians who are appropriate for the style of the production. *Tommy*, *Les Misérables*, and *The Band's Visit* have very different musical styles. Aside from being excellent musicians, it helps if the musicians have a keen understanding of the show's music style, because their personal experience contributes to interpreting the music.

For every Broadway musical, the musician's union requires that one of the production musicians serves as an "in-house contractor." The position is separate from the music coordinator, is arranged with the music coordinator and the general manager/producer, and comes with a 50 percent premium over their salary. The in-house contractor handles day-to-day issues such a payroll, acts like a shop steward, and answers to the music coordinator.

So far the discussion has focused on musicals, but often music can be composed and recorded for a play. Some plays have a musician onstage. In those instances, the music coordinator is hired for the recording session and for hiring a musician who can be featured in a play. The same union rules apply.

It has been discussed in other segments how today Broadway ensembles are disbursed throughout the theatre for several reasons. Sometimes it is the director's vision to use a musician onstage; sometimes the producers want a couple more rows of paying seats. Whatever the reason, one of the theatre areas that have not been renovated since the nineteenth and early twentieth centuries is the orchestra pit.

Once the makeup of the orchestra is set, the serious question is whether the ensemble fits in the pit. Several department representatives (music, coordinator, props, sound, and general

manager) meet in a rehearsal room to determine if all the instruments can actually fit in the pit. A mock-up of the pit's exact
measurements and the instruments are taped on the floor to
judge if all the instruments would fit. If they do not, can they be
split up into multiple rooms? Most importantly, is there going to
be another room available?

In addition to placement, musicians need chairs, music
stands, and somewhere to store their instruments for safekeep-
ing at the end of a performance. The music coordinator works
with the props department, which is responsible for setting up
the chairs and music stands, and finding the backstage storage
space for the instruments. The coordinator understands the
number of storage lockers needed, such as five large and ten
small lockers.

The sound department is involved because that department
needs to know the number of musicians and the instrumental
makeup. The musicians are equipped with microphones, monitors, and headphones. The sound designer is responsible for
reinforcing the sound of the instruments and coordinating the
many locations. The musicians can be ensconced in an unused
third-floor dressing room.

The director enters this process usually if the artistic concept
is for the band or a band member to be onstage. Another recent
innovation is the actors actually playing the instruments onstage as part of the production concept, which does not involve
the music coordinator. It is at the discretion of the director, with
perhaps the choreographer and the conductor.

A new line item for the producers is COVID-19, which is
now a percentage of the budget just as wardrobe, sound, and
music. Each Broadway show has their own COVID-19 manager who sets the COVID-19 policy for their specific show. This
policy governs the cast, musicians, and audience. The policy
fluctuates as COVID-19 increases or subsides.

Once the production is up and running, the producers think
of ways to grow their audience. Planning a show recording,
participating in the Macy's parade, doing an HBO documentary,
doing a radio or television spot for advertising, flying to Miami
for a publicity event—they want to know what each of those

possibilities would cost. They rely on the coordinator's expertise to create budgets for each option.

The music coordinator's job does not end when a show opens. They are hired to manage any and all musician issues that crop up during the run. That pertains as well to possible subsequent tours. A music coordinator can be involved with a production for as many years as the show runs since there is always some issue to be solved or a question to be answered.

When a Broadway show goes on tour, they play in large theatres in various cities. The coordinator is in charge of making sure there are musicians in each place. A Broadway tour usually travels with a core group of four musicians, and the full ensemble is completed in each city with local musicians. Each city has its own local contractor, operating within the jurisdiction of the local union with which the coordinator communicates. Over time, the coordinator has acquired an extensive list of local contractors and musicians throughout the United States. Usually, things go smoothly until they do not, and then the calm gene is an asset for a coordinator. This is a tale related by music coordinator John Miller:

> I had a call from the conductor from City US at about 10:30 in the morning. The rehearsal was supposed to start at 10 and the conductor says, "Well we're here in the rehearsal room and there are no local musicians, there are no music stands set up, no chairs, there's nothing. What shall we do?" And he was everything you want with a traveling conductor, very calm, not susceptible to the anxiety of the urgency. A very good quality you're either born with or you're not born with.
>
> So I said to him, "Well, are you prepared to commit to what I'm going to commit to, which is somehow or other by 8 o'clock at night we will have a band and the curtain will go up. I don't know how we're going to do it, but we are going to do it. Are you committed to the same?" He said, "Absolutely." So I did two things. First of all I called the producers to let them know what the situation was. They spoke to the main presenter who had either misread the contract or was going to pull a fast one. They [the presenters] thought the show was coming self-contained, where you bring all your traveling

musicians. So they took the position they thought the show was self-contained. Whether it's true or not we'll never know, nor did I particularly care. My mission was simple—have the show open at 8 o'clock that night.

So the conductor and I start making calls to local musicians we knew within a 100 mile radius. This is how we were able to put the full ensemble together: I spoke with him around 11 o'clock, "I've got a tympany player coming from bababa, and a cellist coming from bababa." He says, "I've got a trumpet player coming from here." We spoke again at 12 o'clock and I said, "OK I found a bass player," and he says that's good. Now it's 3 o'clock, everyone is assembled, they started rehearsing and this was the sweetest thing I've ever heard from a conductor on the road. He said, "Well, we have everyone here except the viola player and she can come right after soccer practice."

So that's basically what they hire a music coordinator for: to make sure that whatever happens, that curtain is going to go up and there's going to be a band there.

10

Sound

Sound Designer

Sound design has become an indispensable element in a Broadway production over the past fifty years, due to many factors. Although sound design for dramatic plays existed for millennia in the form of sound effects (thunder sheets, rain sticks, found objects, etc.), sound design for musical theatre only started to come into focus in the 1970s. The influence of film, television, rock concerts, and the evolution of music styles has carried over to theatre and affected audience expectations.

The decibel level of most popular music has increased a lot, resulting in a more in-your-face experience for the audience. In early sound systems it was either high fidelity or loudness. Today with technological advancements, it is both. Also, with the proliferation of jukebox musicals, the volume of the show is part of the audience memory of the songs or bands that are the focus of the story. People have a great capacity to adjust and accept.

There was a time when audience members knew how to listen. There was an oral tradition of storytelling and good conversation, and the skill of listening takes concentration. Until the early twentieth century, the world itself was quieter and less distracting. Today people multitask ad infinitum and attention spans are shorter. They hear but they do not really listen.

Generally speaking, new generations of theatre performers are not trained the way they used to be where the actor could project their voice to the last row in the theatre and not be hammy about it. This is partially due to the influence of film and television. There certainly are actors who can project quite well, but performing for theatre requires more vocal development and training than film or television, and switching between media requires adjustments for the actors. Simultaneously, many acting programs focus less onstage acting and more on performing for the camera.

With these combined stylistic and environmental changes, the increase of sound reinforcement in theatrical productions has become the norm, and that's where the sound designer comes in.

Often a sound designer played an instrument or has a musical background, was trained in critical listening, or had experience in sound recording. It helps if their musical background is wide-ranging. The knowledge of acoustical engineering is a critical asset for a sound designer. Sound is affected by the size of the theatre, the distance sound travels, an audience in a room, and the loudness in an enclosed space.

Sound for a play involves more interlude, transitional music, or soundscapes to bring people to different environments. It adds to the mood, tension, or supports other elements in the play. Some playwrights are very specific about music and others are not. A play can have a composer for such incidental music, or a sound person can find prerecorded music for specific scenes. The sound designer can create soundscapes, which are compilations of sounds that support a scene and are inserted at certain points in a play to take the action from one point to another throughout the play. It could be people chanting, a train whistle, a train moving along the tracks, or a car horn blaring.

The sound designer can be approached for a new project a couple of years before it goes into production or as quickly as just a few months. Sometimes the initial offer is contracted quickly, but there are other instances where the sound designer starts work in earnest before a contract is even signed. So much of Broadway depends on the availability of a theatre, so often a project waits and waits for the right theatre, even though the production has been in development for several years. Like everybody on the creative team, the sound designer usually works as a freelancer and can be committed to multiple projects at different stages of development. If schedules change, the designer might have to abandon a project or perform a very delicate balancing act.

In the past, the sound designer was hired significantly later than the other designers, resulting in situations where the set and lights were well into the design phase before the sound designer became involved and had to negotiate loudspeaker placement. It is far easier to collaborate and make logistical and spatial decisions when all design departments are included in early meetings. As sound designers create relationships with directors and composers and as sound becomes increasingly recognized as not only a practical but artistic discipline, sound designers are being brought onto projects earlier and earlier. Some directors prefer to have early interactions with the sound designer, especially on shows requiring many sound effects or soundscapes. Other directors might not give sound much focus until everyone is in the theatre.

The sound designer can be recommended to a project by the director, composer, musical director, orchestrator, or producer, based on prior experiences or simply by hearing one of the designer's existing shows. The sound designer is then responsible for choosing some of the sound team, which usually consists of an associate or assistant designer, the sound mixer or Audio 1 (A1), one or two backstage sound crew or Audio 2 (A2), and often a production sound engineer. The associate sound designer or assistant are considered part of the creative team, and they assist the designer often attending meetings with or without the designer, creating paperwork, preparing sound effects, and interfacing with the rest of the team.

The associate is most often a member of United Scenic Artists Local 829 IATSE. The mixer (A1), A2, and production sound engineer (also referred to as production sound person) are members of Local One under IATSE (which represents stagehands on Broadway) and hired by the production under a pink contract.

Or they can be a member of another local from around the country that is affiliated with IATSE.

The production sound engineer's tenure in the theatre is usually limited to the preview process, but they can be on a retainer throughout the show run to handle training schedules and/or sub for the A1 or A2. Generally, the associate's work is complete by opening night.

The jobs of sound mixer and A2 are discussed in detail under the mixer and Audio 2 sections. Both positions are essentially an extension of the sound design team. The mixer (A1) is responsible for adjusting microphone levels for the actors and orchestra, as well as maintaining the sound experience of the show consistent from performance to performance, given the parameters of what the sound designer and the creatives have determined during rehearsals and previews. The mixer's talents are critical to the sound design, and many sound designers have a few people they rely on in that position. As in many disciplines, when people work together, they develop a shorthand and method of working that makes every new instance a little bit easier.

The backstage sound person (A2) is responsible for maintaining the cast microphones, troubleshooting problems as they happen during a show including intercom and video issues, interfacing with the orchestra about sound-related issues, and often will train on the mix of the show to be available to cover when the A1 takes time off.

The production sound engineer is responsible for coordinating the equipment installation and leading the sound labor crew throughout the tech and preview processes. The production sound engineer interacts most with the production electrician and production carpenter; for example, all three might be responsible for hanging the equipment on a lighting truss, which is a hanging structure from which lighting and sound equipment can be hung. The production sound engineer will interface with the production electrician to ensure that there are no conflicts between lighting and sound equipment (often also done by the associates for each department), and the production carpenter is needed to ensure that weight limits and rigging points are sufficient for the truss. The production sound engineer works with the sound team to execute their vision but has less creative input. Early in the process, the assistant/associate and the production sound engineer work closely together preparing sound equipment paperwork needed by the rental companies down to the last cable.

Once hired, the sound designer reads the script, listens to music demos, and meets with the director to discuss general concepts, ideas, dynamics, and desired style of the show. Some directors are quite specific about sound effects and soundscapes, especially for transitional moments, so the sound designer can work ahead by preparing some of those elements in advance of getting into the theatre.

There are meetings with the composer or music director/supervisor to discuss the overall musical style, the instrumentation of the show, and any complications they may foresee. These conversations continue as the preparation progresses. There are also ongoing communications and discussions between the design teams and the production teams to facilitate the installation of the show once they are in the theatre.

As soon as a theatre is selected for a show, the sound team conducts a site survey to assess the building itself. If an existing show is already running, that can be a great opportunity to listen to how the theatre reacts acoustically to reinforced sound, even if the existing show style and sound system differs greatly from what the sound designer's present objectives are. There are more detailed discussions as to speaker placement and focus.

As has been mentioned previously, a Broadway theatre is totally empty when a new production moves in. It is the responsibility of every design department and their crews to ensure that all hardware, cabling, motors, and mounting hardware are brought to the theatre at load-in. The same is true for all of the sound equipment, which must be rented (occasionally a production can choose to purchase the sound equipment outright).

As with sets and lighting, there is a bid process for sound. The designer and the team create the equipment list for the bidding process, which includes all the equipment suitable for the show. Some designers rely on manufacturer-specific software to aid in selecting the best loudspeaker type for a particular

212 / Chapter 10

purpose. Other designers, based on prior experience and comfort level, have their favorite types of equipment, and that knowledge influences their choice of the loudspeakers required to provide the best quality and coverage throughout the theatre for a particular show.

There are three major sound shops in New York City, and the equipment list can be bid to one or more of them. There can be a gentlemen's agreement between general managers and rental companies, and sometimes the designer has a little bit of input as to which sound shop is preferred for a particular project. The sound shops submit their numbers as a weekly rental and a "prep fee," and the management team reviews and compares the numbers.

It is the sound designer's responsibility to select the best equipment for the show, so many designers stay current on new technology; however, new technology usually means more expense. Consequently, the sound designer works closely with the rental houses when concessions and equipment substitutions ensue (it is more cost-effective to use a piece of equipment the sound company already owns, rather than have them purchase something new) until the budget lines up. An experienced sound designer knows when a particular piece of equipment is worth fighting for and when it is not.

A sound system is more than loudspeakers: it is also the microphones for the cast and orchestra, and different orchestrations can require different types of microphones. There is the mixing console that interfaces with the entire sound system, equipment to play back sound effects, and various audio processing tools to sculpt the sound coming out of the speakers to best reproduce the original sound sources. A microphone that is well-suited to a trombone, for example, may not be appropriate for a violin. The same is true for performers' microphones. There are a handful of different types of small microphones generally used for musical theatre sound reinforcement. They all have different characteristics, not only in size, but how they are placed on the actor, their sound quality, their durability, and their resistance to water and sweat. A sound designer might have to experiment with different types of microphones if there are particularly challenging circumstances on a certain actor.

Once the bid is mostly confirmed, the sound designer and team create paperwork to illustrate the best physical locations for the speakers to discuss with other design departments and to negotiate the physical space required for sound, lighting, scenery, and projections. There can be an immense amount of paperwork generated, and most of these duties fall to the associate, but some of it can also be generated by the designer or production engineer.

After the rental bid is awarded, the sound team with additional crew spends two to four weeks at the rental company assembling the equipment necessary for the show. Every piece of equipment, cable, and hardware to be used in the theatre is pulled, labeled, tested, connected, and packed for delivery. There is usually just enough time to install the equipment in the theatre before rehearsals onstage begin, so it is important to test all the elements before they even get to the theatre. This paradigm is slightly different in other countries where theatre rentals—the actual cost of the theatre building and crew—are far less expensive.

Trucks of scenery, lighting, sound, and video equipment arrive at the theatre in a precisely choreographed dance over a number of days during load-in. The production heads coordinate each day of load-in with production management—there's nothing worse than multiple departments trying to work in the same area of the stage! The associate sound designer may also be onsite to answer more design-related questions (in what direction does a particular speaker point, at what angle?) and to work with other design departments if, for example, a lighting instrument needs to shift a little bit to accommodate a speaker or vice versa.

Closer to and before the cast starts rehearsals in the theatre, the sound designer allots time in the theatre to listen to the sound system often using some sort of computer-based measurement tool to make the speakers respond in a predictable way. Different designers have different methods of doing this. Ironically, this listening time for the sound department is called "quiet time" or "system tuning." Adjustments can still be made to the physical position of loudspeakers if it is necessary, but mainly the goal is to ensure that the sound system is evenly balanced and sounding good throughout the theatre before the cast arrives.

In addition, the designer often creates some sort of sound plot or rough rehearsal sound effects and/or soundscape to be played back during rehearsal so that sound moments can be refined early in the process.

Although most Broadway theatres have an orchestra pit, sometimes producers and directors choose not to use the pit and replace it with seating, adding a couple of audience rows closest to the stage. It has become quite common to attend a Broadway musical and never actually see the musicians, as they may be scattered throughout dressing rooms, the basement, the trap room, or some combination of those locations. Sometimes they are part of the visual picture onstage as well.

Many sound designers want to be involved with the music department and the orchestra placement/layout, because the sound designer needs to consider how best to reinforce the musical sound regardless of where the musicians end up. For the music department, it is optimal for musicianship to place the musicians together, so that eye contact and ensemble listening can occur, but other creative decisions can impact this decision. Then the sound designer is tasked with ensuring that musicians in disparate locations can see and hear each other in appropriate ways. It is a knotty logistical puzzle. The musicians and cast must see the conductor in some way (often off a television monitor), and the conductor must see everyone. Not having acoustical sound coming from musicians in an orchestra pit requires the sound designer to address reinforcing the orchestra in an entirely different fashion.

As some shows become more pop/rock-based, more techniques learned in the recording studio are being applied to live reinforcement, such as computer plug-ins. A more "processed" sound can be the goal for a particular show rather than a more "natural" feel. Contemporary composers often do most of their composing using headphones sitting in front of a laptop and thus rely on electronic music instrumentation rather than acoustic instruments. Many pop/rock shows require more technology from the sound department to allow for click track playback.

At the basic level, a click track is a metronomic click that is generated either by a simple metronome or via the sound or music department's playback computers. It is only heard by the conductor and some or all of the musicians in the orchestra, and it can be used simply to ensure that the tempi of certain songs remain consistent night after night. Or a click track can be accompanied by prerecorded or sequenced electronic music tracks that are part of the orchestration. Those music tracks can include extra layering of instruments or more elements typical of pop/electronic music, and those tracks are blended with the live musicians for the audience to hear. Essentially, the click track remains to guide the conductor and musicians to stay in time.

There are now personnel devoted to "electronic music design" who are responsible for programming keyboards with the appropriate sounds and who also take care of other electronics-intensive work. These electronic music designers work hand in hand with the sound department to create the appropriate experience.

As the show approaches technical rehearsals, the sound mixer programs the sound console, which is discussed under the mixer (A1) section. The designer decides which type of console is best for the show in question, but the mixer is the one who ultimately programs and mixes the show according to the guidelines set by the designer.

When the cast arrives at the theatre, they have rehearsed a month or so in a rehearsal studio, developing the bones of the musical. Once in the theatre, all the technical and artistic elements come together. The sound department works with the costume and hair departments to get the best physical location for a microphone so it is comfortable for the actor given their costume and hair designs. Some sound designers work diligently with costumes and hair to hide the microphones as much as possible. Other designers prefer a microphone position that optimizes a more direct sound from the actor, which usually means the microphone position is more visible.

As rehearsals in the theatre take place, it is time for the mixer to fully learn the structure of the show and the designer, in conjunction with the director and music department, to construct the aural parameters of the show. How loud is it? What is the balance of the solo vocals to the ensemble vocals to the rehearsal piano? How do sound effects weave in and out of scenes? Do sound effects need to sound as if they are coming from specific places on the stage? Most importantly, is the sound essentially the same all over the theatre?

It is very expensive to have an orchestra in the theatre for rehearsals, so generally the musicians are brought into the process late in the technical rehearsals. There can be a few sessions of just the musicians and sound department (no cast) to get baseline balances of all the musicians by themselves, and then a couple of rehearsal sessions with both the cast and the musicians but no audience.

Once a musical is in previews the sound designer can do their most valuable work in refining the sound of the show. Not only is the cast and orchestra performing together more regularly, but the presence of the audience in the theatre affects the sound in the theatre, so the sound designer can make adjustments based on real conditions. Is the orchestra too loud in the balcony? Are the vocals clear enough? Previews are the time to adjust these factors, making minor changes and fine-tuning the production.

At some point during the previews, the show is frozen and no more significant changes are made to the show's script, staging, or music. Hopefully, this occurs late in previews and allows the cast time to just run the show unchanged over a number of days. This date usually occurs a couple of days before the first critics come to the show. (Critics tend to see the show a few days before official press opening, which gives them time to write their review and go to press so a review can come out immediately following the official press opening.) Hopefully by that point, the show is a well-oiled machine, and if the show is well-received, it can hopefully last for a very long time.

The sound designer's job essentially ends on opening night, but they will occasionally check in on a running show especially to audit new mixers or listen to a new cast.

Sound Mixer (Audio 1)

With all the technical devices available for people today, how we listen has changed dramatically from the past. As the sound mixer Elizabeth Coleman recalled:

> My dad's generation would have friends come over, they would all sit together, listen to a record together, and consume what they heard in a very thoughtful way. They would discuss the recording techniques and it was very much a mindful activity. It was not passive. Today music is consumed on various devices in the background while they eat, study, and drive. It becomes a rather passive pursuit without active engagement. The appreciation is not there.

How people interact with sound is different. When musicals used only foot mics and people were trained to sing and project their voices, there was a more lean-in connection the audience had with the performance. Although today's audience is not aware of the change; technology in some ways interjects a bit of distance between the audience and the performers. If a show has a gentler sensibility like *The Band's Visit*, there is a lean-in quality. The pop and rock shows require the technology because they represent recordings we all have heard and expect in that type of show.

During the run of a Broadway show, the sound department consists of the mixer/head (A1) and one or two assistant sound persons (A2). The mixer and assistant frequently alternate their positions during the run. They learn each other's job so there is always a backup person available if someone is ill. It also gives the mixer temporary relief from a very stressful task.

The mixer is the person who usually sits at a large computer console and manages the entire sound system for every performance of the run of the show. The placement of the sound console depends on the structure of the theatre. It is most often at the back of the orchestra section, in the mezzanine, or even in the center of the orchestra section. The mixer is controlling three computers: a main and backup sound effects machine, and the sound console computer, which is interfacing with a couple of devices backstage.

Unlike a mixer in a recording studio, the Broadway mixer is actively monitoring every microphone and speaker in the show throughout the performance. The mixer listens to and balances all the sounds in a show—the actors' voices, the orchestra instruments, the environmental noises, and sound effects—to support the storytelling and create an emotionally satisfying evening for the audience.

All of the sound people I spoke with for this book had a musical background either playing one or more instruments or singing. A musical background trains the ear and develops the art of listening. Mixing requires attention to detail, concentration, understanding engineering concepts, and proficiency in technology.

The mixer is the one who programs the sound console, which is a complicated task. Because technology keeps changing so rapidly, the mixer must stay current with the changes and the new equipment. Depending on the timeline of the show, the programming can begin in the rental shop or sometimes in the theatre during load-in.

Once the sound bid process is complete, the mixer, assistant, and production sound person (if there is one) go to the rental shop and build the system entirely. This takes about two or three weeks full time. They build the sound system from the ground up. The designer may stop by to check on the progress and answer any questions that arise. There are racks of equipment in the shop from which they construct everything including the cables needed for the system to function. Once the system is together, they test every speaker, microphone, and whatever else is included while they are in the shop, because there is no time when they load into the theatre. This is a daunting task.

During load-in, the mixer helps the stage crew with some of the sound equipment and must organize their own limited workspace. The mixer arranges where to put the equipment, where to put the monitor, where to put the script until it is not needed, and how to make the space maneuverable.

Not to get into the total weeds of this procedure, the basic structure of the console is how the system is going to send audio out to the entire sound system throughout the theatre. Sound is sent to the stage so the performers can hear the music. The music director and orchestra needs to hear the performers and each other, especially if the orchestra is in separate areas of the theatre. The audience needs to hear the performers. The sound department needs to hear all of it to monitor it.

A play is simpler and is not usually as elaborate as a musical, but if body mics or foot mics are being used, programming the sound system is the same. Programming is specifically for running the show, scene to scene, character to character.

The mixer programs the console according to scenes, so the people in that scene and their microphones are put together as a unit. When that scene is playing, it can be brought to the middle section of the console for easy access for the mixer to adjust the sound during the performance. They can mute and unmute individual actors' microphones and maintain the sound balance. When programming the console, the mixer is hyperaware of inputting the scene data into the console to afford ease and efficiency for hand movements moving the faders (levers that move up and down, similar to the lighting faders) when running the show. This programming makes re-creating the sound of the show every night as consistent as possible throughout the entire run of the show.

When mixing Broadway-style musicals, the goal is to have the minimum number of microphones open at one time. The sound structure is worked out between the designer and the mixer. Today microphones are everywhere in a Broadway musical. What the mixer does at the console is if two actors are having a conversation, as one says his line, his mic goes up and then the mixer takes it out; when the next person speaks, their mic goes up and then it is taken out. Throughout the show, the mixer basically adjusts the sound of the actors, the singers, and the orchestra to make sure all are audible to the audience and the sound is balanced. Sometimes within songs the mixer switches between people who have solo lines and the ensemble and back again. Each of those changes are cued, which the mixer programs.

Sound is rarely used in workshops. If it is used, the sound designer will reach out to any mixer who is available. The sound designer approaches the mixer and sound assistant they would like for the production when there is a fully mounted tryout or when the production enters the Broadway production phase. That is when they formally join the production.

Every designer has their core people, but mixers and assistants may work with several sound designers depending on the availability of work. Mixers often work with the same sound designers, because over time the communication channel has been established. The mixer knows what the designer wants, and the designer can trust the mixer to enact their wishes.

The sound designer recommends their team for the show's run, who are paid by the producer. There is one rate for the mixer (A1) and one for the assistant (A2), which is usually a fair rate. If the show is particularly difficult, those rates can be negotiated by the mixer and the assistant.

The mixer and assistant belong to a union local. There are many locals in various towns throughout the United States, each has a number specifying its location, and all are under the umbrella of IATSE (i.e., Local 82 refers to Wilkes-Barre, Pennsylvania; Local 2 is Chicago). To work on Broadway, the sound people must belong to one of the unions under the IATSE umbrella.

Initially, the mixer confers with the sound designer about what the sound concept for the show is, based on what the creatives want. They also confer about the console, since the mixer is the one who physically operates the console during the performance. Aside from the mixer's ease in operating the console, it is essential the equipment produces the sound the designer wants for the show. There is another console for special effects, which the mixer also operates, and it has a channel capable of sending those effects to all the speakers in the house.

Once hired, the mixer contacts the stage manager for a copy of the current script. If it is a new show, the script is still being tweaked. The mixer reads the script from beginning to end, then rereads it again and breaks it up into scenes. If it is a complex show, there may be a third reread and time to think about how they want to program the scenes into the console. Depending on their individual process, a mixer can create an Excel spread-sheet to identify who is or who is not in a scene, who is singing a solo, or if it is an ensemble number. This is preparatory work for programming the console and takes time. The mixer's goal is to break the script into manageable segments that are control-lable in the heat of a performance. This work is done in a sort of console vacuum.

Now the mixer must learn the show by attending rehearsals to hear who says and sings what. Since during performances, the mixer's job is to manage the microphones for everyone, the learning process requires spending additional time in the theatre after regular rehearsals to practice the cues, which can take two to three weeks. In the beginning of a run, the mixer uses the script at the console to execute the cues. Depending on how hard a show is, it might take six weeks before the mixer can put the script down and run the cues from memory.

Once in the theatre, the rehearsal changes are kept current by the stage manager, who maintains the script page changes and passes them on to the mixer. These changes happen constantly until hopefully the sound is set by the last couple of preview performances and certainly by opening night. The mixer repro-grams the console according to any changes and new cues that affect actors' lines or new songs or music.

During the tech there will be a designer run-through of the show, which for the sound department includes the designer, the associate, the mixer (A1), and the assistant (A2). During tech, the mixer creates sound cues, sometimes from the script or the stage direction, or there can be light cues that need to synchro-nize with the sound.

The *sitzprobe* with the musicians and cast is the first time ev-eryone hears each other. It also gives the mixer the opportunity to sit, hear, and see the shape of the show without having to deal with the console.

Pre-show, the mixer checks in with the stage manager to get a rundown of any actor changes for that performance. The mixer checks with the music director to find out if there are any changes in the orchestra makeup (i.e., a substitute musician) and which instrument is affected. When the show is ready to begin, the stage manager flashes the mixer's cue light, which causes them to pick up their headset, and the stage manager says, "OK we're ready to go. We've got places." The conductor comes out at the same time. The stage manager says, "All right, let's begin." From then on, the mixer has no interaction with the stage manager, unless there is some problem.

There are technologies that contribute to theatrical sound production. An Astro Spatial Audio unit is a spatial placement device that allows the ability to make sound as if it is coming from a specific place. Sound uses an equalizer that evens the loudness for certain frequencies for a particular room. If the placement and position of the microphone on the actor can cause a bit of muffling, the equalizer can clear up the voice. Lastly, there are fail-safe measures built into the entire system.

However, all this technology is operated through computer systems and even with fail-safe and redundant measures built into the entire system, computers can crash. One mixer had the entire system crash during a show and the backstage assistant did not know how the system worked. The mixer notified the stage manager that she had to go backstage, which stopped the show. She phoned a tech expert who walked her through the problem, and she got the system back up and running. Something like that is rare.

The mixer has ongoing conversations with the actors, stage managers, music director, and musicians during a long run. Issues crop up that need to be addressed, for example if an actor is not saying their lines correctly or has started to mumble. That affects the sound and the mixer's cues. If the mixer takes a cue off an actor's action, but the actor has stopped that action, that affects the mixer's work.

The mixer works with the music director if a person is starting to have pitch problems. The theatre is not like a recording studio where a mixer can manipulate a voice to improve the pitch and the voice quality. In the theatre, the mixer can support and complement the sound, but the performer must sing in tune. The mixer does make sure the voices sound as clear as possible and as natural as possible. Most importantly, the sound designer and the mixer stay in touch during a long run. The designer might spot check a performance to make sure their sound design is intact.

During the run of the production, sometimes tweaks to the sound system are necessary. For three or four hours over a day or two, after cast and crew leave the theatre, the sound department does a system balance assessment. There are several computer programs for this assessment. One is called SMAART (System Measurement Acoustic Analysis Real-Time Tool). Microphones are placed in different parts of the house and noise is run through every section and part of the system. Then music is played. Noise and music alternate to hear what it sounds like in each part of the system and whether the equalizer needs to be changed.

If so, then the delay system has to change. Sound travels, so with speakers at different distances, the speaker closest to you arrives faster than the speaker further away. The sound department runs the noise and music, and they figure out what the time delay is for each speaker. That information is then put into the system so that the sound arrives at the same time no matter where the audience is sitting. The decibel level is monitored as well.

There are many variables with a sound system, some of which can be countered and others that cannot. The number of people in a house changes the sound and if the house is somewhat empty, it will sound empty. A mixer cannot change that. Temperature or humidity changes, cast changes, or substitute musicians—all those variables affect the equipment and sound of a show, and the mixer's job.

The mixer's primary goal is to try and maintain the designer's sound. The job is one of constant adjustment and is a concentrated two-and-a-half hours eight times a week. The intensity of the job is shared with the backstage A2 person who learns how to mix and run the show. When A2 is up to speed, A2 and A1 swap jobs maybe two or four shows a week. This allows the show to have a cover for the mixer, in case of illness or life, and gives the mixer(s) a break.

The speakers used in a Broadway show are determined by the musical genre of the show. The designer chooses speakers that create the best sound for a pop show like *Ain't Too Proud* or a traditional show like *Carousel*. Speakers are not the only essential equipment for a show's sound; microphones are essential as well.

Every microphone has its own personality, so again the designer chooses microphones that are appropriate for the particular show, the voice, and the instrument. Not only are microphones worn by the actors, but they are in the pit with the orchestra or wherever the instruments are located. Instrumentation differs greatly between pop and traditional musicals. Some microphones work best with brass and others with strings.

Lavalier microphones are the type used on Broadway, and they are the same as what we see on a newscaster or their guests. They are small and black and usually attached to the collar or neck area. They are considered perishables because they often break with the wear and tear of a performance. On Broadway, the sound department works with the hair, wig, and wardrobe departments to figure out the best placement for the microphone on an actor, and when necessary helps with costume changes that affect the microphones.

Mixing a Broadway play is a different job than mixing a musical. It is mostly playback of preset music and moving foot mics. Actors are infrequently outfitted with mics, so there is not that much equipment. The primary job for the mixer is making sure the words can be heard. The sound designer has the say and the stage manager calls the cues. For a mixer's work, a play needs less input from the mixer and is perhaps less creative than a musical.

The mixer on a Broadway musical has a more immediate influence in how the music is heard and the sound is shaped. The mixer is the one controlling the balance of the performers' microphones and the orchestra's instruments. When a performer is singing with emotional experience appropriate to the role, there are many other people who have some sway over that performance—the music director, the sound team, the director, and the composer. It can be more interesting for a mixer because they have more input and artistry in shaping a song and contributing to the experience for the audience.

During the run the mixer has a certain amount of work to execute even when not in the theatre. Microphones are considered perishables and frequently break. It is the mixer's responsibility to answer emails, order equipment and supplies (such as microphones, rechargeable batteries, and tape for sticking microphones on actors), payroll, and helping with an outside event for the show.

In the years without microphones, performers learned how to speak and sing and project their voices onstage. There are still some performers who are well-trained in vocal technique, but there is increasingly a generation who is not. They think technology replaces that technique. It does not. Microphones are a support aid, not an alternative to those techniques. It is one reason so many poorly trained performers end up with nodes on their vocal cords. Just like vocal projection where a person supports air to go over the vocal cords to make them vibrate, so a microphone has an element inside that needs air pressure to make it vibrate and work. If the actor is not singing or speaking, the microphone will not work. The mixer cannot improve that.

An interesting side point is that the mixer is literally listening to the show every night and some pop shows today can be very loud. The loudness can be the result of the music style or a producer or director who wants it loud. Some audience members are used to being blasted with sound from rock concerts and movie surround sound. Constant loud volume affects one's auditory nerves. Since mixers do not use headphones because they need to listen to the show, some mixers have special earplugs to protect their ears. One has a pair that are molded to her ears with a special filter that can be changed and can go from low to high.

The mixer Charlie Grieco pondered, "You have to try and please at least ten different people in ten different ways—the audience, the music director, the lyricist, the composer, the director, the producers, the cast, the musicians—and ultimately the story." Although the sound is set by opening night, it is never quite set for the mixer. For some mixers that challenge is what makes the job exciting. It is never boring.

Assistant Sound Person (Audio 2)

Similar to the music department, there is a certain fluidity in the sound department between the jobs of the mixer (A1) and the assistant (A2). Depending on how skilled the person is, a sound person in a production can wear several hats. At various phases of the production, an A2 can be the production sound person, the mixer (A1), or an assistant (A2). This section is focused on the A2, but in truth the job is intertwined with the mixer's. No matter what position, the A2 must stay knowledgeable with sound technological changes.

The assistant sound person or A2 is the person who works backstage and coordinates with the mixer during a performance. There is usually one assistant on a show but if it is a complex musical there may be two. Like the mixer, the assistant belongs to a union local under IATSE, has a musical background, and loves music. The A2 is recommended by the sound designer and paid by the production. As mentioned in the mixer chapter, there is a general rate for assistants, which can be negotiated if the show is particularly difficult. The A2 joins the production at the same time as the mixer, which can be at a tryout or Broadway phase.

Often mixers and assistants have worked together on previous shows, and they switch jobs during an eight-performance week. The mixer can work backstage two shows a week while the assistant mixes the show. Sometimes it can be evenly split, switching four shows each. Especially on current musicals, both jobs are extremely exacting and tense, so changing positions helps break the monotony, keeps the mind fresh, and guarantees there are backups for both jobs.

The A2 joins the mixer and production sound person (if there is one) in the rental shop building the sound system. This process takes about two or three weeks. The A2 also participates in the load-in and installation of the sound equipment.

In the rental shop, it is easier to test the system in its entirety, working out all the bugs and kinks possible for several reasons. The team can focus on the equipment and accessibility to the equipment is simplified. Tens of thousands of feet of wire and cable are run in the theatre during installation. Any problems are easier to fix in the shop when you have both ends of the wires in front of you, rather than in the theatre when one end is five hundred feet away from the other end. And by the time the equipment is loaded-in to the theatre, the theatre is teeming with all the departments and labor unions become an expense.

The job of the A2 is to monitor all the microphones and video monitors backstage during a performance. That includes all the actors and the musicians who have microphones and/or monitors. The A2 works backstage or more correctly at the home base usually under the stage in the trap room. Racks are set up with equipment for them to listen to the show through wired speakers the entire night. Essentially, the A2's job is monitoring all the show microphones during the performance and heading off any problems before they happen.

Before and sometimes during the show, the A2 helps to attach the microphones on the actors correctly every performance and makes sure they are hidden. Because of wigs or costumes, some actors require more help than others.

The A2 learns the show, where the cast enters or exits the stage, whether stage right or stage left, and listens to their microphones two or three minutes before their stage entrance. If a microphone has gone bad, usually the actor is not aware of it. The A2 goes upstairs, tries to find the person, and deals with the issue in any way possible. Sometimes it is a wire in the microphone that breaks, which becomes a logistical coordination with the hair and costume departments. If there is time, the actor has to strip down to where the microphone and transmitter can be swapped out if necessary, which involves hair or wig and clothes. This may read as a simple description; however, if this occurs in the middle of a performance, there is a limited time to correct the issue. Backstage is swarming with cast and crew, and the hair, wardrobe, and sound departments work together to resolve the issue as quickly as possible under duress.

The A2 is not in the basement all the time and works with various crew members throughout the show. If speakers onstage have to be turned on and off, the A2 is required backstage to do that. Other times it might be a monitor that needs to be turned on or off. In *Beetlejuice*, a speaker was offstage in the wings where scenery was constantly coming and going at that spot, so the A2 had to rotate the speaker out of the way to allow the scenery to be moved on and offstage.

If it is a strenuously active show like *Beetlejuice*, the assistant stayed close to the stage to blow air into a group of actors' microphones as a preemptive strike. The microphones were not broken, but with the vigorous staging there was a lot of moisture from perspiration. If water gets in the microphone, it sounds muddy or dull. The mixer can try to brighten it through the equalizer, but keeping it as dry as possible is better to avoid the problem.

The A2 communicates with the mixer via text message or walkie talkie throughout the show, especially if there is a problem the A2 cannot resolve. One mixer said the assistant's job was like a firefighter hoping nothing goes wrong and when it does, the fire has to be put out as quickly as possible. The mixer then tries to find an expedient solution. If the microphone breaks and is crackling, staticky, and not usable, the mixer attempts to work off another actor's mic who is nearby as a temporary fix.

Although I am writing about the A2 person, the assistant and the mixer (A1) actually work as a unit. Once the show is up, the A2 starts to learn the finger choreography on the console and the mix of the show, which takes about two to three weeks plus a lot of homework during the day. When an A2 joins a running show and is learning to mix a show from someone else, it is a full-time job and more. The new A2 gets to the theatre early to learn the cues, practice the mix, and listens to the score all the time. Then it may take a month or two to learn the intricacies of the console and coordinate it with the action onstage. The A2 uses the script at the console when beginning to mix the show, but eventually is able to put the script away, just watch the stage, listen intently to the performance, and mix the show. That can take another month.

When two people mix a show, the ultimate goal is they mix the show identically or at least very close, but they are two people who hear different things. During production, levels are set, the system is tuned, and it is refined for days with only a couple dozen people in the house. Once the show is up and running, fifteen hundred bodies are introduced into that theatre, and that can have a dramatic impact on the sound.

As mentioned, there are shows where the orchestra is placed at different locations backstage or in the house, so video monitors and microphones are used so the musicians can communicate with each other. When troubles arise, this separation complicates resolving the issues. In one show the cello had a mic, but the cable partially dislodged from the speaker, which caused buzzing. The A2 had to reconnect it.

With *Moulin Rouge*, the conductor is in the pit pretty much by themself playing keyboard, and everybody else is scattered throughout the theatre. The wind instruments and brass are in a room above the lobby. The drummer has their own little room in the trap. The guitars, bass, keyboards, and string instruments are all within the same big room. It is all connected by remote video and remote sound so they can all hear each other and talk to each other with the conductor as well.

The irony is that musicians are trained to play together; placing them in different areas of the theatre can produce various results. Some musicians may not mind it depending on their instruments. If one is playing a synthesizer, the sound is pretty much controlled by the mixer. If one is playing an acoustic piano or part of a rhythm section, that distancing can have an effect.

The pertinent question is how are band members really able to hear and play together as if they were all together in the pit? The answer is they wear headphones with personal mixers, use video monitors, and communicate by text. Cameras are placed all over, so band members who need to can see each other, can hear each other, and often can talk back to one another. If a little more is wanted from the bass player, the musician can adjust the mix on their personal mixer.

Foremost, the dialogue and lyrics need to be heard. If there is a full orchestra in the pit, that kind of placement makes balancing the orchestra and the vocals easier because the conductor has more control. If everyone is in different locations including the conductor, it is more difficult. To hear the dialogue, the orchestra needs to be toned down so the performer's voices are not overpowered by it. Even though an orchestra can be in the open orchestra pit, that acoustic information needs to be balanced with what is coming from the sound system.

Today, all the sound in a Broadway show is fed through a sound system, somewhat resembling the surround sound in a movie theatre. It does not quite have the same acoustic sound coming from the orchestra pit as in years past, but this is due to several contributing influences.

The styles of musicals have changed. There are more sung-through musicals where a lot of dialogue is sung like an opera or where music plays under the dialogue. There is the rise of the pop and jukebox musicals, which have more brass and percussion, and the energy of the music keeps building. The audience wants to hear what they heard on the recording and expect the same energy they get at a rock concert. More of the audience is used to their living room television sound and their remote control, but this is live theatre with a storyline (hopefully). A director, writer, or producer can have input and urge for louder sound. All of this affects sound on a Broadway stage.

Generally speaking for an A2 on a play, there are area microphones or foot mics around the stage that have to be turned on and off to give a little support to the cast. There can be a sound console, but it is smaller than for a big musical. There is certainly less equipment. If there are any wired microphones, it is a mere handful, whereas a musical can have thirty to forty. On a play there is usually only an A2; sometimes there can be an A1 and A2. An exception is *Harry Potter*, which had a full sound crew.

Production Sound Person

A production sound person works with the designer, the associate designer, the mixer, and however many assistants there are. Once the sound equipment has been sent out to bid and approved, they join the production to help supervise the building of the sound system, the installation of it, all the way up typically to opening night, when their contract ends and the job ends. Not all shows have a production sound person.

The production sound person works with the production manager to come up with a labor budget to build the system, a time schedule as to how long it will take, when to build the system, and coordinate when exactly the system needs to be loaded into the theatre. Part of the job is to facilitate and coordinate with the departments (i.e., electrics, props, carpentry) if any sound department needs cross into their domains.

After the system is built and the show opens, a production sound person can return to the show and sub as an A2 or an A1. They can learn the backstage track or sometimes that person can take over in front of the house to mix as well.

Although the unions are very departmental, occasionally it all goes out the window. Charlie Grieco relates an example:

> I was an hour out of the city and there was a snowstorm, so I left at 3 o'clock for an 8 o'clock curtain. By 9:15, I just made it to the Lincoln Tunnel and I never made it into work. At least three or four other crew members didn't either. There was an audience and there was a show that was going to happen. Essentially anyone who did make it to the theatre pitched in wherever they could to make the show happen.

Theatre, in general, is a very collaborative community until it is not. One sound mixer was working a Broadway tour out of town and her routine was to check all the equipment before the show. At the incident time some years ago, five flat foot mics were used for backup in case of an emergency. When the mixer, who was African American, checked the mics, someone had cut all the cables attached to the microphones, which meant she had to reattach all the cables with little time to spare before the show began. A local stagehand on the show told the mixer who had done it and unfortunately it was a white stagehand. This is the exception in theatre, but sadly it does happen, and there was a double target: an African American woman.

11

Lighting

Lighting Designer

Lighting design is an elusive art, and there is no one way to design lighting for a theatrical production. There are the mechanics of light fixtures and the equipment and the process a lighting designer goes through during a production, but it all starts with the script that inspires the designer's imagination. Lighting designer James Ingalls said there are also three essential requirements for a lighting designer: flexibility, good eyes, and diplomacy.

The primary objective is to illuminate the stage, either the action, a character, or the story with or without calling attention to the lighting itself. It is a collaborative endeavor eventually involving the director and all the other production designers and departments.

Lighting design is everywhere today—at rock shows, concerts, clubs, churches, film, television, and small and large venues. Over the last thirty years, the technical changes in theatrical lighting have affected the entire entertainment industry, including Broadway, and some of that evolution is discussed in the lighting associate section.

Today there is so much discussion about communication but how does a director convey what they have in their mind and a lighting designer show what they imagine in their mind. As the

233

lighting designer Allen Lee Hughes relates: "If I say the lighting is going to be warm, what does that mean? My warm may not be your warm. Even if I show the director pictures, he or she might look at one thing and think I'm talking about that, whereas I may be looking at something else entirely."

The director's recommendation of lighting designer has considerable weight in a Broadway production, as does the set designer. It is the producer who gives final approval. The lighting designer is hired after the director and set designer, and somewhat later in the production process. Before they are formally hired, the lighting designer reads the script and meets with the director, who describes their concept for the production. If the show is appealing to the designer and negotiations with the producer are satisfactory, they are hired.

The lighting designer works closely with the director, as well as the set, sound, and projection designers, so it is valuable to be included in the early production meetings, perhaps six months before opening (ideally before the sets and costumes are completed). More often the lighting designer is hired late, perhaps six weeks or later before opening.

In theatre, nothing profoundly affects a scene as much as lighting and sound, which function interdependently because many sound cues are coordinated with light cues. Although lighting seems fleeting, it establishes time, creates a mood, and enhances the atmosphere of a scene. Often the audience is not consciously aware of lighting. Usually, theatre lighting is subtle and tries not to call attention to itself, but that depends on the show and the staging. Allen Lee Hughes relayed lighting *K2* on Broadway:

> The way we did *K2*, there was a sunrise at the beginning of the play set to music and seemingly no actors on stage. I had a certain amount of time where basically it was just a light show. Now in that case, the lighting *wanted* to call attention to itself by being interesting and spectacular enough to hold the audience's attention. At a certain point, the sun broke across the ledge where the actors were and that was the first time the

audience realized there were actors onstage. From that point on, the lighting and the show became about the actors.

The lighting design team consists of an associate, an assistant, and a computer programmer, who the designer recommends. The lighting team and equipment must fit within the show budget otherwise the plan must be revised. The designer's fee is negotiated separately with the producer. Everything is subject to approval from the producer. On Broadway, a lighting designer and associate is a member of the United Scenic Artists Local 829, which is under the umbrella of International Alliance of Theatrical Stage Employees (IATSE).

Design Prep

Independently, the lighting designer spends time developing ideas to bring to the first production meeting, but some light fixtures are attached to the set. An early hire allows the lighting designer to have some input with the set designer's drawings, because the anticipated set construction informs the designer's vision. The lighting designer can assemble ideas, but without the set drawings they cannot really begin work.

Awaiting those drawings, the designer studies the script, breaks it down into scenes, and imagines how to light each scene. When completed, a set of the scenic design drawings are given to the scene shops for bids and a set is given to the lighting designer. Now the lighting designer goes to the drawing board to create their own set of drawings.

From the set drawings, the lighting designer learns what set pieces dress each scene and calculates how many instruments are needed to cover that space. If the fixture is attached to the set, they can compute the fixture's measurements and the appropriate height for attaching it to the set.

The lighting prep phase consists of a volume of paperwork done together with the designer and the associate.

The light plot is a series of drawings that shows the pipes, instruments, and where they should be hung for each scene in the play. The drawings are like an architect's drawings of a house specifying measurements. The light plot is broken into the deck plot (stage), a ground plot (bird's-eye view from above), and a section plot (the stage cut in half and viewed from one side or the other). The light plot shows every light, its assigned color, and its control number. It indicates where the audience sits and if lights are to be hung on the balcony or from the box seats. If you ever sat in the orchestra section, you probably saw the light rigs hung on the balcony or the boxes. The plot is used to determine how much cable is needed, what type of instrument is hung, and how much hardware is required.

There are a number of other pieces of paperwork the lighting team generates besides the light plot. There is the channel hookup, which is a guide for the electric crew specifying each channel, the position where it is hung, the unit number, the purpose, color, and other information. For example, channel one is hung on the first electric (which can be at the proscenium). It might be unit number one, and its purpose is upstage front lighting. It has a certain color and a certain gobo (a specific pattern like rain or a city skyline). There are several channels, and each unit can have a different type of light. There is another document called the instrument schedule, which is similar to the channel hookup but sorts the lights out by position on the rig.

Some designers draft their plots by hand and give them to their associate to put into a computer. Some designers start drafting the light plot on the computer and then the associate takes over. All of this paperwork is eventually given to the programmer to input into the lighting console.

When the drawings are completed and before the lighting design is finalized, the designer consults with the set designer, director, and the producer. After approval by the producer, the designer's drawings are submitted to several shops for bids, much like the set designs. Once a bid is approved by the producer, the lighting designer submits a shop order for the equipment (number of lights, various cables, equipment, and hardware needed).

The script governs light—the time of day, the time of year, the location of the action, and from where the light is coming which determines its angle (a room, a window, the side of the stage, day, or night). Light moves in a straight line, but ultimately what is being lit is a lot of angles to highlight something onstage (i.e., a person[s], a room, a sofa, a cup, a chair) or even air (atmosphere). James Ingalls related:

> Lighting design is alchemic in a way because you have to figure out how illuminating air is going to help tell the story. You are essentially lighting air. There's nothing to hold onto. I have to use my imagination of what the show might look like to someone, to assemble enough pieces of metal with lenses in them to be in the right place in the right colors, to create some kind of clarity. I really don't know how to describe how I do that.

On Broadway there is a computer control board much like the sound computer board you see in the back of a theatre, but it is smaller. The programmer is the one who programs the console. It takes only one person to operate (the head electrician) the light board because the show cues are locked in and changes have been decided and timed. A light cue can be set in split time: all the lights coming up in two minutes and then going down in three seconds.

The lighting designer works with the production head electrician of the crew who will install and run the show. The paperwork gives the production head electrician all the necessary information to hang the show. If there are electrics attached to scenery or light-up signs that are part of the scenery, all of that is mapped out and made very clear for the head electrician to direct their crew when installing the show.

Today there are software programs that allow a designer to show in two or three dimensions what lighting they are imagining. These programs show the lighting on the stage in each given scene. It is used for film and big arena shows like the Super Bowl as well.

To this point, the lighting designer's work is based on what has been discussed with the director and design teams early on. The actual implementation of the lighting design begins during load-in when the set is placed on the stage, the lights are hung, and hopefully before the actors start rehearsing in the theatre, which is somewhat late in the production.

By the time the lighting designer is working onstage, sets are complete, the costumes are almost complete, and actors have rehearsed. As with all the departments on Broadway, each original brilliant idea has morphed into something quite different. The real conundrum for all Broadway designers is how to design and build a show six months in advance that is going to evolve from the idealized version. The designer trusts their assembled team to be adaptable to execute the light plot, make adjustments when necessary, and find solutions to problems that arise to maintain their vision.

Load-in and Installation and Tech

Each Broadway theatre has a house electrician who is hired by the theatre owner. Their primary job is the house lights and overseeing that the production electrical work preserves the rules and integrity of the theatre. For example, a Broadway theatre has a house electrician who knows the theatre, turns the house lights on, runs the house lights when the house goes to half, and at intermission brings the house lights back up. Depending on the show, they may be responsible for one cue in the show. That is governed by union rules.

The head production electrician supervises the production electrical crew in running the show and is hired by the producer through the production management company. The producer may have a preference for a head electrician with whom there is a previous work relationship. The head electrician may have an assistant and a crew of eight to ten people consisting of the production hires as well as some over-hires (temporary hires) for the purposes of hanging the lights.

On a Broadway show, all the lights are rented. Once the head electrician gets the lighting plot, they contact the lighting shop that won the bid. The lighting associate and the electrician's crew assembles the equipment for the entire show at the shop and packs it in road boxes. This includes all the physical hardware, cables, and machinery needed to hang the show. The boxes are labeled with crucial information such as these units on the first electric, these units on the second electric, the first electric needs to be twenty-two feet long, etc. The boxes are delivered to the theatre.

The next stage is the load-in process, during which the lighting designer and the associate work with the head electrician and lighting crew to install the lights. Once onstage, the lighting designer is like a conductor working with an orchestra. One light crew group may hang lights on the balcony, while another group hangs lights over the stage or at the boxes, while some are affixing lights to the scenery. Once hung, the lights need to be focused, which can take a day or two, depending on the size of the production. All the information for color, value, and light cues are being input into the computer by the programmer.

As equipment is being installed, the designer and/or associate works with the scenic team if adjustments are needed. For example, working from the set drawings, the designer prescribed five feet offstage for a fixture, but the shop had to adjust the set designer's plan and there are only four feet offstage. For another fixture they may get the extra two feet they need, or the scenic crew says they can only have a foot. There is a mixture of art and mechanics involved in lighting a show, so things have to be reengineered to function and still achieve the designer's vision. The problem-solving requires creativity, imagination, and adaptability.

Before the cast transfers to the theatre, there is a dry tech where all the stage crews start at the top of the show and work through to the bottom of the show to practice every department's moves for the entire production. This is complex but important to see how everything works together.

A revival of a show is less complicated because the script is known. With a new play or musical, there is an element of organized bedlam approaching opening night. More often than not, things are not quite ready. With the sets, lighting, costumes, electrical, and sound being pulled together once they are all in the theatre, the next serious issue that affects the crew work time is when to bring the actors onto the stage to rehearse.

About three weeks before previews for a play (for a musical, it could be five weeks or longer), the actors are brought to the theatre. Then the actors and lighting merge. While actors are getting used to the actual playing area, the lighting designer may have to rehang lights. The actors begin to use props and the director can make changes. It can be a stop-start process so that the scene is run, the actors stop and freeze in place, and the designer adjusts the focus of the lights, the timings for the cues, and the actual value of each light. The director says, "You know, that's great, but it's a little too dark too soon." Change. "Actor Z, that entrance is awkward. Try coming in downstage in one." Change. While all this is happening, the associate and programmer are trying to keep up with these changes and constantly updating the data into the computer.

Once in the theatre, the entire staff and cast of a Broadway show is on ten out of twelve hours a day, sometimes until opening night. During daily notes call, the associate confers with the head electrician concerning any changes. Making changes is a challenge for the crew because the tech people have only about three hours in the morning to work and clean up the stage before the noon rehearsal. With the actors onstage, changing light focus, density, and cues is formidable. A drama is usually frozen relatively early in rehearsal, but a musical may not be frozen until opening night.

When the real tech occurs close to previews with the cast and all the departments, the sooner the production can get through tech the better it is for the production. There is more time for run-throughs to practice all the elements together, see what's working, and see what's not working. Ideally it is hoped to complete at least two run-throughs before there is an audience. Once previews begin, things can change during the day's rehearsal with a performance that night.

As first preview draws nigh, everyone involved in the production is actively trying to finish their task—stagehands, sets, costumes, sound, props, lights, orchestra, actors, director—so pre-preview onstage is usually a heightened, stressful mess that somehow resolves by previews due to the magical expertise of the entire production staff.

Previews/Run

The light cue lists are a tool for the stage manager to use to stay current with changes occurring during rehearsal and previews. Since there is so much going on at the same time, communication among the departments is critical. The stage manager may have Johnny coming in upstage right, but that has changed and the light cue has changed, and now Johnny is coming in downstage left.

Although the lighting is somewhat set by previews, a preview audience can expose something that could be improved. A director can decide a scene that was midstage should be pulled downstage. During the second week of a musical preview, the opening number can be cut and the entire opening restaged. Then the lighting designer and the team scramble to make those adjustments. Such changes so late in the production are rare, but if a show is having trouble it can happen.

The lighting industry keeps evolving, so constant brushing up on computer programs and keeping in touch with the lighting community to know what is new is a must. Refocusing lights and color values during rehearsal and previews will make those changes and maintenance much easier with the evolving technology.

There is a great deal of difference between lighting a drama and lighting a musical. Specifically, for a drama there may be twenty cues, but for a musical it could be well over eight hundred. What propelled Tharon Musser to push for a more computerized lighting board when she was lighting the original *A Chorus Line* was the dancers. There was constant motion and a multitude of angles.

Once the show opens, the designer, the associate, and the programmer are gone. Then the head electrician assumes the responsibility of running the show, maintaining the light instruments, and the lighting console.

If it is a long run, gels burn out and lights drop focus because of the city vibrations, so the designer must return to the show about every six months to bring it back to opening night standards. This is a negotiated comeback fee. It is an additional cost for the producer, but the producer wants to keep the show in shape, especially with a long run.

Lighting Associate:
Lighting Programmer and Technology

As with lighting designers, there is no one way to be a lighting associate. On Broadway, lighting designers often work with one associate and usually one assistant, two assistants if the show is big. The lighting designer recommends their associate and assistant(s), but all are paid through the production company. Both the lighting designer, the associate, and assistants are required to be members of United Scenic Artists 829, the Union for Theatrical Designers and Scene Painters under the IATSE umbrella.

The duties assigned to the associate are governed by the designer's work style. Some designers are more hands-on and work directly with the scenic and electrical crews. Others rely on their associate to facilitate the design and adjustments as they occur, while the designer is engaged with the other department designers. If they are a delegating type of designer, the associate becomes the go-between person for the designer, the head electrician, and their crew. The associate represents the designer and oversees that the designer's ideas are executed. In that scenario, the associate can make design decisions when working with the crew without the designer present. However, they are in constant communication with the designer to keep them informed of any changes.

A lighting assistant does not have the authority to make decisions and must consult with the designer before responding to queries from the electrical crew. It all depends on the designer. An assistant on a Broadway musical manages the follow spots for the show.

The designer reaches out to the lighting associate early; it can be six months and often more in advance of opening. General management advises the designer what the budget allowance is for the associate's hire. A lighting associate is hired for a certain number of weeks. If some pre-production weeks early in the process are partial weeks, such as two days in one week and three days in another week, those days can accrue as one week.

Once hired, the associate and the designer figure how many weeks they need for their team from the start of preparation to the opening or when the production is frozen, as well as post-opening archival time, if required. Today, designers document their designs for future reference. If the associate is included in early design discussions, they have a better understanding of why design decisions were made. If during tech a light has to move three feet to allow a chandelier to fly in, the associate should have enough understanding of the lighting plot and the designer's intentions to be able to know where to put that light and how to solve the specific problem.

The pre-production phase occurs early in the production, well before load-in to the theatre. During this period, the associate often works directly with the designer as the designer is creating the paperwork: the light plot, the channel hook-up, and the instrument schedule. As mentioned in the lighting designer section, the light plot is basically a giant drafting showing every single light, where the lights are hung, if and where it is specifically attached to scenery, and if there are individual signs that light up. The channel hook-up is a guide that organizes all the lighting information by the control channel number associated with the lighting fixture, including specific information for each instrument such as color or gobo (pattern). The instrument schedule is similar to the channel hook-up but is sorted by the positions where the instruments hang on the rig. Then all the basic information needed for the console (the circuit or dimmer number, soft-patched to the channel number) is eventually fed into the lighting console by the programmer.

Some designers make only hand-drawn drawings and others initially use computers, but whatever method is used, the drawings are handed over to the associate for input into a computer (not the lighting console). The paperwork is an enormous task for the lighting associate. Ultimately, all the documents are given to the head electrician to execute their work.

Once the lighting bid has been awarded to a shop, the head electrician and their crew starts to assemble, pack, and label all the lighting equipment for the entire show in preparation for load-in. The associate participates representing the designer.

During the load-in, the associate works with the head electrician. Once everything is loaded-in, the process of installing the lighting instruments begins. The designer might actively participate part of the time directing the installation crew, but more often they are dealing with other design departments and must rely heavily on the associate to honor the design vision. This is a period of organized mayhem in the theatre. As Aaron Porter said, "It's all kind of an organic amoeba that changes form and slowly takes shape."

During rehearsals, the associate created a cue list for the lighting department, which they update and maintain until the show is frozen. This is a herculean task because as repeated throughout this book, everything keeps changing. As lighting cues change an updated cue list is given to the stage manager for their call script. Sometimes the stage manager asks the associate for clarification if a cue has changed. For example, if a cue was tied to an actor's line, but now the actor enters earlier, the stage manager and lighting designer find another place to call the cue to make the cue work.

The lighting designer's assistant on a Broadway musical is typically in charge of keeping track of the follow spots. There are two or three follow spots up in the lighting booth, and a track sheet is made for each follow spot. The track sheet creates a road map of cue information for the spot operator to follow. The lighting assistant has information such as "at the top of the song, pick up Sherry in the red dress and fade out on Martha as she exits stage left. Spot 2, you are going to stand by and pick up Johnny's entrance in the middle of the song." There may be a deck (backstage) electrician who is positioned for when a scenery piece moves offstage. They run that track and during the show unplug and replug the light for that move. Sometimes there are two of them—one on stage right and one on stage left.

As with home computers, a computerized lighting board can crash during the show, so there are two consoles. The head electrician builds the system, and it must be sustainable. There is also a complete protocol if the console crashes. The primary console and the backup console sit side by side. If the primary console crashes, the electrician swings around to the backup console and continues. If there is time while a scene is playing, they may be able to troubleshoot the problem on the primary console and correct it. There are always updates on the computer hardware and software programs. The entire lighting industry is evolving so everyone keeps learning.

A young person can learn lighting fundamentals in university theatre programs. College is a limited experience because there often is an abundance of current equipment at the student's fingertips. In the past, that knowledge could be applied doing summer stock, where the student could gain practical experience. Summer stock was often a seat-of-the-pants situation, where a person did one show a week for a season of ten or twelve weeks. It could be a baptism of fire, but skills were really honed. Summer stock has virtually disappeared now, so the next step during and after college is internships at some regional theatres where the student can work with skilled artisans in a professional setting. There is also community theatre. These are opportunities to build relationships with working professionals and grow a reputation.

Lighting Programmer

A Broadway show is run on a lighting console. It is much like the sound console that usually sits at the back of the orchestra section, but it is smaller and located backstage. The lighting console is programmed by the lighting programmer who is selected early in the production. The lighting programmer, a position necessitated with the arrival of computers, is specially trained in the various lighting software programs. The programmer takes the associate's ever-changing documents and inputs all the information including updates into the lighting console.

The programmer is a highly specialized job, carries a massive responsibility, and must be accurate. Running the show relies on their work. The programmer's job is usually from load-in to opening, after the crew is sure all the instruments are operating properly and the designer's color choices, values, and focus are correct. The job is somewhat like that of a script girl on a film. As mentioned previously, cues for a drama are far fewer than for a musical. If the designer needs to know where a light source is, what color it is, and what unit it is hanging on, the associate or programmer can relay that information.

During load-in the programmer closely communicates with the head electrician regarding data they are inputting (e.g., needing clarification about the entire second ladder lighting rig, only to be told by the electrician, "Oh, we pulled that down a fourth").

The jobs of the designer, associate, and programmer end when the show is frozen and there are no more changes. That is when the head electrician takes over and runs the production lights from the lighting console. The stage manager calls the light cues during the show, but the head electrician is the person who is responsible for maintaining the lights on the show and executing the cues for every performance.

A Partial Evolution of Theatrical Lighting Technology

Until about thirty years ago, lighting technology had remained essentially the same since the early twentieth century. There were light boards that could handle one light cue at a time. Then came the ability to preset cues for two scenes or ten scenes in advance. The operator could set the faders (levers that slide up or down to light or dim a scene) into positions for the cues in advance. Presets took more time to execute lighting cues and were cumbersome.

There was one electrician who became something of a legend in the theatre world. He was so dexterous he could move the levers and change multiple cues rapidly using his hands, elbows, and forearms, making the preset board operate quickly and smoothly. He was a technical artist and in constant demand.

Today on Broadway preset boards are still used but they are called submasters or independent masters. They are usually used to light something that does not need to go through the computer console, such as work lights backstage. If there is a crash during a dark transition backstage, the submaster can be thrown on to make sure everyone is okay. Broadway house lights are on a submaster, not run through the console.

The preset lighting boards were replaced by digital memory consoles. Although more expensive and less cumbersome than preset boards, scenes could be designed, recorded, and stored in the digital memory console. There was less room for human error and less time between lighting cues, so productions preferred them.

Today there are a myriad of light boards in use. There is a company called ETC Lighting Company (Electronic Theater Controls Company), which specializes in all sorts of lighting products. They have an EOS family of computer consoles, which is a series of light boards made with the same lighting control hardware, software, and programming layout that provides an operator consistency when recording lighting cues. The operators do not have to learn a new program. During the run of a show there is a board operator who works the console initiating the cues at the command of the production stage manager.

The real revolution in stage lighting came in the 1970s, when Tharon Musser was designing *A Chorus Line* on Broadway. She wanted a computer control board that acted like a road board. Meaning if she set the light at 50 percent, it would stay there until she wanted to bring it to another level. Until then, that move was not possible. She approached Strand Lighting to create it for *A Chorus Line*. The first computerized board was called the Light Palette. That board was used on the show.

Perhaps the biggest innovation in lighting has been the computer. Producers were slow to embrace computers because early computers were expensive and constantly changing. However, the most expensive cost is manpower. A producer doing a musical requiring three or four men to run a show department can reduce that expense to one man using a computer. Eventually, using computers began to make sense financially and artistically.

Today another development is the moving light, in which a light no longer has only one purpose but may have forty uses. It is a flexible, versatile fixture that has a movable beam, as well as prisms, irises, and shutters that are controlled through the computer. As audience members we have seen the use of moving lights on awards shows where lights swoop up and highlight someone or something specific. Moving lights can create a myriad of looks in one fixture instead of several fixtures on a rig. These lights are computerized and automated internally so they can mix colors to create new colors. They have wheels within to get different patterns or sharp or blurry edges. An iris inside can enlarge a circle or make it smaller. A gobo can make an entire stage appear to have rain or leafy shadows.

Musicals are a lot about movement so moving lights are used more frequently, even though they are expensive. The advantages outweigh the expense since they are controlled through the computer. If a director or choreographer has changed an actor's or dancer's position, an entire light rig with moving lights can be refocused through the computer. All the changes can be made without having a man up on a ladder rehanging and refocusing the light. For musicals moving lights can be brighter than traditional lights, which adds to the razzle-dazzle. Moving lights are evolving to include some of the versatility that LED lights already have. Change is always incremental, so traditional lights that need to be hand-focused are still used.

The next significant progression in the twenty-first century is LED lights. Conventional lights use gels, which are pieces of colored plastic that fit into them and light bulbs. During a run, the lightbulbs burn out and need replacing. Over time gels get brittle, the colors fade, and they need replacing. Traditional lights also require more people to operate, struggle to provide the same light subtleties, and cannot produce the same speed or reproducibility achievable with the newer technology.

LED lights are completely computerized, so the color, intensity, and focus are controlled by the data programmed into the light board. There are no gels or replaceable light bulbs. If the green is too intense, the quality of the green can be changed via the computer. With conventional lights you had shutters (like blinders on a horse) to create sharper optics. Since the shutters are inside the computer, the designer can create stripes and sharp lines without having to change the instruments. Spotlights can create squares and shapes. An LED spotlight can be pinpointed on a cup and saucer. LED allows for new developments in the art of lighting design, providing subtleties that never could be achieved by preset boards.

On Broadway, LED lights are rented from various stage lighting companies. At this time, they are expensive to buy, but the cost will come down and savings in manpower, bulbs, and plastic gels will make purchasing financially feasible. The Goodman Theater in Chicago is starting to buy some to be part of its inventory. The incorporation of such lights will be slow in most regional theatres because of the cost. Rock concerts have been using LED lighting for some time.

There are textbook differences between drama, opera, modern dance, and ballet, but attending all performances is a group of people sitting out front watching a group of people moving onstage. The visual focus for a musical is constant motion. There are more transitions, scenery, and bodies moving on and offstage. In *42nd Street*, the action moves from New York to Havana. Lighting design is not only about movement, but angles as well. Dancers' bodies are a constant whirl of moving angles all over the stage. The LED development allows for a larger and more flexible lighting palette to respond to that movement. For a drama, the action can have one or three sets, but the action is more static.

Theatres are structured differently. There is the proscenium (stage and audience), thrust (audience on three sides of stage), arena (audience surrounds the acting space), and black box (square room that can be configured any way desired). It is possible with lighting a proscenium with the audience in front of the stage, lights can be hidden in the wings and not have shadows. A thrust stage has fewer walls and less room to hide lighting fixtures, so you can get shadows. The arena is perhaps the most difficult because there are no walls to hide anything. All of this technology is fascinating to create and play with, but for a Broadway stage, it always returns to the story being told. The lighting scheme must fit the script and illuminate the action. The lighting designer's primary purpose is the story.

12

Hair/Wigs and Makeup/Prosthetics

Hair and Wig Designer

Hair design is important in life as well as storytelling on Broadway. The hair designer is often recommended by the costume designer, the director, or the producer. The hair designer works most closely with the costume designer, and their job is to complement and complete the costume designer's vision. The director has some input, but it is the costume designer who has the concept of the characters' looks and the hair designer who helps express that concept.

Most Broadway productions use wigs rather than the actors' own hair for very practical reasons. There are serious maintenance differences between wearing a wig and using an actor's own hair during a run. A person's hair can be unpredictable depending on the lifestyle, weather, and humidity. If an actor is using their own hair in a show, that requires styling it for every performance. They must live with that style in real life during the show's run. If someone is wearing a wig, the maintenance of the wig is done during the day by the hair staff and the actor comes in at half-hour for the wig to be placed on their head.

The combination of wigs and real hair can also complicate the hair department's pre-performance timing. Legally, actors are called for half-hour, but if the hairdressers need more time, the actor may be asked to come in a bit early. Depending on the situation, sometimes this can be a problem due to union rules that would require an actor to be financially compensated.

A hair designer can be hired six months in advance of a production or two months before rehearsals begin. It is important for the wig designer to begin their design along with the costume designer, director, and anyone else who is involved, so there is a consistent vision. Today, press work begins well in advance of the opening, so the hair designer needs enough prep time to prepare the wigs for photographs.

The hair designer receives a fee for their designs, which includes early prep time. Separate from their design fee, they must submit a budget for the wigs and hair, which includes every item necessary for wig and hair maintenance. The hair designer receives a royalty for their designs, as well as on Broadway tours and international productions under the original producer. Those royalties end when the production ceases. There are generally no royalties for regional productions due to smaller budgets and operating costs.

When the hair designer knows they are working on a production, they sit down with the costume designer and other creatives who want input. The costume designer has already created sketches and idea reference points, which they share with the hair designer. The hair designer then does their own research for hair style, hair color, and period if applicable, and shares their ideas with the costume designer and director. Before any wig work begins, the costume designer and director must approve. Once a cast is engaged, the hair designer measures and notes the shape of the actor's head so the wig making process can begin. A more thorough discussion of wig making is at the end of this segment.

On Broadway, there are very strict union rules governing hair, makeup, and costumes. Costume people do not touch hair, and hair people do not touch costumes. Determining jurisdiction of costumes and hats onstage takes time, so it helps if the teams have worked together so some issues have been smoothed out.

The costume designer designs the hats, which go to the wardrobe department. Hats go on top of wigs, which the hair department has constructed. The hat must be put on and taken off by a hair person. This specificity is important because if a wig worn in one scene is worn in the next scene, there are tricks as to how hats are kept on people's heads. When taking off the hat, the hair person must not cause the hair to fly away and look unkempt.

To a non-theatre person, this may seem rather extreme, but backstage there is low light, confined space, and time is expedient. The crew is working under pressure, so each person needs to know their job. When you have a thirty-second change from street clothes into a ball gown, there is no time to check things or for mishaps.

During the design period until opening, the hair designer usually has an associate who, as one designer said, "is another me." If the designer is dealing with other departments or is involved in other design projects, their associate steps in, supervises the hair department, and makes sure that the designer's concept is adhered to. The show is run by the hair supervisor (see the next section).

Although a hair designer prefers to work with someone they have worked with before, the availability of an associate for the designer can be limited. Many hair associates work in television and film as well, because there are only so many theatre jobs. Once the show opens, the designer's responsibilities are minimal unless the production requests their presence or there are new principals going in, especially if it is a celebrity. If the designer is unavailable, the associate will step in, give notes, and answer any questions the hair supervisor or production may have.

Hopefully, final wig fittings happen two weeks before moving into the theatre for tech. Wigs are made offsite, styled offsite depending on the designer, and brought to the theatre by the designer and their associate. Sometimes, the styling happens at the theatre with the associate and the hair department.

When the production is in tech, it is ten- to twelve-hour days for crews. Tech is a grueling process. Although the wigs have been prepared before tech, tech is the first time the director sees the wig onstage with costumes and under lights. The director and the hair designer evaluate what does and does not work to determine potential changes. This period lasts three to four weeks. Toward the end of tech and once previews begin, the hair designer begins to focus on understudies and swings, especially with musicals. In the first week there often are injuries with dancers and the show must go on.

To be a hairdresser, a person needs to be licensed in whatever individual state they are working. In Chicago, fifteen hundred hours are required to graduate from a beauty school to get a license. In New York, working in film, theatre, and television, a hair stylist must be a member of the Hair and Makeup Union Local 798, which covers the Eastern Region and is part of International Alliance of Theatrical Stage Employees (IATSE). Originally, Local 798 was divided into theatre, television, or film. If a person worked in theatre, they could advance toward television, and after television they could advance toward film. That condition has now been eliminated. Today if you are a member of the union, you can work in any of those jurisdictions. It is interesting to note that some hair supervisors on Broadway may oversee the designs of the makeup designer.

Hair is very personal, and actors want to feel comfortable. There are always going to be individual opinions, and the designer will try to compromise as much as they can while still maintaining the integrity of their design. An actor can have specific requests or health issues such as allergies or want products that are not tested on animals. The designer incorporates these concerns as much as possible.

In general, musicals are more likely to incorporate wigs in the production as opposed to plays. The hair designer David Brian Brown reflected:

> The wig work for a play has to have more detail, be delicate, and look natural. In a play you often use an actor's own hair because they like the freedom of having their own hair, so they don't have to be aware of it. Others prefer a wig, so they don't have to bother with their hair for a performance. Whatever the reason, a wig in a play has a much higher quality than a musical because the theatre is smaller, the audiences are closer, and plays are generally more about real life and real situations.

Although the hair designer's responsibilities mostly end on opening night, they are still expected to oversee the production depending on their availability. This is part of their royalty obligations. Most cast changes during the run of a show are managed by the hair supervisor. If a new wig is required for a new actor, that is the designer's responsibility. There are times with a long run the designer's presence is required. If it is a celebrity or important principal replacement, the designer will return if they do not have a conflict. If the work entails several hours of time, they will be paid a day rate according to their original contract negotiations. When the new wig is completed, it will be sent to the supervisor for restyling.

Making Theatrical Wigs

There are several wigmakers for pop icons, arena shows, and large spectacles, but there are few theatrical wigmakers left in New York. Bob Kelly and Paul Huntley, two icons in the industry, have both passed on. Now either the designers are also their own wigmaker or there are many small shops that can handle individual pieces. There is a wigmaker in Los Angeles named Victoria Wood and a wigmaker in London named Ray Marston who are frequently used for theatrical wig building.

Budgets for some services have shrunk, and a production is always watching the bottom line. Wigs for principal actors and stars require more detail work and consequently are very expensive. Musicals have large ensembles who also use wigs. The cost of fifty wigs from a large wig company is daunting to a show's budget.

Necessity became the mother of invention for hair designer David Brian Brown, who learned how to make wigs and started his own small shop. It is not a commercial shop, but he is able to make wigs for his Broadway productions allowing him creative and financial control. It also affords a designer the ability to create wigs for small productions or for friends who have miniscule budgets, where some cost can be absorbed and the designer can continue to create.

In designing a wig, the designer chooses the materials to be used in the construction of the wig. They measure the actor's head and make a mold of it using cellophane or transparent tape, which is transferred to a head block. Then a lace foundation is made to weave in the hair. This requires knotting one hair at a time to the lace, a very time-intensive procedure, generally taking about forty hours to finish. Once the wig is completed, it is styled for the show. For a musical, endurance is a major factor, especially for dancers. The wig must be secure enough on the head to withstand the choreography, so the dancer does not worry about it coming loose.

There are different ways of learning how to make a wig. It can be at a beauty school, university, wigmaking schools in London, or private training. Even YouTube videos can give you an idea of the process, but learning in person is better. A hair person can also absorb a lot of information working with different wigmakers on many different productions.

Hair Supervisor

The hair supervisor is the person who runs the hair department during the run of the show. The position functions similarly to the costume supervisor. The only difference is that the hair supervisor on Broadway runs a track during the show, which means they follow a lead actor's exits and entrances throughout the performance to help with any wig or hat requirements that are needed.

Who recommends the supervisor can vary, but usually it is the hair designer who suggests who they want to supervise the show and if the producer approves, the production hires the supervisor. During the run of the show, the supervisor is fundamentally the designer's eyes and ears. The hair supervisor is the person who runs the show, keeps the hair work consistent, and maintains the designer's design.

Some supervisors negotiate their own contract and others have an agent. The supervisor negotiates a budget for their department, which can include the entire team. Other productions have an overall budget for all the hair department salaries, which the supervisor then apportions to the team. Still for other shows each team member's salary must be negotiated and backed up by the supervisor.

During a performance, the supervisor runs a track, supervises the hair department, and monitors hair issues backstage. It is difficult for the hair supervisor to have eyes on the team the entire show, so the supervisor has an assistant often with whom they have worked to make sure the hair room operates smoothly in the supervisor's absences. In addition to the supervisor and assistant on a big musical, the hair team consists of three or four additional people. The assistant is recommended by the supervisor or the hair designer, and is part of the hair budget.

The supervisor is responsible for setting up the entire hair department backstage, making sure the room is an efficient working space for the team, buying all the equipment and supplies for maintaining the wigs. Like the costume supervisor, a hair supervisor maintains their own kit of tools they are comfortable with, which consists of brushes, curling irons, hot tools, and blow dryers. Specialty items such as disposable pins, wig caps, and blocking supplies need to be purchased. Before purchasing new equipment, the supervisor checks to see if any shows are closing, not going out on tour, or are selling their room kits. Those show kits sell at a discounted rate, which is much less than buying it all new.

Once the supervisor is hired, they consult with the designer to collect all relevant information as to the hair needs of the show: how many actors are in the show, how many wigs each actor wears, and actors' head sizes. The most important item purchased for the hair department are the canvas wig blocks. If there are twenty actors who wear five different wigs, the supervisor must be sure to have five wig blocks to match the head size for each actor in the cast. That is one hundred wig blocks.

When the supervisor joins the production depends on the designer. There are times when all the wigs have been styled and the designer and the designer's associate bring all the wigs to the theatre. There are other times when the supervisor loads everything into the theatre and they and the team help the designer and associate to style the wigs. Again, it depends on the size of the show, how many wigs need prepping, and when rehearsal starts.

From the stage management team, the supervisor is given the script broken down into scenes for the entire show and a separate chart for every actor in the show. The supervisor then inputs that information into their computer organizing a separate track for each actor. Next the hair supervisor assigns each team member a specific actor(s) to track throughout the show. The track documents indicate what scene the actor is in, where the actor enters and exits the scene, and whether the actor is on stage left or stage right. All this information is printed out for the team member to follow, then highlighted and color coded for each actor, so the team knows exactly where they have to be at every point in the show to aid the actors with their wig(s).

During tech, moving from one scene to another takes time because the team must figure out if there is a quick change and where they must be with the next wig for the actor. The actors run off, the wig is removed, costume is changed, and the wig is replaced for the next scene.

Hair people handle anything to do from the neck up, which includes hats. The costumers bring the hat to the hair people, who put it on the actor's head and secure it. If the hat is put on improperly, there can be an accident with someone's head being hit with a sharp pin or the wig being untidy.

Sometimes the hair crew has to handle both wigs and real hair, as in *Mrs. Doubtfire*. All of the children did not wear wigs, and those who did not had to have their hair styled for every performance. It is a challenge for hair people working with real hair because they never know what they are going to get on any given day, and it happens just before curtain. As mentioned, real hair is different every day depending on the lifestyle, weather and humidity, and the amount of time showering. A wig is easier to maintain consistently. It can be tweaked when taken off, so it is ready for the next time it is put on. The actor does not have to sit in the chair the whole styling time. Wigs are touched up and restyled for every performance. The hair department is at the theatre an hour and a half before each show to prepare the wigs for when the actors arrive at half-hour.

Wigs are not washed every day, and each wig reacts differently to washing. Maintenance of the wigs is the responsibility of the entire hair staff to keep their specific actors' wigs clean and fresh. As supervisor Victoria Tinsman said, "Hair has a memory and when it loses its memory and doesn't want to go into the place where you're telling it to go, it's time to get washed."

If it is a heavy dance show and the actor is sweating profusely, that wig gets disheveled. That wig must be washed more frequently than a wig that is put on someone's head who just walks across the stage and then takes it off. So a very active wig must be washed a couple of times a week versus once a month for an inactive wig.

A show that uses period hairstyles versus modern hairstyles can require more maintenance. Period hair has a specific look because it is representing a historical period. Wigs in modern hair designs are more difficult to make look natural because after it has been washed and dried, the wig does not look like real hair. So different techniques of styling are necessary. Victoria Tinsman said:

> A really good hair stylist is never done learning and there's *always* another way to do something. It might not work in your hand. It might work better in someone else's hand, but there's always a new way to do something. You just always have to be open to getting notes and even taking critiques, because a critique at the end of the day is just going to teach you something new. It's not personal.

The hair supervisor belongs to the Hair and Makeup Union Local 798, which is for New York City and under the umbrella of IATSE. The union always covered television and film, but not necessarily theatre. Before in the theatre field a hair member was not required to belong to the union to work on Broadway if they were working on wigs, but that has changed. Now the union has ruled that all hair people who work on Broadway must belong to the union. To join, a person accrues a certain number of work hours on Broadway to qualify. Even if the person worked in regional theatre or other theatres, those hours do not carry over for Broadway. A new applicant must submit the application form, reference letters, and verification of working hours to prove eligibility. A cosmetology license is also required.

If there are cast changes, the production contacts the designer, because it is the designer's job to make new wigs if required. Once the wigs are completed, they are sent over to the supervisor who restyles them for the new actor.

Allergies are more in the supervisor's area. Hair sprays can be a very sensitive area for people because of the scent or allergies. Since wigs are usually styled prior to the show, hair spray is rarely used in front of the actor and the smell has dissipated by the time the wig is placed on the actor's head.

When the show closes, the hair department is part of the load-out of the show. The department staff takes all the wigs and washes them, dries them, bags them, and labels each one with the name of the actor who wore it and the character name. Then all the wigs are sent back to the designer or to storage, if the production is going straight to tour. All the purchased supplies for the show now belong to the production. The supplies are packed into boxes, labeled, and most likely put into storage to reuse for a tour. The supervisor's personal kit is also packed and returned to them.

Some hair supervisors have studied hairdressing as well as makeup and are qualified to do both. Sometimes it is possible for the supervisor to be hired as both a hair and makeup supervisor. If it is a very heavy makeup show, the production will hire a makeup supervisor and a hair supervisor. However, that is another salary and an added expense, and if the production can hire one person qualified to do both jobs, the production is happy to do so.

Some shows hire a separate makeup supervisor whose job is makeup and maintaining the supplies. Whether a hair/makeup supervisor or a makeup supervisor, they do not do the makeup for the show. Once the design is complete and the makeup designer has left, it is the hair/makeup supervisor's job to check the actors and make sure they are doing what the designer wants and what should be onstage. For a heavy makeup show like *Cats*, the makeup supervisor had to teach the cast how to do their makeup. The hair/makeup supervisor orders all the makeup and makeup supplies once the show is up and running, and always makes sure the supplies are readily available for the actors.

There are several schools throughout the United States that teach makeup, but as of this writing, there are only two schools in the United States that have a particular major for both wigs and makeup. They both have a bachelor's and master's program. Those schools are the University of North Carolina School of the Arts and Cincinnati Conservatory of Music.

Makeup Designer

Unless it is a style-specific show, like *Moulin Rouge*, the makeup designer is often one of the final design positions hired on a Broadway production. A makeup designer typically begins their work when rehearsals are scheduled to begin. The style of theatrical makeup has changed considerably over the last thirty or more years, even in opera. In the past, stage makeup was heavier and more stylized. The modern camera technology and lighting of film and television has encouraged a more natural stage makeup image.

The union is Hair and Makeup Union Local 798, which covers film, television, and theatre. On a film or television production, hair and makeup are distinct departments. On a Broadway production, makeup and hair departments are very much connected and work in tandem with the costume designer.

Hair and makeup are so related to one another because it is about the entire look of the head (the face and the hair) that often the hair and wigs designer on Broadway also designs the makeup. An interesting side issue is that currently there is a Tony award for costumes, but not separately for hair or makeup.

The costume designer or director can recommend the makeup designer. The makeup designer recommendation is reviewed, approved, and hired by the producer. The designer or their agent negotiates a designer fee, but the production has a separate budget for supplies.

Once hired, the makeup designer meets with the costume designer, the hair designer (if separate from makeup designer), and the director. They review the research that has already accrued. The color palette is important, so that the makeup supports and is congruent with the style and time period of the costumes and the hair.

The makeup designer does their own research and is in a continuous dialogue with the costume and hair designers as the production progresses. Depending on the schedule, the director can be involved with the makeup imagery as well, more so during tech, when they can see all the elements fully together under the lights.

There are two parts to theatrical makeup design. First the aesthetic design, based on the show's story and the characters who inhabit that story. Then through research and images, the designer develops an ideal for how they want the characters to look. The practical side of how the makeup looks is that it must function within the show. Whatever the designer envisions has to be specific to the story, but also achievable for the performer to do on their own and in a short time period. During a Broadway run, performers almost always do their own makeup, with supervision from a designated makeup supervisor, who can often be a member of the hair team.

As mentioned earlier, on Broadway the makeup designer can be brought in as early as when rehearsals begin or as late as when tech starts. In the past, stage makeup was much more stylized, heavy, and exaggerated, whereas today it is primarily more natural like street makeup. Unless a show uses makeup as an integral part of a period look or the overall design of a show as with *Moulin Rouge*, frequently makeup design does not get the same level of production support as costumes or scenery.

On a big production, a large cosmetic company can have an interest in a makeup sponsorship as a means of showcasing their products. Makeup on *Moulin Rouge* was very much part of the aesthetic and the storytelling, so it was a positive opportunity for a cosmetic company to make a relationship with the production.

The designer consults with the producer to estimate how much product is needed for the designs and what they think the sponsorship amount should be to support the show. The producer and makeup designer then work with the company to refine the sponsorship arrangement. The company's products are usually donated to the production. Then there is a separate production budget for items the sponsoring company may not carry, as well as for specialty items such as face wipes and expendables. In essence there are three budget items: the design fee, the sponsorship allotment, and the expendable makeup budget.

There is not much difference between designing for a drama or musical today, because both categories use more naturalistic makeup. An exception can be a highly stylized or energetic musical, with the added challenge of requiring makeup to withstand choreography and quick changes.

Once the style and color palette are established and the show is cast, the makeup designer starts to work with the performers. The makeup designer might have an assistant during the tech process, when the actors are doing their makeup for the first time. Especially on a large musical where there can be a large cast, it can be difficult for the solo designer to help all the actors, who might need extra support with their makeup in the beginning. That is when an assistant is helpful to field questions and help supervise the makeup application.

The makeup designer often has a personal supply kit they work with for the fitting process. Before placing a large makeup order for the production, the designer has a one-on-one fitting with performers in a show. This introductory fitting is to set up the makeup look, to make notes for each actor (i.e., the color of eye shadow and lipstick), and to determine what makeup products are needed. If the prominence of the visual element of the makeup in the show is essential, the designer will make a kit for each actor to control the palette and the products being used to achieve the look. Other times, the actors are asked to use their own foundations and mascara, and any specialty colors or products will be provided for them.

Once the designer evaluates what additional makeup the actors need, the designer estimates supply costs and submits it to the company manager. Replenishing makeup products during the run of the show can be the performer's or the production's responsibility, depending on the arrangement determined by company management.

The prep time for the makeup designer varies from over a month to just a few days, depending on when they were brought on to the production. In addition to the fittings, the designer makes a face chart for the individual makeup plots. The face chart is the illustrated picture of the makeup design, and the makeup plot is the list and description of makeup products used to create the look. If there is time, the makeup designer gives lessons to the actors on how to do their makeup. The designer also attends rehearsals to get a sense of the show's timing and flow, and where characters enter and exit the stage. However, during the rehearsal process the actors are not in full hair and makeup.

If there are prosthetics or extremely quick changes, there might be one makeup crew position hired for the production, but that is rare. Stars may have their own personal makeup artist. However, even celebrities can often do their own makeup for productions, taking part in the theatrical ritual of the makeup transformation. Theatre is magic.

The tech process is an essential phase for the makeup designer to assess their design. That is when all the production elements come together. It is the first time the cast is in full costume, makeup, and hair/wigs on the set and under stage light. Tech is extremely important because it gives the designer a chance to see how the makeup looks in context with all the other design elements, and to offer support and adjustment as things change.

Makeup designer Sarah Cimino said that makeup design is like painting a picture and all the components must be harmonious. How does the actor's skin tone appear under the lights with the makeup? Does the lipstick look right under the lights or with the costume? Do the wig and makeup complement each other under the lights?

The designer goes through the same procedure of makeup fittings and kits for the understudies and the swings. Swing performers can cover four or five character tracks in a show, so they need the makeup kit for each character they cover.

If there are cast or ensemble changes, the designer does not need to create a fresh design but can return to help teach the performer(s) the makeup specifics. The design has already been set, though color and product selection can change for the new performer(s). The designer will make a face chart and give the new actor a brief lesson on the makeup application.

As mentioned on Broadway the hair and makeup departments often work together. There is almost always a hair supervisor on a Broadway show, but less often a makeup supervisor. Since the performers almost always do their own makeup, it falls to the hair supervisor or a designated makeup supervisor from the hair team to monitor the actors to make sure the integrity of the makeup is maintained throughout the run. It is also the hair supervisor or designated makeup supervisor who reorders the makeup and maintains the makeup stock.

The makeup designer does not work the show's run. After completion of the tech and if there are no notes after previews and the looks are settled, the designer can step away. They remain available if assistance is needed or there is a big cast change.

Prosthetics

When we hear the word prosthetics, we usually think of body limbs. Prosthetics in theatre is the responsibility of the makeup designer because it deals only with the face. Most often it might be a scar or wound.

Unlike movies, there are very few shows on Broadway that require prosthetics. The most recent use of a true prosthetic in a Broadway show was in the production of *Mrs. Doubtfire,* and it is a good example of the process of a prosthetic in a theatrical production.

It can take three to four hours each day on a film shoot to prepare an actor in a prosthetic. An actor in a stage production has a half-hour to get ready for each performance. When such a musical is made of an iconic and favorite movie, the audience wants to see onstage what they remember from the movie. The designer for *Mrs. Doubtfire,* Tommy Kurzman, had worked with the costume designer for the production and originally was told the production was not thinking of using a prosthetic, but they wanted someone who would figure out how to make it all work.

Mr. Kurzman was approached when the production was scheduled to have a tryout in Seattle. Before the production left for Seattle, he consulted with the costume designer, the director, and the actor. The director did not want to lose the fact that the same actor was portraying the role of father and Mrs. Doubtfire, which would have betrayed the premise of the story. Onstage the character had to be believable to his children when they stood in front of him and did not recognize him as their father.

The first information the designer needed to know was how the prosthetic needed to function and what were the expectations for it. Did it go on? Did it come off? How many times? There was no time for tape or glue. The mask could not completely cover the actor's face because he needed to be able to emote. A certain amount of choreography and space is needed when someone helps an actor take off a prosthetic, especially in the middle of a scene. This all had to be planned carefully. In the heat of a performance, there is zero room for error.

Eventually it was decided that some kind of prosthetic was going to be necessary. The designer had about four weeks to figure out a solution. He researched people who knew about prosthetics, researched photos of older Scottish women, and photoshopped the actor's face using different shapes to figure out an aesthetic look. Through referrals he found a woman who worked in television and was able to make a prototype, which the designer took with him to Seattle. Silicon was used to make the mask. A life cast of the actor's face was made, and a mold was created.

Perhaps the most important criterion for this prosthetic was the actor is in and out of the prosthetic, going from Mrs. Doubtfire to father, almost twenty times in the show. Although experimenting during a production is not ideal, the prototype was an opportunity to learn what worked and what did not. Fortunately, the Seattle theatre was huge, so the distance between the stage and the audience helped make the prosthetic work because the visual distance blurred some of its imperfections. It also provided many lessons for the production as to what needed to change for Broadway. The experiment allowed Mr. Kurzman to learn about functionality and what he would finesse for the move to New York. Most importantly, the production learned the mask needed durability to last eight shows a week over a period of time.

The production returned to New York where there are shops that produce prosthetics. What developed from the prototype was a cowl mask that the actor dives in and out of, and there is a snap at his neck that holds the cowl tight. The glasses go on separately, which hide the seam under the eye and makeup is applied around his mouth, so he looks like he's wearing lipstick.

Usually, the designer would have to make a budget for a bid for this type of item, but it was a single item, not twenty. Mr. Kurzman knew the company he wanted to create the prosthetic for Broadway, and the producers approved it.

In the production there is an understudy, so the understudy had to go through the same process. The stage management team on a show is always diligent in rehearsing understudies, but with the role of Mrs. Doubtfire preparation was absolutely necessary. Not only for it being a dual role but also having dexterity in manipulating the prosthetic at a moment's notice. Currently there is a national tour and anyone playing Mrs. Doubtfire will have their own mask and will go through the entire process.

Once the makeup looks are set, after the show is frozen, after official press opening, and after formal opening, the design part of makeup is done. If there are cast replacements, the designer is usually called back to assess the makeup for the newcomer. As previously mentioned, how everyone's complexion responds to the lighting is crucial. In essence, the designer's job does not end with opening night.

Sometimes, not always, a makeup designer can receive a royalty on their design work depending on how integral the makeup design or prosthetic design is for the production.

Although there are shops that create prosthetics, there really is not a theatrical school program that teaches the skill of prosthetics. For Tommy Kurzman, it was solving a puzzle.

Furthermore, the skill of theatrical makeup is not taught at most colleges or universities today. The lack of in-depth makeup training is partially due to budget cuts in colleges and perhaps not thinking makeup is an essential element for theatrical training. The real issue is that although theatrical makeup has become more naturalistic, there are subtleties in makeup that contribute to a character expressing a story.

There are at least two schools in the United States that have a particular major for both wigs and makeup, and both have a bachelor's and master's program. Those schools are the University of North Carolina School of the Arts and Cincinnati Conservatory of Music. Juilliard in New York City does teach a fifteen-week makeup class to third-year students. There is a workshop at New

York University, but it is outside the main curriculum. There may be other universities that teach the art of theatrical makeup as well. In addition, there is the Make-Up Designory, which has a variety of programs for makeup students.

Theatrical production can become focused on technology and forget the importance of theatrical makeup, but no one wants to go to the theatre and see an actor *au naturel*. The inventiveness of makeup contributes to and is an important element of the storytelling.